International Political Economy Series

Series Editor
Timothy M. Shaw, University of Massachusetts Boston, Boston, USA;
Emeritus Professor, University of London, London, UK

The global political economy is in flux as a series of cumulative crises impacts its organization and governance. The IPE series has tracked its development in both analysis and structure over the last three decades. It has always had a concentration on the global South. Now the South increasingly challenges the North as the centre of development, also reflected in a growing number of submissions and publications on indebted Eurozone economies in Southern Europe. An indispensable resource for scholars and researchers, the series examines a variety of capitalisms and connections by focusing on emerging economies, companies and sectors, debates and policies. It informs diverse policy communities as the established trans-Atlantic North declines and 'the rest', especially the BRICS, rise. NOW INDEXED ON SCOPUS!

More information about this series at
http://www.palgrave.com/gp/series/13996

Agnes Gagyi · Ondřej Slačálek
Editors

The Political Economy of Eastern Europe 30 years into the 'Transition'

New Left Perspectives from the Region

palgrave
macmillan

Editors
Agnes Gagyi
University of Gothenburg
Göteborg, Sweden

Ondřej Slačálek
Charles University
Prague, Czech Republic

ISSN 2662-2483 ISSN 2662-2491 (electronic)
International Political Economy Series
ISBN 978-3-030-78914-5 ISBN 978-3-030-78915-2 (eBook)
https://doi.org/10.1007/978-3-030-78915-2

This Palgrave Macmillan imprint is published by the registered company Springer Nature Switzerland AG
The registered company address is: Gewerbestrasse 11, 6330 Cham, Switzerland

Foreword

This book makes an important and wide-ranging contribution to understanding social change in Central and Eastern Europe.

In line with the open and grounded sharing of experiences that has characterised the making of this volume, the editors and the individual contributors have avoided the temptation of producing a prescriptive book, of the sort that has proliferated in past decades in the field of left politics and to which many scholars continue to dedicate their efforts. They do make general assumptions about the political actors and strategies of the new left forces in Eastern Europe, but the methodology used to reach the conclusions is based on a thorough empirical examination and analysis of the experiences of each country, rather than simply applying a monolithic theoretical model to the realities of different political processes in the diverse countries of the region.

It always helps to know the origins of a collaborative project. For us, fellows of the Transnational Institute (TNI), the roots lie thirty years back when in June 1990, six months after the collapse of the USSR, we convened in Amsterdam a meeting of activists from Eastern and Western Europe. From what was then Czechoslovakia came students who had joined Charter 77 on Prague's Wenceslas Square. From the former German Democratic Republic came feminist and peace activists who had been in Alexanderplatz as part of the movements that brought down the Berlin Wall. A peace movement supporter came from Hungary, along with a sociologist from an independent network of academics researchers.

A member of a local organisation supporting Solidarity came from Poland along with someone from a newly formed feminist group. And a young intellectual came from the former Yugoslavia, active in building social movements across the Balkans.

Around the oval table of TNI's old offices opposite the Van Gogh Museum, they sat with feminists, peace, green and other civil society activists from Western Europe. We discussed shared concerns: the meaning and scope of personal and social engagement; how to build or strengthen democratic institutions rooted in peace and justice; how to combine pluralism with egalitarianism; and how to restructure our ideas and practices as means that pre-figure the end goals, rather than the goals justifying the means. All of us were active in social movements committed in different ways to democracy and acting independently of the state, the market, private companies and political parties. We drew on our contrasting experiences to shed light from different angles on the common concerns. Respective understandings of rapidly changing politics, economics and social relations in both parts of Europe was a hundred times greater than had each person continued to stare at these relationships only from her or his own experience. There was a visceral sense of excitement at having a shared quest. We were all searching for, and experimenting with ways of transforming unequal and increasingly authoritarian societies while avoiding the fantasy of a benevolent centralised state and its corollary, a single benevolent political party. By learning from the failings of social democracy in what was then called "the West", we were also searching for social and co-operative means of wealth creation rather than relying on the state or private corporations. It was a collaborative quest we all wanted to deepen and expand.

But anxiety also permeated the discussions. Even in 1990, there were already menacing threats that in the following years would make exchanges and collaboration between "Eastern" and "Western" activist-scholars in Europe very difficult. In the former communist countries of Europe, there were signs of new forms of authoritarianism, made more toxic by appeals to nationalism. On the capitalist side of Europe, there were signs of a determined class war against trade union power and the welfare state. These threats became all too real, almost fatally closing the spaces for transformative practice both in the east and in the west of Europe, destroying the strength of movements that depended, paradoxically, on the social democratic policies that the activists and thinkers meeting in Amsterdam so derided.

Fast forward two decades, and TNI convenes another, more global, encounter in Amsterdam in February 2016 around that same oval table. The purpose was to jointly draft a research agenda for a decentralised New Politics think tank on counter-hegemonic politics. Across Latin America, progressive governments—which had been a beacon of hope for much of the left everywhere—were in retreat or losing their original democratic and participatory credentials. In the United States and Europe, reinvigorated authoritarian forces and corporate interests had accumulated power at levels unprecedented in recent history.

An outcome of that 2016 encounter, and a subsequent meeting in Amsterdam in 2018, was an invitation to TNI from a group of enthusiastic and mainly young activists from former communist countries in Europe to co-organise a conference in Prague in 2019 which would analyse the new political developments. The two of us jumped at the opportunity to renew the quest that had begun three decades ago, now with a new generation that had learnt hard lessons and developed sophisticated analyses from which activists worldwide have much to learn.

The idea of this book was born of the Prague encounter. It contributes much-needed insights into the evolution of left political imagination in Eastern Europe since 1989, addresses acute biases in the global sense of European left politics and offers fresh ideas about how to achieve democratic and emancipatory alternatives that hold lessons for us all everywhere. Perhaps most importantly, it contributes to the efforts of left activists from across the region to meet, share and build a common emancipatory project.

Amsterdam, The Netherlands
January 2021

Daniel Chavez
Hilary Wainwright
Co-convenors of the TNI New Politics Project

Daniel Chavez is a Dutch-Uruguayan Activist-Scholar. A Transnational Institute Fellow since 2005, he earned his Ph.D. in Development Studies from the Institute of Social Studies of Erasmus University Rotterdam in 2001, subsequently joining the Institute as a staff member. He cut his activist teeth at Uruguay's United Federation of Mutual Aid Housing Cooperatives (FUCVAM). He has published extensive research on emancipatory politics and public policies, including the co-edited books *The New Latin American Left: Utopia Reborn* (2008), *Repensar lo público.: Estado, sociedad y servicios básicos en América Latina* (2018) and *Public Water and Covid-19: Dark Clouds and Silver Linings* (2020).

Hilary Wainwright is a Feminist Sociologist who works as an independent activist-researcher and journalist. Transnational Institute fellow since 1986. She is a founding editor of *Red Pepper*, a British political magazine. She is a senior Research Associate of the Institute of Development Studies, Sussex University. Her books include *Arguments for A New Left; answering the free market right*(1994) and *A New Politics from the Left* (2018). She is a Member of the editorial collective of *Socialist Register*.

Contents

Introduction 1
Agnes Gagyi

Life in Transition and in Crisis. The Political Autobiography of a Generation 17
Dana Domşodi and Florin Poenaru

When Did a Transition to Capitalism Start in Serbia? 41
Vladimir Simović and Tanja Vukša

The Restoration of Capitalism in Slovenia and Croatia 65
Marko Kržan and Dimitrije Birač

Bosnia and Herzegovina After the Transition: Forever Postwar, Postsocialist and Peripheral? 81
Danijela Majstorović and Zoran Vučkovac

Ukraine and the (Dis)integrating "Empire of Capital" 97
Yuliya Yurchenko

Reconfiguring Regimes of Capitalist Integration: Hungary Since the 1970s 115
Agnes Gagyi and Tamás Gerőcs

Czechia 30 years On: An Imperfect Oligarchy Without Emancipatory Alternative 133
Ondřej Slačálek and Daniel Šitera

Post-dissent and the New Right: Problems and Potential of post-Communist Dissent in Slovakia and Beyond 151
Joseph Grim Feinberg

The Shame Movement in the Context of Georgia's 30 years of Transformation: A Gramscian Analysis of Civil Society 169
Nino Khelaia and Tornike Chivadze

The Roots of the Moralization of Politics in Post-1989 Bulgaria and What It Means for the Left 187
Georgi Medarov

The New Protest Movements and the Left in Russia: To Overcome the Crisis of Hegemony 205
Oleg Zhuravlev

Fear, Doubt and Money. War of Ideas, Production of Ignorance and Right-Wing Infrastructures of Knowledge and Hegemony in Poland 223
Andrzej W. Nowak

Conclusion: Seven Excursions into the Ideological Landscape of Eastern Europe 251
Ondřej Slačálek

Index 267

Notes on Contributors

Dimitrije Birač is a Croatian Economist, graduated on Marx's theory of surplus value in the course of economic theory and is currently attending doctoral studies on Faculty of Political Science in Zagreb, where he focuses on the making of the Croatian political and economic system during groundbreaking years 1989/1991. His interests are economic history, the history of economic thought, political economy and political theory, with an emphasis on the Marxist perspective. As a political activist, he is an executive board member of parliamentary party Nova ljevica (New Left).

Tornike Chivadze graduated from the Social and Political Faculty of Tbilisi State University and is currently doing a sociology M.A. at Corvinus University, Budapest. His working areas and experience include tax policy, pension policies, industrial policies and economic issues. He is a member of the editorial board of the analytical media portal "European.ge", before which he worked as an invited specialist for the Georgian Social Democrats.

Dana Domşodi is a Lecturer in Sociology at the Faculty of Sociology and Social Work at Babeş-Bolyai University. Her research interests include modern theories of property, class studies, social history and classical political economy. She holds a Ph.D. In Politics, Human Rights and Sustainability, obtained in 2018, from Sant'Anna School of Advanced Studies, Pisa, Italy.

Joseph Grim Feinberg is a Research Fellow at the Philosophy Institute of the Czech Academy of Sciences and is editor of *Contradictions: A Journal for Critical Thought*. His current research involves the history of social thought in East-Central Europe, the problem of citizenship and non-citizens, and the notion of internationalism. His book *The Paradox of Authenticity*, on problems of performance and the reconceptualisation of "the people" in post-Communist Slovak folklore, was released in 2018.

Agnes Gagyi is a Sociologist, working on politics and social movements in Eastern Europe from the perspective of the region's long-term world-economic and geopolitical integration. She is a Researcher at the Department of Sociology and Work Science, University of Gothenburg, and member of the Working Group for Public Sociology "Helyzet" in Budapest.

Tamás Gerőcs is a Political Economist who is currently doing his Doctoral Studies at the State University of New York, Binghamton. His research field of interest is semi-peripheral dependent development in Eastern Europe and labour relations in the Hungarian automotive industry. Gerőcs is a Research Fellow at the Institute of World Economics, Centre of Economic and Regional Studies in Hungary. He graduated from the Corvinus University of Budapest in 2008 with the M.A. degree of International Relations. Gerőcs is a member of the Budapest-based Working Group for Public Sociology "Helyzet".

Nino Khelaia is a Doctoral Researcher in Political Science at the Department of Social Sciences at Humboldt-Universität zu Berlin and Analyst at the Georgian Public Broadcaster in Tbilisi. Her research focuses on post-socialist state, society, economy, and social movements. She is also part of the Tbilisi working group on the Evolution of State and invited lecturer at the Tbilisi State University programme "Post-Socialist transformation: Politics, Economy and Society".

Dr. Marko Kržan is a Slovene Sociologist specialising in Marxist theory of value and modes of production, especially with regard to really existing socialism. He has been professionally involved in politics as an advisor to Združena levica (United Left) parliamentary club in the Slovenian parliament (2014–2018). Currently, he is a freelance Researcher, Translator and Publicist.

Danijela Majstorović (M.A. 2003, Ohio University; Ph.D. 2006 University of Banja Luka) is Professor of English Linguistics and Cultural Studies at the University of Banja Luka's English department. She is also a Humboldt Experienced Research Fellow studying social protests and third-wave migrations in and from post-2015 Western Balkans at Justus Liebig University in Giessen, Germany. She was a visiting researcher at Lancaster University in 2006, a Fulbright fellow at UCLA in 2012–2013, a Canada Research Chair in Cultural Studies Postdoctoral Fellow at the University of Alberta in 2014 and a visiting researcher at Indiana University in 2016. Her research interests involve critical discourse analysis, critical theory, feminist theory, post- and decolonial theory and post-Dayton Bosnia. She published over 25 journal articles, co-authored *Youth Ethnic and National Identity in Bosnia and Herzegovina* (Palgrave, 2013), authored *Diskursi periferije* (Biblioteka XX vek, Belgrade) and *Diskurs, moć i međunarodna zajednica* (FF Banja Luka, 2007). She edited *Living With Patriarchy: Discursive Construction of Gendered Subjects Across Cultures* (John Benjamins, 2011), *U okrilju nacije* (CKSP Banja Luka, 2011) and *Kritičke kulturološke studije u postjugoslovenskom prostoru* (Banja Luka, 2012). Her new book *Discourse and Affect in Post-socialist Bosnia and Herzegovina: Peripheral Selves* is due to come for Palgrave in 2021.

Georgi Medarov is a Sociologist based in Sofia, Bulgaria. He works as a Researcher at the Institute of Philosophy and Sociology at the Bulgarian Academy of Sciences and teaches sociology at the University of Plovdiv. He is also a Member of the Collective for Social Interventions (KOI).

Andrzej W. Nowak is a Philosopher, University Professor and Researcher at the Faculty of Philosophy, Adam Mickiewicz University, Poznań, Poland. His current research focus is on (social) ontology and social studies of science and technology. Propagator of Immanuel Wallerstein's theory of the modern world-system, particularly interested in the study of semi-peripherality. Tries to merge the ontological sensitivity of post-humanism with the Promethean promise of modernity and Enlightenment. Author of books: Ontological Imagination. Philosophical (re)construction of phronetic social science (2016, in Polish), Agency, System, Modernity (2011, in Polish) and co-author of Whose Fear? Whose Science? Structures of knowledge and socio-scientific controversies (2016, in Polish). An active participant in public life, occasional columnist, blogger and a devoted bike tourist as well as a marathon runner.

Florin Poenaru is a Lecturer in Sociology and Anthropology in the Department of Sociology and Social Work, University of Bucharest. He has a Ph.D. in social anthropology from Central European University, Budapest and was a Fulbright Visiting Scholar to City University of New York. He works on issues related to class, post-socialism and global history of Eastern Europe and teaches classes on contemporary theories in sociology and anthropology. He is a co-editor of CriticAtac, founding member of LeftEast and regular contributor to Bilten. His latest book is *Locuri comune: clasă, anti-comunism, stânga*, Tact, 2017. He also took part in over a dozen of election monitoring missions across Eastern Europe, the Balkans and the Middle East.

Vladimir Simović is a Sociologist. His research and theoretical work focuses on Yugoslav self-management and theory of remembrance. He is one of the founders of the Center for the Politics of Emancipation (CPE), Belgrade based think tank. He is one of the editors of the research publication "Balance Sheet of Transition—Contribution to the Analysis of the Restoration of Capitalism in Serbia" (CPE, 2015). With other CPE members in 2016, Vladimir established the educational programme "Studies of Socialism". He writes analysis for various online and printed media on a regular basis.

Daniel Šitera is Head of the Centre for Global Political Economy of the Institute of International Relations, Prague. He published in *Journal of International Relations and Development* and *New Perspectives*. His work is located in the areas of the International Political Economy of East-Central Europe and the European Integration.

Ondřej Slačálek is Assistant Professor at the Department of Political Science, Faculty of Arts, Charles University, Prague. He has published various scholarly articles on the history of radicalism, social movements, national identity and nationalism in journals such as *Patterns of Prejudice*, *Slavic Review*, *Czech Sociological Review* and others, and essays in *Eurozine* and *A2larm*.

Zoran Vučkovac is a Ph.D. Candidate at the Graduate Center for the Study of Culture at the Justus Liebig University in Giessen, working on entangled histories of labour and violence during the breakup of

Yugoslavia. He holds an M.A. from the University of Alberta's English and Film Studies programme and has presented conference papers on memory politics and published articles on horizontal political decision-making and social activism. He worked as a researcher at the Centre for Democracy and Transitional Justice and was one of the founders of the Banja Luka Social Center, an independent platform dealing with historical revisionism, social justice and feminism.

Tanja Vukša graduated Sociology at the Faculty of Philosophy and has a master's degree in the Department of Culture and Gender Theory at the Faculty of Political Sciences in Belgrade. She is a Member of the Center for Politics of Emancipation (CPE). Her theoretical interests are economic theories and analysis and, in particular, feminist critique of political economy. Areas of interest include also the history of Yugoslavia with a special focus on self-management as well as questions related to the possibilities of building a socialist project in the twenty-first century.

Yuliya Yurchenko is Senior Lecturer in Political Economy at the Department of Economics and International Business and a researcher at the Political Economy, Governance, Finance and Accountability Institute, University of Greenwich, UK. She researches state, capital, society relations, public services as/and commons. She is author of *Ukraine and the Empire of Capital: from Marketisation to the Armed Conflict* (Pluto Press, London 2018).

Oleg Zhuravlev is a Researcher at the Public Sociology Laboratory (Russia), which he and his colleagues founded in 2012. He earned his Ph.D. in Sociology from the European University Institute in 2018. He has been involved in research dedicated to social movements in post-soviet countries and beyond, armed conflicts and labour under neoliberal conditions. He is a part of the Russian Socialist Movement.

Introduction

Agnes Gagyi

By the 30th anniversary of the fall of the Berlin Wall, across Eastern Europe,[1] high expectations associated with the promises of transition to free market and democracy have given space to feelings of disillusionment. While expressions of this disillusionment are getting entangled with various social movements and political conflicts of an ongoing global crisis, international discussions on Eastern Europe mostly focus on new illiberal regimes, and interpret their rise in terms of a backslide on an otherwise predetermined route from dictatorship to liberalism (e.g. Cianetti et al., 2018; Greskovits, 2015; Rupnik, 2007). Formulated from the perspective of a transatlantic power coalition in crisis, this narrative reiterates the Cold War framework implied in the normative story of

[1] The book follows the vocabulary of discussions around socialism/postsocialism, and applies the notion of "Eastern Europe" to countries of the former Soviet bloc. It does not engage in the complex debates about the region's definition, but highlights differential trajectories of postsocialist global integration, including intra-regional hierarchies implied in that process (like in the chapters on Ukraine or Bosnia).

A. Gagyi (✉)
Department of Sociology and Work Science, University of Gothenburg, Gothenburg, Sweden
e-mail: agnes.gagyi@gu.se

A. Gagyi and O. Slačálek (eds.), *The Political Economy of Eastern Europe 30 years into the 'Transition'*, International Political Economy Series,
https://doi.org/10.1007/978-3-030-78915-2_1

transition, this time with a negative edge. Illiberal outcomes of postsocialist transition are depicted as a time-loop in history, where authoritarian tendencies inherently associated with the past make a sudden comeback in Eastern Europe, a backlash that even impacts Western liberalism's core. As one of the most influential recent formulations of this narrative, Krastev and Holmes' (2019) The Light that Failed put it: Trump's USA follows Putin's Russia through the force of reverse imitation.

This new version of the transition story obscures decades of empirical critique of the transitology narrative, which by today constitutes the mainstream consensus among researchers of the region (e.g. Kubik, 2013). It artificially separates East European politics from its global context by defining local development as primarily shaped by its the socialist past, obscuring connections with a global transformation that produced similar instances of right-wing authoritarianism across the globe since the 1980's, including the recent wave of Western right populism. Beyond that, it also misrepresents political development in the region. While highlighting most spectacular cases of illiberalism, it omits contemporary cases of intensification of neoliberal reforms, and invisibilizes the continuity of populist conservative agendas in postsocialist power struggles.

Academic research less visible in public political debates has provided more complex approaches to the questions above, throwing light on connections between economic deprivation and class-based dynamics of postsocialist populism (e.g. Ost, 2005), continuities between socialist and postsocialist elites (e.g. Eyal et al., 1998), transnational links between socialist and capitalist policies (e.g. Bockman, 2011), continuities of long-term processes of modernization across local socialist and capitalist regimes (e.g. Lampland, 1995; Verdery, 2003), comparative regional intellectual history (e.g. Trencsényi et al., 2018), or global relations of socialist regimes beyond the East–West divide (e.g. Mark et al., 2019). Growing dissatisfaction with neoliberal reforms in Western contexts supported a growing tendency for researching transition in terms of capitalist reintegration (e.g. Drahokoupil, 2009; Dale, 2011; Shields, 2014), reviving earlier traditions of Western left academic interest in the region. Meanwhile, even if marginalized by mainstream paradigms, several East European left intellectuals discussed socialism and transition from the perspective of global capitalist history, and criticized normative transition narratives on that ground (e.g. Barša, 2020; Boatcă, 2006; Böröcz, 1992; Buden, 2010; Kagarlitsky, 2008; Kiossev, 1999; Krausz, 2015;

Melegh, 2006; Močnik, 2019; Przeworski, 1991; Sowa, 2018; Szalai, 2005; Tamás, 2000; Todorova, 2009).

This volume aims to amplify a specific voice in this debate: that of a new generation of left intellectuals from the region, whose lifetime largely coincides with the transformations of the postsocialist period. In a context where left critiques of the transition had been suppressed by postsocialist anti-communism, and where the global left—itself weakened by neoliberal hegemony—paid little attention to post-socialist East European perspectives, building a new left orientation in Eastern Europe constituted less of an evident choice of a political line, but rather a laborious process of collective learning, debates, and practical experimentation. By today, this work bred new forms of analysis and political thought that combined local left traditions and their critiques with various threads of international left perspectives and their contemporary applications, to make sense of how socialist and postsocialist histories connect to global processes, and how left politics on the ground can relevantly address those contexts. The rare examples of local left thought such as mentioned above constituted an important resource in this process. Needless to say, the formation of a new generation of new left intellectuals is only one aspect of the potential of new left politics in the region. This book aims to visibilize the former; a further task is to analyze its relations with popular and institutional actors.

Building Dialogue

The field of East European new left thought is not homogenous; as the articles in this collection show, approaches vary both in their theoretical frameworks and empirical foci. However, what is probably more significant than a momentary snapshot of convergences and differences is the process of dialogue in which individual standpoints are formulated and debated. Within this process, this book aims to serve a specific function, reacting to a particular type of obstacle. While subsequent waves of the formation of East European new left have connected to European and global initiatives—from the alterglobalist movement of the 2000's to post-2008 anti-austerity movements or new municipalism—integrating local perspectives with broader international left political frameworks has been a challenge. After the global left's disillusionment with state socialism, East European politics has not been considered as a significant site informing left theory. Local new left activists looking for alliances were met with political frameworks born in different global contexts—like the alterglobalist critique of global neoliberalism based on the experience of the Global South, or the post-2008 wave of anti-austerity politics that used social gains of postwar Western welfare states as a main point of reference. Specific aspects of East European experience, like local histories of state socialist systems and their crises, the shock of deindustrialization, privatization, and austerity coupled with an ideological victory over socialism, or the humiliating aspects of European integration conditions, did not seamlessly fit with such narratives.

For those new left actors who engaged in academic research, existing infrastructures of academic knowledge production constituted a similar setting. Despite renewing attempts by local actors to work together and build common frameworks of understanding, new left research on the region has been dominated by objective conditions of academic funding and hierarchies, with the typical outcome that researchers individually join scholarly programs defined by agendas of Western scholarship. Even in cases where local researchers successfully set up local research collaborations, efforts to synchronize these across the region met limitations of funding interest. The by now significant volume of internationally available research on the region by members of the local new left[2]has been typically carried out from Western universities, and allowed for little cross-regional coordination. Meanwhile, an even larger scope of new left research published in local languages remains hardly accessible for cross-regional or broader international debates.

One effect of the above conditions has been that specific characteristics of local development have been linked to different branches of general frameworks circulating in international critical debates. While such gestures provide a possibility to grasp the significance of local processes in an internationally communicable way, they imply a risk that the steps of generalization are made too fast, ignoring local aspects that fit those frameworks less, as well as intra-regional variations that would disturb respective broader narratives. For example, while for Georgian or Romanian new left actors, neoliberalization through deregulation, privatization, and liberalization is an analytical frame that reflects the practice of contemporary regimes, for those in Hungary or Serbia it has a limited

[2] E.g. Gabor (2010), Halmai and Kalb (2011), Dolenec (2013), Horvat and Stiks (2015), Unkovski-Korica (2016), Ban (2016), Mikuš (2018), Szombati (2018), Yurchenko (2018), Kirn (2019), Cucu (2019), Scheiring (2020), Djagalov (2020), Pixová (2020).

analytical capacity. Differences of the experience of late socialism—varying widely from Yugoslav self-management to oppressive austerity states like in Romania—are reflected in similar variations of new left narratives of the transition.

In this context, new left actors recognized the potential of cross-regional comparison from early on. Since the beginning of the 2010's, regional new left meetings served as high-energy events of lasting inspiration, resulting in recurrent efforts to maintain cross-regional dialogue. A main insight from these debates has been that in order to theorize regional development as part of global processes, details of cross-regional comparison of global integration need to be taken seriously at the level of conceptualization. Unlike models that directly combine general theoretical insights with local cases, thinking through comparison makes it possible to take into account a broader variety of factors and constellations, and examine them in terms of possible dynamics of concrete struggles, a necessary condition of political thought. As Simović and Vukša argue in this book, the concrete process of contradictions that serves as the field of political action is not visible from a highly abstract level. Or, as Cardoso and Faletto put it, speaking about the stakes of regional comparison in *Dependency and development in Latin America*, mere applications of general theories of capitalism

"do not offer accurate characterizations of social structures, nor do they grasp the dynamic aspect of history actualized by social struggles in dependent societies. (…) It is diversity within unity that explains the historical process. If the analytical effort succeeds, general platitudes and reaffirmations about the role of capitalist modes of production can turn into a lively knowledge of real processes" (Cardoso & Faletto, 1979: xv–xviii).

Conceiving the region's global integration through the concrete diversity of local constellations enables local analysis to join global dialogues not in terms of competing general theories, but in terms of a collective process of political reflection on interconnected but diverse forms of systemic contradictions. On behalf of East European new left circles, initiatives for such dialogues include the English-language platform Left East and its summer meetings that bridged East, South European and Middle Eastern perspectives, the Zagreb Subversive Festival that worked as a hub of communication between regional and international movements, or a recent proliferation of thematic networks like Essential Autonomous Struggles Transnational (EAST), a new East European left media network, initiatives like Dialoguing "Between the Posts" or Decolonizing Eastern Europe, or practical collaborations like the regional housing cooperative network MOBA.

This book aims to serve a specific function in this process: to enhance the visibility of regional new left perspectives across the region and internationally, by providing a first English-language collection of new left diagnoses on the region's postsocialist development. While many of the arguments presented in the book will be familiar to specific new left actors in the region, the lack of a regional outlook on new left analyses regularly surfaces as a barrier of comparative work in regional conversations. Similarly, while several authors' arguments are embedded in various international academic and political networks, the idea of an East European new left as a relevant voice in debates on the region hardly appears on the map of international discussions.

The book's selection of authors does not aim for completeness in terms of any pre-fixed criteria. We aimed to bring together authors well embedded in local left debates, and showcase their analyses as examples of relevant new left perspectives developing in the region. The list is topics is not exclusive either; several important topics of recent debates, also involving some of this book's authors—like women's labor and anti-gender politics, reconfigurations of regional integration into new geopolitical shifts, continuities, and ruptures with earlier left traditions, or the region's relation to colonialism—remain undeveloped. We invite readers to see the book as material for later debates. In order that articles provide a better insight on new left contexts, we asked authors to place their arguments within local new left debates and their relevant references. For the same reason, we included a process of peer review with authors with expertise on respective topics and familiar with their context in local new left debates.

Despite not aiming for an exclusive overview, the book offers several substantive insights on potential contributions from a comparative East European new left perspective. One way it does this is by making visible common threads in local new left analysis, that discern a specific standpoint in broader international debates on postsocialist transition and the politics of the current crisis. One such common feature is the adherence to basic tenets of the historical materialist tradition. Despite differences in the choice and application of various left traditions of social analysis, all pieces in this collection share the conviction that ideas and institutions do not move history on their own, and that the ideational and institutional aspects of transition need to be understood in their relation to broader processes of socio-economic change. In the substantive analysis of transition and postsocialist development, this emphasis implies major differences from research agendas dominated by liberal political and economic theory, changing the scope, stakes, and narrative of what is conventionally treated as the story of postsocialist transition. A related emphasis is that instead of a transition from dictatorship to democracy, measured in changes of political institutions, these approaches look at transition primarily as a process of integration into global capitalist circuits in a subordinated position. Consequently, structural hierarchies implied in that process are taken into account in the evaluation of democratization.[3]

A third common thread is a shift of attention from institutional changes performed in the immediate process of regime change to asking how late socialist crisis and ensuing transformations prepared and enabled those changes, how the relations implied in them informed postsocialist development after the phase of institutional regime change, and how this long process of socialist crisis and postsocialist integration connects to the global context of capitalist crisis and its management since the 1970's. This shift of attention makes it possible to highlight aspects of global transformations within the specific local processes of the transition, and to view East European histories of post-1970's crisis management in their relation to other semi-peripheral and peripheral cases, instead of the more conventional practice of comparing regional performances vis-a-vis a unidirectional East–West axis of developmental hierarchies.

Fourth, in line with the above considerations, the approaches featured in this book conceive ideological and power struggles as relations that mediate the conflictual process of global integration. This view also impacts authors' periodizations of political history: instead of clear-cut breaks marked by institutional changes, periodizations follow the rhythm of reconfigurations in local regimes of external integration. Finally, this view highlights the aspect of continuity in the relations of conflict and cooptation between competing blocs of internal–external elite alliances and various forms of popular contention. Authors point out that nationalist and globalist ambitions have always been part of postsocialist elites' competing agendas, including former instances of local right-wing hegemonies. From this perspective, in their relation to popular contestation,

[3] For a comparative analysis of East European and Latin American neoliberalization that approaches the issue of democratization from a similar angle, see Madariaga (2020).

shifts between late socialist, nationalist, and liberal regimes are not interpreted as shifts between oppression and democracy, but as shifts between various modes of constructing hegemony over expressions of social discontent. In this sense, analyses of popular contention featured in this book diverge from Western narratives of neoliberalization, which explain populist tendencies by the "crisis of democratic capitalism" (e.g. Streeck, 2014). Instead, they stand closer to what Kumral and Karatasli (2020) offer as an alternative reading of global right populism based on the experience of the Global South, where successive right-wing populist and globalist regimes have been part of changing modes of authoritarian governance that served to coopt and hold in check local popular struggles in the process of neoliberal transformation.

Next to common threads of analysis, the other comparative aspect the book highlights is specific ideological constellations of postsocialist transformation. Such are the various versions of anticommunism and their effects on the development of the local left, the conflict of Westernism vs. nationalism, or different aspects of antipolitics—from dissidents' moral politics to the politics of anticorruption, or the ideas of civil society or technocratic governance in contemporary movements. The issue of the socialist idea of modernity, and its relation to capitalist modernity and its right-wing critiques, is also discussed. The scope of ideological issues addressed in the book is not exclusive: the analyses serve to give an impression of the specific reality of the ideological terrain on which local left political thought operates. Instead of taking Western paradigms of ideological orientation for granted, these analyses show how notions of communism, corruption or civil society gain their significance as part of real ideological processes that mediate global integration in the region.

The Structure of the Book

The argumentation of articles varies from broader narratives of socio-economic and political transformation to analyses that address the issue of postsocialist transition through the prism of specific ideological concepts. The order of articles in the book does not separate these two approaches. Instead, it aims to facilitate understanding through successively introducing perspectives that are important for the book's overall approach, as well as through reflecting territorial and historical closeness between cases. The collection starts with Dana Domsodi and Florin Poenaru's introduction of a generational perspective on new left analysis of the region, which they discuss in the case of Romania's late socialist and postsocialist development. Domsodi and Poenaru trace new left generational experience across this period as marked by three overlapping crises of structural processes: the profitability crisis of the post-1945 global cycle, the crisis of the socialist model of forced industrialization; and the social crisis built up by global neoliberalization, into which postsocialist societies enter with high hopes in 1989. Against the narrative of a general "backslide" into illiberalism, they emphasize the process of sense-making through which members of this generation came to understand their own life experience of disillusionment through a broader critique of capitalism.

The following piece by Vladimir Simović and Tanja Vukša conceptualizes transition in terms of a longer process of structural struggle between socialist and capitalist logics of social organization. They conceive Yugoslav socialism as a system established by efforts to replace capitalist relations with socialist self-management, that worked as a battlefield on which the capitalist logic finally emerged victoriously. This definition of socialism not as a homogenous system, but as a sphere of structural struggle inserted into global capitalist dynamics, remains an important point throughout the book in the interpretation of the political levels of decisions. Marko Kržan and Dimitrije Birač's analysis of the transformation of Slovenia and Croatia follows up on this approach to discuss the particular conditions of Slovenian and Croatian transitions to capitalism. Starting from an analysis of late socialist bureaucratic and technocratic elite fractions, they explain how different elite coalitions came to mediate different routes of the transition in the two cases, and how both models fared in the aftermath of the 2008 crisis. Writing about Bosnia and Herzegovina after the transition, Danijela Majstorović and Zoran Vučkovac add a further perspective to this analysis. Adding the aspect of biopolitical governance to the notion of peripherality defined in terms of political economy, they characterize Bosnia and Herzegovina's case as a colonial, postwar, and postsocialist condition, where economic hierarchies of capitalist integration combine with EU and UN protocols of control integrated with internal regimes of clientelism, salariat, police brutality, and undemocratic ethnonationalist rule. Against the background of three stages of economic and political restructuring after the war, Majstorović and Vučkovac present three cases of resistance, asking how models of sociality implied in acts of resistance can escape the logic of peripherality instead of reinforcing it.

Yuliya Yurchenko's piece on Ukraine's postsocialist development also focuses on the interaction between internal state-society relations and global capitalist geopolitics, with a neo-Gramscian emphasis on tracing connections between local oligarchic and lobbyist groups, international organizations, and different fractions of transnational capital. She presents a chronology of Ukraine's postsocialist development in terms of phases of a struggle between competing oligarchic networks and their transnational alliances. It is this context in which she unpacks four ideological myths around the politics of Ukraine (the myth of necessary transition; democracy; the "two Ukraines"—East and West—and the Russian/communist "Other"), and in which she places the history of the 2004–2005 Orange Revolution, the 2013–2014 Maidan protests, the war in Donbass, and Volodymyr Zelensky's successful 2019 presidential campaign. Following links between internal regimes and external integration, Agnes Gagyi and Tamás Gerőcs analyze how reconfiguring regimes of state–society relations in Hungary are linked to changing modes of world-economic integration since the world-economic crisis of the 1970's. They distinguish three main phases: the dismantling of a "bridge" position built on Western technological imports and Soviet raw material exports in the context of the 1970's crisis, the Western FDI-based model of the 1990's, a debt-led integration model in the 2000's, and a post-2008 model of integration which combines a dependent integration subservient to the needs of Western and Eastern investors with the support of oligarchic national capital in non-tradable sectors.

Ondřej Slačálek and Daniel Šitera's chapter addresses the present crisis of democracy in the Czech Republic as a long-term result of postsocialist politics, characterized by a competition between two factions of the Czech capitalist class and their political projects: neoliberal nationalism and liberal globalism. The chapter presents a chronological analysis of three periods of rule of respective factions, as well as three interregna. Slačálek and Šitera characterize the interests and composition of the factions, their main challenges and main competing discourses, showing how their struggle kept the socialist alternative in a permanently subordinate and suspicious position that prevented it from developing. Writing about the other half of former Czechoslovakia, Joseph Grim Feinberg follows up on the idea of depolitization of social critique, showing how the legacy of dissident moralization of politics worked in the context of post-socialist Slovakia. Feinberg argues that anticommunist dissident legacies were used by an alliance of conservatives and liberals in a symbolic struggle against "populism" and the "legacy of communism" and in support of a depoliticized struggle for "decent politics", used as tools for discourse policing to silence social criticisms of the transformation. Feinberg calls for a dialectical critique of this dissident legacy in order to formulate a new dissident position adequate for the situation of real capitalism.

Tornike Chivadze and Nino Khelaia delve deeper in the analysis of depolitization of postsocialist dissent, and investigate the recent Shame Movement in Georgia in the context of a Gramscian analysis of state-civil society relations throughout Georgia's 30 years of postsocialist transformation. Chivadze and Khelaia claim that the Shame Movement has been reinforcing the hegemonic neoliberal order in Georgia, and take this conclusion further as an agenda for a left-wing analysis of Georgia's post-socialist state–society-economy relations. Georgi Medarov offers another account of the moralization of politics as an element of postsocialist political economy. Starting from asking why Bulgaria, despite having one of the highest rates of social inequality in the EU, has not produced a strong left political alternative, he analyzes local versions of antipolitics: discourses of anti-corruption, the moralization of politics, technocratism, and the discourse of "Europeanization". He shows how, in the relation between changing governments and successive forms of social contestation, these ideologies worked to depoliticize economic policies and to naturalize and dehistoricize social inequalities, channeling critique away from structural relations and towards a personalized critique of "dishonest" and "corrupt" politicians. Tracing the transformations of political economy after the fall of socialism, Medarov illustrates how depoliticization facilitated the unchallenged implementation of neoliberal policies, and discusses the difficulties that the radical left faces in this context.

Speaking about Russian protest mobilizations between 2011 and 2014, Oleg Zhouravlev further deepens this line of analysis, applying a Laclauian lense on the formation of protest politics in terms of hegemony formation. He offers an empirical political sociological account of the protests, explaining why existing fractions of the local left were unable to influence protest frames, and how, in their effort to create a hegemonic political subject from diverse left-wing and right-wing constituencies, protests limited their claims to an idea of "democracy" emptied of social content, and to a "politics of authenticity" focused on the moment of protest and the facing of repression. Zhouravlev argues that these characteristics of the protests were alienating to a majority of the Russian population, something that was skilfully made use of by Putin and his political technologists.

In the last empirical article, Andrzej W. Nowak turns towards the issue of populist anti-scientism, analyzing infrastructural conditions of major transformations of morality and rationality in Poland since the 1970's. Nowak describes how the Catholic church's rising influence on moral and political issues has been coupled with the Solidarity movement, and with a wave of international criticism against the emancipatory idea of reason and science implied in socialist ideology. Nowak traces the techniques of the conservative counter-offensive, its ability to learn from both Lenin and Gramsci, and to create networks of influence and promote its own hegemony under an anti-hegemonic rhetoric. In face of this process, he argues, the Left is weakened by its anti-institutional and anti-statist stance, and needs a focus on the material conditions of production and the promotion of ideas.

In the concluding chapter, Ondřej Slačálek discusses five nodes of postsocialist ideological struggles that the book's authors addressed: anticommunism, Westernism, nationalism, irrationalism, and antipolitics (through its three aspects of anti-corruption, civil society, and technocratism). Slačálek characterizes these as discourses that are applied to obscure real social conflicts, but which at the same time rely on elements of real experience which can be critically reconstructed, and which can contribute to left-wing analyses and programs. He addresses anticommunism's paralyzing effect on the local left together with the traps Ostalgia presents for new left politics; speaks of nationalist ideology as a means of autocratic and xenophobic politics, yet also a prism through which essential global power relationships become visible in popular politics; and investigates irrationalism as a powerful tool of neoliberal and neonationalist politics, yet also a ground of conflict that makes visible the political usages of reason and the need for the Left to develop a dialectical and self-critical rationality as a basis for its politics.

Without claiming any primacy in the process of the development of East European new left perspectives, we hope that by highlighting regional new left analyses of postsocialist transformation, this book will help strengthen regional and international debates, and contribute to the larger process of conceiving the contemporary crisis as one of a common global history, which can be faced by collective power.

We thank the Transnational Institute for the partnership which made possible the writing of this book, as well as the Rosa Luxemburg Foundation and the European Cultural Foundation for their support of the project at various stages. We are grateful to our internal reviewers, whose deep engagement with the arguments in the chapters made the editing process a constructive debate on its own. In some cases, this process led to co-authorship. Our thanks to those internal reviewers who remained in the background go to Wiktor Marzec, Jana Vargovčíková, Stanislav Holubec, Volodymyr Ishchenko, Albana Shala, Goran Musić, Madlen Nikolova, Ilya Budraitskis, and Gal Kirn. Finally, we are equally thankful to the editors of the Palgrave International Political Economy series and our anonymous reviewers for their thoughtful comments and support.

References

Ban, C. (2016). *Ruling ideas: How global neoliberalism goes local*. Oxford University Press.

Barša, P. (2020). Trapped in false antitheses: Timothy Snyder's analyses of the global authoritarian turn are crippled by his anti-totalitarian framework. *Czech Journal of International Relations, 55*(2), 47–64.

Boatcă, M. (2006). Semiperipheries in the world-system: Reflecting Eastern European and Latin American experiences. *Journal of World-Systems Research, 12*(2), 321–346.

Bockman, J. (2011). *Markets in the name of socialism: The left-wing origins of neoliberalism*. Stanford University Press.

Böröcz, J. (1992). Dual dependency and property vacuum. *Theory and Society, 21*(1), 77–104.

Buden, B. (2010). Children of postcommunism. *Radical Philosophy, 159*, 18–25.

Cardoso, F. H., & Faletto, E. (1979). *Dependency and development in Latin America*. University of California Press.

Cianetti, L., Dawson, J., & Hanley, S. (2018). Rethinking "democratic backsliding" in Central and Eastern Europe–looking beyond Hungary and Poland. *East European Politics, 34*(3), 243–256.

Cucu, A. S. (2019). *Planning labour: Time and the foundations of industrial socialism in Romania* (Vol. 32). Berghahn.

Dale, G. (Ed.). (2011). *First the transition, then the crash: Eastern Europe in the 2000s*. Pluto.

Djagalov, R. (2020). *From Internationalism to Postcolonialism: Literature and Cinema Between the Second and the Third Worlds*. MQUP.

Dolenec, D. (2013). *Democratic institutions and authoritarian rule in Southeast Europe*. ECPR Press.

Drahokoupil, J. (2009). *Globalization and the state in Central and Eastern Europe: The politics of foreign direct investment*. Routledge.

Eyal, G., Szelényi, I., Szelényi, I., & Townsley, E. R. (1998). *Making capitalism without capitalists: Class formation and elite struggles in post-communist Central Europe*. Verso.

Gabor, D. (2010). *Central banking and financialization: A Romanian account of how Eastern Europe became subprime*. Springer.

Greskovits, B. (2015). The hollowing and backsliding of democracy in East Central Europe. *Global Policy, 6*(1), 28–37.

Horvat, S., & Stiks, I. (Eds.). (2015). *Welcome to the desert of post-socialism: Radical politics after Yugoslavia*. Verso.

Kagarlitsky, B. (2008). *Empire of the Periphery: Russia and the World System*. Pluto Press.

Kalb, D., & Halmai, G. (Eds.). (2011). *Headlines of nation, subtexts of class: Working class populism and the return of the repressed in neoliberal Europe*. Berghahn.

Kiossev, A. (1999). Notes on self-colonising cultures. In B. Pejic, & D. Elliott, (Eds.), After the wall: art and culture in post-communist Europe. *Moderna museet*, 114–117.

Kirn, G. (2019). *Partisan ruptures, self-management, market reform and the spectre of socialist Yugoslavia*. Pluto.

Krausz, T. (2015). *Reconstructing Lenin: An intellectual biography*. NYU Press.

Krastev, I., & Holmes, S. (2019). *The light that failed: A reckoning*. Penguin UK.

Kubik, J. (2013). From transitology to contextual holism: A theoretical trajectory of postcommunist studies. In J. Kubik & A. Lunch (Eds.), *Postcommunism from within: Social justice, mobilization, and hegemony* (pp. 27–94). NYU Press.

Kumral, S., & Karatasli, S. S. (2020). Capital, labour and the global populist radical right. *Global Labour Journal, 11*(2), 152–155.

Lampland, M. (1995). *The object of labor: Commodification in socialist Hungary*. University of Chicago Press.

Madariaga, A. (2020). *Neoliberal Resilience: Lessons in Democracy and Development from Latin America and Eastern Europe*. Princeton University Press.

Mark, J., Iacob, B., Rupprecht, T., & Spakovska, L. (2019). 1989. *A global history of Eastern Europe*. Cambridge University Press.

Melegh, A. (2006). *On the East-West slope: Globalization, nationalism, racism and discourses on Eastern Europe*. Central European University Press.

Mikuš, M. (2018). *Frontiers of civil society: Government and hegemony in Serbia*. Berghahn.

Močnik, R. (2019). What is New in New Forms of Nationalism? The case of Hungary. In Vladimir Milisavljević & Natalija Mićunović (Eds.), *Xenophobia, identity and new forms of nationalism*. Institute of Social Sciences.
Ost, D. (2005). *The defeat of solidarity: Anger and politics in postcommunist Europe*. Cornell University Press.
Pixová, M. (2020). *Contested Czech cities: From urban grassroots to pro-democratic populism*. Palgrave.
Przeworski, A. (1991). *Democracy and the market: Political and economic reforms in Eastern Europe and Latin America*. Cambridge University Press.
Rupnik, J. (2007). Is East-Central Europe backsliding? From democracy fatigue to populist backlash. *Journal of Democracy, 18*(4), 17–25.
Scheiring, G. (2020). The retreat of liberal democracy: Authoritarian capitalism and the accumulative state in Hungary.
Shields, S. (2014). *The international political economy of transition*. Routledge.
Sowa, J. (2018). Populism or capitalist de-modernization at the semi-periphery: The case of Poland. *Nonsite,* 23. https://nonsite.org/populism-or-capitalist-de-modernization-at-the-semi-periphery/. Accessed 1 February 2021.
Streeck, W. (2014). *Buying time: The delayed crisis of democratic capitalism*. Verso.
Szalai, E. (2005). *Socialism: An analysis of its past and future*. Central European University Press.
Szombati, K. (2018). *The revolt of the provinces: Anti-gypsyism and right-wing politics in Hungary*. Berghahn.
Tamás, G. M. (2000). On Post-Fascism: How citizenship is becoming an exclusive privilege. *Boston Review, 25*(3), 42.
Todorova, M. (2009). *Imagining the Balkans*. Oxford University Press.
Trencsényi, B., Janowski, M., Baár, M., Falina, M., Lisjak-Gabrijelčic, L., & Kopeček, M. (2018). History of Modern Political Thought in East Central Europe. Volume II/1: Negotiating Modernity in the "Short Twentieth Century and Beyond (1968–2018). Oxford University Press.
Unkovski-Korica, V. (2016). *The economic struggle for power in Tito's Yugoslavia: From World War II to non-alignment*. Bloomsbury Publishing.
Verdery, K. (2003). *The vanishing hectare: Property and value in postsocialist Transylvania*. Cornell University Press.
Yurchenko, Y. (2018). *Ukraine and the empire of capital: From marketisation to armed conflict*. Pluto Press.

Life in Transition and in Crisis. The Political Autobiography of a Generation

Dana Domşodi and Florin Poenaru

The original impetus for this text came when we realized during one of our conversations, sometime around the thirtieth anniversary of the 1989 events, that this period of time largely overlaps with most of our lives (we were both born in the early 1980s). What appeared to be an abstract and indefinite historical period—the transition after 1989 of the central and eastern European countries—that constituted the fulcrum of our research and writing in the past decade, in keeping with the preoccupation of an entire academic field of study, took on a different meaning. Transition was in fact our life or, to put it differently, we have lived our lives so far in transition. Hence, thinking back to the last 30 years of post-Communism and further back to the last decade of Communism took a very (auto)biographical turn. In this text we want to give a sense of

D. Domşodi
Faculty of Sociology and Social Work, Babes-Bolyai University, Cluj-Napoca, Romania
e-mail: Dana.domsodi@ubbcluj.ro

F. Poenaru (✉)
Department of Sociology and Social Work, University of Bucharest, Bucharest, Romania
e-mail: florin.poenaru@unibuc.ro

A. Gagyi and O. Slačálek (eds.), *The Political Economy of Eastern Europe 30 years into the 'Transition'*, International Political Economy Series,
https://doi.org/10.1007/978-3-030-78915-2_2

this (auto)biographical prism; to reflect on the historical transformations leading up to and after 1989 from our perspective as subjects and objects of these transformations.

Wright Mills (1959) described the sociological imagination as the ability to understand together the life of an individual and the history of society. Otherwise, seen in isolation from each other, we either get methodological individualism, (or, even worse, psychologism), or abstract empiricism. Mills' argument is compelling and biography and history should come together in order to understand trajectories, social formations and structuring structures in historical motion. This is what we intend to do in this text. In order to do so, we want to bring to the fore the sociological category of "generation". We believe it to be a theoretical and empirical device that responds to Mills' call to avoid the twin traps of simple biographization and abstraction.

However, at the same time, we are fully aware how fraught with contradictions, misunderstandings and loaded significance this term is. What constitutes a generation? What are its boundaries? Is the concept of generation inevitably bounded with big events (the first and second world wars, 1968, 1989) or, more problematically, linked to age, that is biological benchmarks of development (18 years, 21 years and so on)? Moreover, this term was further brought into disrepute as a sociological concept when it entered mainstream media debates, especially in the US, with the occasion of the so-called "generational war" between the "boomers" and the "millennials". Even the names of the respective generations are as contested as they are problematic.[1]

We want to signal, from the outset, that we have no intention to engage in these debates here. Our focus is elsewhere, namely to describe a "structure of feeling"[2] that emerges from complex historical transformations and is common to a generation of people born in the last decade of Communism in Romania. One might call them the "Communist millennials" or "the last Romanian Communist generation",[3] but irrespective

[1] See the key text for this orientation, Howe, N.,Strauss, W. 2000. *Millennials rising. The great next generation.* New York: Vintage Books.

[2] A term coined by Raymond Williams (1977).

[3] The "last soviet generation" is a term introduced by Alexei Yurchak to describe the experiences of Soviet citizens born between the 1950s and early 1970s. Hence, both in terms of temporality and conception our understanding is different. We refer to the last

of the name, they share the fact that they came of age in the turbulent 1990s and began their mature lives with the new millennium.

In our understanding of "generation" we take a cue from Karl Mannheim (1952). He wrote that belonging to a generation is similar to occupying a class position. Both entail a form of objective localization, and both are structurally inevitable. Belonging to a class entails a form of situatedness in an economic structure, while belonging to a generation means a particular location in the historical time in which social processes unfold. To belong to a generation, just as to belong to a class, entails a particular predisposition towards a series of experiences, lived moments, events and affective structures. They are simultaneously subjective and collective, individual and shared.

Moreover, for Mannheim, belonging to a generation is intimately linked to a problem of social knowledge. To occupy a certain position in historical time delineates the type of historical experiences and the kind of embodied knowledge available by virtue of this particular positioning. It is not at all a form of biological reduction (certain events are understandable only by those who lived them), but a way of saying that the position from which we experience and live through historical time fundamentally structures the way we feel, understand and value the events we live through.

At the same time, we do not want to jettison differences of social class, gender, education, geographical location, profession, etc. of the members of the generation. Rather we want to highlight the fact that these determinations are themselves situated in a particular historical time and have more (or less) relevance particularly in relation to this historical time. To put it differently, it is one thing to be born in a rural family in southern Romania in the 1950s and completely another to be born in a similar family at the end of the 1980s. The historical trajectories and historical experiences will be completely different.

By bringing to the fore the concept of generation, our real focus becomes then a broader historical sequence (early 1980s to the present) rather than disparate events. We look at broader forces and outcomes, and seek to notice how they reflect on and interlace with concrete biographies, sometimes in unexpected configurations and with unforeseen outcomes. This brings us back to Mannheim. For him, generations are produced

Communist generation in order to speak about people roughly born in the last decade of Romanian Communism, during its terminal decline. See Yurchak (2006).

in fact by "dynamic destabilization", that is rapid historical changes and ruptures. A new generation emerges "as a result of an acceleration in the tempo of social and cultural transformation, basic attitudes must change so quickly that the latent, continuous adaptation and modification of traditional patterns of experience, thought and expression is no longer possible" (1952: 309). This gives rise to a new generational style or a new "generational entelechy". What enables us to speak of the generation is precisely the destabilization brought about by the historical sequence we analyze here.

But we start with a detour. We begin by discussing Ivan Krastev and Stephen Holmes volume (2019) in which they try to explain why liberalism failed in central and eastern Europe in the subsequent decades after 1989. We remain unconvinced by their argument and this gives us the opportunity to put forward our own understanding of communism and post-communism. However, we believe the book has merit because it puts its finger on something we also share among ourselves and with our generational peers: an immense feeling of disillusion and disenchantment with our society and our lives 30 years after 1989.

Krastev and Holmes focus on how this feeling derives from the crisis of global liberalism, which, in turn, gave rise to illiberalism, and the reign of the extreme-right in contemporary central and eastern Europe. By contrast, we argue that in fact the reason is to be found in a series of overlapping and continuing crises that fundamentally shaped the trajectory of the world in the past 30 to 40 years. They were especially transformative for the post-Communist subjects who are now in their early to late thirties. Also in contrast to Krastev and Holmes' pessimistic view that blankets central and eastern Europe as a right-wing illiberal inferno, we highlight precisely how members of our generation have been engaged in intellectual and political projects that contest liberalism with a view to rearticulate a radical left-wing alternative.[4] The generational experience was salient in this regard. While we make our arguments in relation to Romania, the site of our research and lived experiences, we know from our interactions that we in fact describe a shared phenomenon across the former Communist

[4] Keir Milburn similarly, and quite tellingly, overlooks this aspect in his investigation of the rise of a new generation of left-wing movements and activists. He sees this trend only pertaining to the West (US, UK and Spain) whereas eastern Europe is, mistakenly, reduced to cohort of youngsters who vote for the extreme right. See Milburn (2019).

space so much so that in fact we can talk of a transnational generational experience that is still unfolding.

The Failure of 1989

Krastev and Holmes aim to reflect on the 30 years since 1989. They specifically want to examine what happened in the past three decades that post-Communist central and eastern European countries abandoned the quest for Western liberal democracy and embraced instead illiberalism, authoritarianism and nativism. Their starting point is the failure of the 1989 revolutions. Hence, they ask: "So, what kind of failure was the revolution of 1989, given that its aim was Western-style normality? To what extent was the liberal and therefore imitative revolution of 1989 responsible for the illiberal counter-revolution unleashed two decades later?" (2019: 90). For the two authors the problem is all the more serious since thinking about the failed 1989 revolutions is in fact a challenge to "think[ing] about a world onto which a high tide of illiberal and anti-democratic 'anarchy' has now been so ominously loosed" (2019: 17). What initially appeared to be only a central or eastern European affliction is indeed more global in scope. In fact, the underlining concern of the volume is to grasp how liberalism—the winner of the Cold War and the undisputed ideological orientation after 1989—ended up a victim of its own success. In short, their aim is to understand how the light that guided the second half of the twentieth century, and the first decade of the post-Communist period, has failed—as alluded to in the title of the book.

Their answer is encapsulated in the manner in which they formulate the problem. Liberalism gave rise to illiberalism precisely because of its success. Emerging as the uncontested ideology of the post-Cold War world, liberalism lacked any alternative, the famous "there is no alternative" (TINA) popularized by Thatcher. It was the dominant global ideological and political force, spearheaded by the triumphant West, the United States in particular, and regarded as the embodiment of the unipolar new world. Initially, central and eastern Europeans willingly imitated liberalism, hoping to transform their societies according to its principles. But to Western eyes, the copy was always imperfect. They kept failing. Their genuine attempts not only to copy, but also to become like the original never materialized.

In addition, the authors argue, the uncontested supremacy of Western-imposed liberalism after 1989 resembled closely the lack of alternative to the Communist ideology imposed from Moscow before the regime change—a different kind of imposition, to be sure, but an imposition nonetheless. Central and eastern Europeans wanted to have their own voice, to discover their own identity. Moreover, inherent in liberalism is the lack of sensibility to local identities and histories. It is global and cosmopolitan, and hence oblivious to any particular features and to any forms of local solidarities. The elites that profess it have no allegiance except to the liberal ideology itself. This is precisely the terrain, Krastev and Holmes argue, where illiberalism in the region thrives. The illiberal ideology seeks to bring back a sense of national pride and a form of rootedness able to resist the deracinating effects of a globalized and uncontested liberalism.

But there is more to it. Because it has no allegiance except to the global sphere, post-Communist liberalism leaves countries defenseless. The migrant crisis of 2015 is a case in point for the illiberal movement. But, in the eyes of the illiberals, the West appears to have lost its way more generally, and earlier than that. Gay marriages, atheism, lack of national identity, etc. are seen as sins that uncontested global liberalism have brought upon the West itself. Once a beacon of hope for the post-Communist central and eastern Europeans, the West appears now inevitably on a path of great decline. Paradoxically, illiberalism appears a form of defense of the West itself from its own liberal decadence.

After the terrain is cleared regarding central and eastern European illiberalism, the two authors go on to explain the trajectories of Russia, USA and China after 1989 in the same mold—that is, as various responses to the uncontested triumph of global liberalism. In short, all these countries developed sui generis forms of illiberal and authoritarian reactions to the liberal post-Cold War dominance that explain their current political configurations and paradoxes.

The analysis offered by Krastev and Holmes has considerable merits. First, it puts its finger on something important when it links the rise of central and eastern European illiberalism to a form of resentment towards the West and to the outcomes of globalization in the past 30 years. Secondly, they are right to see in Orbán and his ilk precursors of kindred phenomena unfolding elsewhere, particularly in Trump's USA and Bolsonaro's Brazil. Always considered backward and forced to catch-up, the region has in fact been in the forefront of the rise of right-wing contestation to global liberalism, at least in the recent period. Finally, the authors are right to see in Putin's policies, especially in the annexation of Crimea, a form of reaction to unfolding global turbulence, and not a type of aggressive imperialism redolent of nineteenth century Tsarist ambitions.

These merits are, however, seriously undermined by the authors' theoretical and methodological choices. They explicitly anchor the analysis in psychology: "The rise of authoritarian chauvinism and xenophobia in central and eastern Europe has its origins in political psychology not political theory". (2019: 286) Consequently, for them, countries become actors with agency and feelings. They feel compelled to imitate, they have inferiority complexes, are revanchist, feel defenseless and react with disgust. Elites with certain characteristics might drag these countries in various directions, but we never learn anything of substance about them. Instead we get psychological snippets derived from biographical sketches of the main culprits, most notably Orbán, Putin, Trump and Xi. Hungary, Russia, United States and China appear synecdoche of their leaders and entirely under their spells.

Throughout the book it is not at all clear if the authors talk about countries or simply about the people that currently rule them and their peculiar biographies and psychologies. Broader social relations, conflicting groups and interests, historical trajectories, classes, institutions and a whole number of other social actors, structural determinants and historical facts are completely absent from their narrative and analysis. Methodological nationalism makes impossible the link to global phenomena and other transnational movements. Even though the two authors regard illiberalism as a more general phenomenon, nonetheless its manifestation takes place within national borders. Societies under the spell of illiberalism appear homogeneous, as if all members participate the same in this political articulation or have equal power.

This fundamentally vitiates the analysis, and it presents illiberalism as the result of yet another failure of the central and eastern Europeans who became fatigued trying to copy liberalism. The idea might appear new in English-speaking academia, but we remember it from our youth in the 1990s. Then Romanian anti-Communist intellectuals similarly blamed the inability of the people for the failure to copy Western institutions and values at a faster rate. They did not use the term illiberalism but crypto-communism to describe the phenomenon of abandoning global liberalism in favor of national retrenchment. People were blamed for being too immature to understand and implement liberalism. Of course, the Romanian intellectuals did not seek to make an analysis; their diagnostic was rooted in very concrete political and class struggles. Krastev and Holmes try to be analytical but at the same time they take for granted and leave unpacked what "illiberalism" actually means, and what it actually does in practice. Is it really the most suitable term to describe the obvious general disenchantment with liberalism after 30 years of post-Communism?

We believe not, and part of the problem is that Krastev and Holmes still employ an "imitative" understanding of the 1989 moment that Jürgen Habermas made fashionable in the 1990s. According to this narrative, what characterizes the 1989 revolutions is an attempt of the central and eastern European countries to "return" to the West, to be reintegrated into its orbit. To do so, they had to get rid of the old institutions and habits and by way of mimetic learning replace them with Western ones. Experts called in to oversee the process would measure progress. They would distribute rewards and punishments according to benchmarks. Krastev and Holmes continue this line of thinking and consider illiberalism as central and eastern Europeans' fatigue and frustration with this mechanism, coupled with fatigue and frustration with liberalism in the West itself. Hence, we are still in the transitology paradigm of post-Communism, only that this time the West itself seems to be afflicted by eastern European ills.

In contrast to Krastev and Holmes, we subscribe to a different approach regarding communism and post-Communism that is rooted in historical materialism and class analysis. Instead of simply seeing post-Communism as a set of radical (neo)liberal transformations of the former Communist states, and hence continue to employ a linear framework of analysis centered around key political moments and actors, we look at post-communism (and "transition") as a political-ideological and cultural formation that is generated, and which, in turn, obfuscates more complex and "longue durée" socioeconomic rearrangements and struggles.

We embed the Communist experience in the wider dynamics of modernity and capitalism in central and eastern Europe in the past three centuries.[5] Also, rather than seeing Communism as a distinct historical period with salient features and bounded margins—as many of the key

[5] A similar effort was employed by Andrew Janos, though we diverge from his perspective since we are indebted to a historical materialist understanding. See Janos (2000).

texts of the transitology paradigm have done (e.g. Dunn, 2004) —we adopt a view that links it to the global experience of capitalism in the second part of the twentieth century (e.g. Arrighi, 2010; Friedman & Friedman, 2008; Kalb, 2005). The case of Romanian Communism is symptomatic here, since its crisis is inextricably linked with the crisis of post-war capitalism, as we will detail below.

Moreover, we regard historical development as driven by the formation, consolidation and struggles of classes and class segments. In contrast to the totalitarian paradigm that reduces the experience of communism to a conflict between the party and the people,[6] we understand communism as essentially structured by class conflicts (Brucan, 1990). Communism produced not only waged industrial laborers out of impoverished peasants but also a class of technical and humanist intelligentsia. The interplay of these classes and the mediation of the Party nomenklatura fundamentally shaped the post-war history of the Communist regimes with important consequences prior to and especially after 1989 (Hopkins & Wallerstein, 1996). Therefore, what collapsed in 1989 was not what is generically called Communism but the particular form of the Party-State, a political device aimed at centralizing power in order to quickly modernize and industrialize the peripheral and agrarian societies of central and eastern Europe (Lazarus, 2007). What enables us to see class as central, beyond a theoretical conviction, are our own lived experiences in Romania since the 1980s, to which will come back in this text.

This theoretical perspective has important consequences also for the manner in which we regard the post-1989 period, the so-called transition. Rather than emphasizing breaks, we look at continuities, particularly in terms of class trajectories and historical becoming. We believe that the post-Communist transition is the continuation of the class struggle already shaping communism, this time in a context fully connected to global patterns of capital accumulation and in the absence of the Party-State (Derluguian, 2005).

At the same time we diverge from mainstream interpretations of the transition that consider it a moment of embracing Western capitalism and market relations after the Communist experience, in a context dominated by (neo)liberalism—as Krastev and Holmes clearly do.[7] Rather, we

[6] There is a vast literature here, but see the classic Arendt (1973).

[7] Examples abound here, but see Mandel and Humphrey (2002).

maintain that the Communist experience was already capitalist in nature and thoroughly linked to global capitalist dynamics well before 1989 (cf. Chase-Dunn, 1982). This in turn allows us to illustrate that explanations of neoliberalism, such as those offered by David Harvey, are important but of limited relevance since they remain too centered on the Western experience, and lack a proper understanding of eastern European communism in the global dynamics of capitalism (Harvey, 2005).

Instead of employing the term transition, with its aforementioned bias towards integration, mimicry and "return to the West", we highlight three overlapping crises of the world in the past 40 or so years that fundamentally shaped the Communist and post-Communist experience and thus the biographical trajectory of people living their lives in these overlapping crises. We discuss them below and some of their radical consequences.

Three Overlapping Crises

1. Accumulation and profit in the capitalist world

This history is well known and well researched so we will only sketch it here. Sometime in the early 1970s, the foundations of the post-war world economy began to alter significantly. The US denunciation of Bretton Woods in 1971, and the first oil crisis in 1973, were events signaling that the previous post-second world war order was collapsing. This was a seismic event, and we can still feel the reverberations half a century later. As it turned out, there were in fact two crises coming together at the same time, one immediate; the other one rooted in longue durée transformations.

The immediate one was a crisis of accumulation in the core of the capitalist system. The postwar military Keynesianism that stabilized western Europe and other parts of the world under the aegis of the American superpower reached its growth limits. The capitalist class began to see its profit margins collapse, and without much room available for extensive expansion within the traditional boundaries of the nation-state, it sought to move to places more amenable to higher rates of profit. The historical conditions were ripe because much of the global South at the time had a huge reservoir of peasants and sub-proletarians willing to transfer into regular industrial jobs at a fraction of what blue-collar workers earned in the developed economies of the West.

This immediately set in motion a race to the bottom between states, in order to attract the floating capital through intertwined incentives: low taxes and a cheap and disciplined workforce. It also pitted the global proletariat against itself. Competition superseded class solidarities and transnational alliances. The overall effect was the stagnation of real wages, if not their suppression across the globe.

This process, with its attendant consequences, has become known as neoliberalism—a term that has been so misused and overstretched as to become quite ineffectual as an explanatory concept. Irrespective of the name, however, the process was successful and throughout the 1980s and 1990s large global corporations (many of them truly stateless and state-like in size) began to accumulate unprecedented amounts of wealth. Despite occasional recessions, these two decades were a golden age for capital, especially for those at the top. This was the moment when inequality levels began to grow, leading to the staggering figures we witness today. In the short term, the capitalist class was having a bonanza.

But neoliberalism was a short-term fix to a short-term crisis. The longue durée crisis was more formidable, less apparent and therefore harder to solve. In fact, it remains unsolved until today. The accumulation crisis of the 1970s overlapped with a more enduring one: a profitability crisis. For over a century (following the great crisis of 1873) the rate of profit for invested capital continued to drop, despite some temporary upturns, and by the turn of the millennium they were expressed in single digits (Carchedi & Roberts, 2018).

The capitalist class blamed this on the workers and on state expenditure—that is, on the feeble, largely authoritarian and deeply imperialistic arrangement after the second world war, devised, largely, to expand US military and economic hegemony globally. As mentioned earlier, neoliberalism was the short-term attempt to solve the issue and it worked briefly. But the decline of profits (and of the Atlantic hegemony, more generally) was a systemic and secular crisis and not (merely) a post-war phenomenon. Neoliberalism worked in the short term with the well-known consequences for workers and state budgets, and significantly enriched parts of the capitalist class via the direct transfers of capital it stimulated. But profitability continued to remain low. Investment in production yielded meager returns. The response to this structural crisis was a well-known trick in the capitalist textbook: financialization (Arrighi, 2007).

This should not be confused with neoliberalism, as it usually has been. It is an entirely different sort of response. Faced with declining rates of profit for invested capital, the capitalist (or to be more precise, the capitalist enterprise) avoids investment altogether and instead seeks to make money through money (the famous relationship C—C' in Marx's framework). This entails a series of opaque mechanisms to maximize profits, which fundamentally rests on the ability to speculate on future gains. The 2008 crisis was generated by such speculative mechanisms that came tumbling down when the bubble they usually create burst. But this did not put an end to financialization and a restart of investment in production. Far from it! Paradoxically, the response of the states, under pressure from the capitalist class, was simply to throw even more cheap money into the system in order to save illiquid banks (Streeck, 2014). This maneuver simply created even more incentives for capitalist enterprises to try to make money from money, since there was so much of it floating around. Who needs the hassle of productive investment when speculating on future price increases can yield greater profits? This longue durée crisis of profitability is far from over, hence financial crises are certain to occur regularly and in shorter cycles.

The overlap between the short and longue durée crises, and the capitalistic responses to it, engendered a global turbulence, uprooting previous arrangements and setting in motion new trajectories and structural pressures (Brenner, 2006). The two crises converged in the 1980s, as an outcome of economic and political events in the 1970s that accelerated already existing tendencies. Hence the 1980s represented the decade in which both neoliberalism and financialization magnified and became the de facto policies of the capitalist class (as expressed by the Thatcher and Reagan regimes) and they remained so, at a global scale, albeit in different configurations, at least until the financial crisis of 2008.

2. The global roots of the communist crisis

Inside the Communist space, this global crisis overlapped with an internal one: the exhaustion of developmentalism led by the political monopoly of the Communist Parties. This did not happen overnight—as the fixation with 1989 suggests. Instead, it was a complex and protracted process, with unforeseen and contradictory outcomes.

To begin with, it would be a theoretical and historical mistake to consider the Communist bloc as something radically different from the capitalist world. Although differences obviously existed between the West and the East (or between the North and South), the socialist East was inextricably part of the post-war global economic system, which was capitalistic in nature. Ideologically, the USSR and its satellites might have presented themselves as an alternative to capitalism, and even, in very limited cases, as anti-capitalist. In practice, however, they were as much part of the same system and, as such, equally prone to being affected by its turbulences and crises.

The political monopoly that the Communist Parties enjoyed over the economy and society enabled them to absorb the pressures differently, and to postpone the moment when they had to deal with them properly. The crisis of the system predated the actual fall of these regimes by at least a decade, if not more. A cocktail of factors such as inertia, repression and central planning averted the inevitable dénouement, at the expense of economic and societal degradation. The Communist regimes collapsed like houses of cards, despite the apparent total control and hegemony the Parties enjoyed. In fact, the internal structures of the state, economy and society were irremediably fissured. They could not cope either with the internal pressures for continued economic growth and reform, or with the external pressures of a global economy undergoing fundamental transformations.

This does not mean that these regimes were unsuccessful. Despite the ideological confusion surrounding these regimes, what they sought to do in practice—and largely achieved—was to speedily develop the agrarian countries of eastern Europe (and of the global South) in the immediate aftermath of the second world war, based on a model coined in the USSR in the 1930s. Variations obviously existed according to local circumstances, but by and large these regimes were really successful in the 1950s and 1960s in temporarily closing the development gap between the West and the East. Heavy industry, mass employment, urbanization, large-scale infrastructure construction and significant social welfare were some of the key features and achievements of these regimes. This severely altered the social landscape of the societies involved and led to the formation, just one generation after the second world war, of radically new social relations, institutions and lifestyles.

However, by the 1970s this model, in most of the Communist countries, was already in crisis. The causes were both internal—largely an exhaustion of the growth rates based on continuous heavy industrial expansion—and external—the aforementioned changes in the global capitalist economy. In addition, the beginning of delocalization of industry from the West undercut the competitive advantages the Communist states enjoyed: their cheap and disciplined labor force couldn't really compete with that of workers in the global South. As companies in the West diminished their costs of production through relocation, the Communist regimes faced increasing costs for labor and resources. Their global competitiveness dropped, and they began to face problems even properly meeting internal demands. Add to this the oil crises of the 1970s and the inflationary pressures they produced; the sudden exhaustion of cheap credit once the US Federal Reserve increased its interest rates at the end of the 1970s; and the technological obsolescence of their industries that by the 1970s was endemic and cumbersome, and it becomes immediately clear why the Communist regimes were in big trouble long before 1989.

After the second world war, the development of communism in Romania followed the general Soviet route of extensive development: the collectivization of agricultural land and the nationalization and expansion of heavy industry. There was enough room for expansion, due to the backward nature of the agricultural economy and the heavy destruction brought about by war.

At the beginning of the 1960s, however, a new trajectory emerged, shaped concomitantly by local pressures and global opportunities. Romania had to export most of its products to the USSR as part of war reparations. This slowed down its post-war development, and subordinated it to the USSR for technology and industrial products. Moreover, the Soviet plans for organizing the division of labor within the Council for Mutual Economic Assistance (CMEA)—usually known as Comecon—envisaged Romania as a producer of raw agricultural goods. In fact, this entailed the continued subordination of local agriculture to Soviet interests, a fact displeasing to the Romanian Communists who sought to modernize the country along industrial lines, and thus justify their monopoly of power. These plans pushed the Romanian Communists away from the Soviet interests and towards an independent policy. But this was done in line with, not against, the Soviet industrializing blueprint. In practice, the Romanians embarked upon the pathway of heavy industrialization and production of capital-intensive goods.

In order to secure capital for its development plans, in 1971 Romania joined GATT, and in 1972 it was the first Eastern Bloc country to join the IMF and the World Bank. Concomitantly, it rebranded itself as a "developing country", seeking preferential treatment from both the West and global South, and a status akin to that of the non-aligned countries. This realignment entailed important shifts in the economy. Western companies were allowed to open joint ventures in the country, and by 1974 Romania was trading more with Western countries than with its counterparts in the Communist world.

By and large, the Romanian industrialization plan worked, so that in 1989 manufacturing accounted for more than 50 percent of GDP, employing half of the working force (Ban, 2012: 752–753). The country had one of the biggest industrial growth rates on the continent, industrial production being 44 times higher in 1989 than in 1950, while in the process the industrial working force grew fourfold (Ban, 2012: 752–753). This "industrial spurt" led to the creation of heavy industry, especially energy-intensive ones, such as steel and petrochemical refineries.

Romania was only minimally affected by the 1973 oil crisis, mainly because it was able to rely on its domestic oil supplies. While as a result of the crisis exports to the Western countries declined, it could reorient exports and seal barter agreements with oil-rich countries in the Persian Gulf. Also, the availability of dollars from the oil-producing countries in the international financial markets allowed access to cheap credits circulated through Western banks, and used for financing further industrial developments, especially in the petrochemical industry which grew exponentially. Higher prices for crude oil meant even higher prices for refined products, the planners of the economy thought. The regime therefore gambled on oil.

However, for most of the 1970s, even though the interest rates were low, Romania was cautious of incurring too much debt. But the pressures exerted by the second oil crisis of 1979 forced the government into extensive borrowing in order to be able to maintain the supply of oil to its petrochemical industry. While at the beginning of the 1970s, Romania was an exporter of oil, by the end of the decade it was transformed into an importing country, due to the expansion of the refining sector. In 1980, the Romanian industry required 16 million tons of oil compared to five million in 1975 (Ban, 2012: 757). But the oil crisis overlapped with a financial crisis, largely triggered by the increase of interest rates on sovereign debt, which signaled a reorientation towards financial speculation for profit accumulation in the Western core countries.

At first, the regime turned towards IMF for help, signing a three-year agreement in 1981. The main goal of the agreement was to improve the efficiency of the Romanian economy. Already in 1979, the new economic policies introduced by the Party sought to reorient production towards value-added targets rather than simply quantitative outputs, trying to address the pressing question of stockpiling in certain sectors. The IMF program aimed at making state enterprises less dependent on the state budget and function on a profit-based logic, within and outside the country, while making them more responsible for capital allocation and investment. The logic behind these "structural adjustment" plans was that by making state enterprises more sensitive to world market relations, their productivity would increase and they would be able to accumulate capital at a faster pace.

In 1984, however, Ceauşescu decided not to renew the agreement with the IMF and embarked instead on a sui generis austerity program. The main reason for this decision was political. By following the IMF policies, the Party was losing its grip on production in favor of market mechanisms. This ran the risk of generating centrifugal reactions and fragmenting political power, especially in favor of the technical intelligentsia.

The austerity program entailed massive cuts in domestic consumption and curtailed virtually all imports. Capital investment was now directed towards debt repayment, which negatively affected the industrial output. In each of the last five years of the Communist regime, industrial production decreased by 1.5 percent, leading to an all-time low in 1989, when the economy shrank by five percent.

The country's advantage of having a cheap, skilled and disciplined work force that could produce cheap products for export was undercut by the technological inferiority of industry, and compounded during the austerity measures by the need to rely on import substitution, which made its products less attractive to foreign markets. In addition, the internal market was too small to compensate for the lack of exports, and—crucially—it could not generate the necessary dollars needed to repay the debts, and buy more technology and energy resources. While the goal of debt repayment was largely achieved, it came at the price of an economy in ruins and a shattered society. The attempt to brutally and radically cut the country off from the global financial flows and credit dependency proved elusive, and ended in disaster, with the regime soon collapsing.

In striving for fast industrialization, what the Communist Party seemed to disregard was the global capitalist context in which it operated, and the fundamentally capitalist nature of the industrialization program. In this context, the economy of the country could not be simply sealed off at will within the national borders and instead remained highly dependent on global capital and vulnerable to its crises and transformations. The gamble on oil failed due to a combination of factors, but most importantly it showed how closely Romania was linked with, and "slotted in" (Arrighi, 2010) the global economy and was thus deeply affected by its turbulence since the 1970s.

As mentioned before, we do not want to dismiss the irresolvable internal contradictions of the Communist regimes, but at the same time their collapse was not generated solely by immanent causes. The dual global crisis of capitalism described above also affected the Communist countries, already facing sui generis problems, and accelerated their demise. More than anything else, 1989 constituted the convergence of these crises, which ushered in a new period of integration in the global economy of the former Communist countries in the absence of the Communist Parties, their developmental goals, their ideology and international forms of cooperation. Neoliberalism was prescribed as a panacea for the post-Communist countries simply because it had already become the dominant form of restructuring the world in the 1980s, as a response to a capitalist crisis.

Looking at these historical developments from a generational perspective, a person born in the 1980s, both in the West and in the East, is a person born in the midst of tremendous socioeconomic rearrangements. For an Easterner, the situation is even more complex because the world in which he or she was born is collapsing. We know this firsthand. When we were born, Romania restructured its debt with the creditors and embarked on its homemade austerity program to fully repay the debt. Our childhood unfolded during the bleak years of shortages and decay everybody remembers so well in Romania. The expansionist, modernist, uplifting character of the regime experienced by our parents' generation was a very distant memory at the end of the 1980s. Whatever we still benefited from the early good days of the Communist rule was through our parents' class and symbolic position within the system, although differences tended to be obfuscated because of the austerity. Even typically progressive institutions of the state, like the kindergarten, were for us a traumatic experience because of the overall social decay happening around us. We were too young to fully register the extent of the crisis, or to articulate a fully conscious political attitude against the Party or against Communism more generally, but we were nonetheless socialized from the early age into an environment of crisis and decay.

Transition was met with enthusiasm for a better future, but also with an equal amount of anguish and tension. We distinctly remember tensions within our families regarding the future trajectories, as did our interlocutors. There was a definite awareness that we lived in turbulent times and that the outcome was far from certain or positive. In fact, our initial experience of transition was one of dislocation, and even a downward slide. Initially, the transition period maintained some of the old benefits of Communism, like free and solid schooling, which for us was crucial, since this was our main milieu in the 1990s and the 2000s. But gradually, we understood that we were growing up in a world that was unquestionably defined by competition, profit seeking and accumulation under the aegis of neoliberalism. With no real memory of the old world to offer guidance, and armed only with the sort of practical knowledge offered by the new world, we continued to be defined by the turmoil of transition.

It quickly became clear that Romanian society was being divided along various class lines of contradictory or complicit interests, where some seemed to be absolute winners and others, at best, struggling survivors. The class composition is heterogeneous and complex and it was in constant dynamic in the past 30 years. Nonetheless, it can be sketched like this: a thin capitalist layer in the upper percentiles simultaneously linked to the state and to global capital and their well-paid and relatively privileged professional and political foot soldiers; a consistent mass of lower-middle class producers and employees (in industry or service, state and private sectors) that is partially emancipated from the spiral of low wages, but dependent on a monthly income in order to sustain a credit-based middle-class utopia, with no significant savings, no valuable properties, and with consumption habits and tastes beyond what they objectively can afford. Finally, there is a large of property-les, in short the poor class, living on the minimum wage or even less, some of them owners of their own dwellings, but nothing more.

This last category, of the so-called "losers" of the transition, is constantly either obliterated from public discourse or invoked by it just to be demonized. Members of it lack proper education and health access, and are constantly depicted as the dangéreuse "other", a social enemy of sorts, bearing the class guilt of poverty. Under the weight of right-wing neoliberal socioeconomic measures, the net of socioeconomic support for vulnerable social categories has basically evaporated under their feet.

From the very beginning, the Romanian transition was a class affair, and here the local version of the enclosure of the commons serves as an argument. For the creation of this capitalist class, the concentration of wealth sitting idle in millions of hands became necessary. Primitive accumulation—or the grand appropriation—took diverse forms, and was possible because a false justifying idea had already taken root in the minds of the newly emancipated Romanians—getting rich by working. This was not completely irrational, given the context of a politically orchestrated process of social pacification. Thus the political constitution of private property took the form of mass allotment, and the creation of a mass of private owners that were ante-festum rewarded for the grand theft of state property that soon followed, and was to have devastating effects on the lives of Romanian people. Basically, everyone was given the chance to buy the apartment in which they were already living, which was supposed to be compensation for the elite feasting on public property they had acquired; from factories and land, to infrastructure and so on.

Hence, our generation was in the unenviable position of growing up and reaching maturity while witnessing these transformations, but without being in a position to influence them in any shape or form. We were too young when Communism fell to be directly involved in its collapse and take an active part in the subsequent rearrangements. By the 2000s, we were already too old not to be affected by the initial transition period, but also, simultaneously too young, to have any meaningful say. We were caught between two worlds, belonging to neither, but at the same time fundamentally shaped by both.

3. A world without the left

From a societal viewpoint, the transition in central and eastern Europe was a full-blown, large-scale social experiment in neoliberalism that was never experienced as such in the West. Also, compared to other parts of the world also ravaged by neoliberal doxa—for example, in Latin America—Russia and eastern Europe were further disadvantaged. They had no protection mechanisms, no tools to fight back. Unlike Latin America, which developed large currents of opposition via a renewed leftist ideology, Russia and eastern Europe went through an intellectual desertification. The left was outlawed and diabolized and "Western integration" was codified as the only viable option. This only exacerbated the scale of the disaster.

This brings us to the third and final overlapping crisis we identify as characteristic for our generation: the global demise of the left in the wake of the collapse of Communism. What started perhaps back in 1968, was exacerbated in 1989 when the fall of the central and eastern European regimes was equated with the definitive demise of any alternative to liberalism, especially one of socialist and radical origins. The left was demonized, and anticommunism became the hegemonic ideology of the transition. In Romania, the Presidential Commission that symbolically condemned Communism prior to the 2007 EU accession orchestrated in fact a wholesale condemnation of left-wing ideas and politics. Krastev and Holmes might wish to investigate the unencumbered role of anticommunism in the affirmation of what they call illiberalism—a glaring omission in their book. The leftist tradition was vilified and censored and so were materialism, empirical study and critical thinking. Anti-intellectualism was a badge of honor after 1989. Inspiration and genius replaced research and arguments. Memory and lived experiences (particularly of right-wing anticommunists) trumped historical facts and accuracy.

We know from experience that a person born after 1980 was immersed from the beginning into a local and global intellectual environment that was structurally averse to the very notion of the left as a legacy of the Enlightenment. If anything it was a perilous legacy that led to the Gulag. How to rearticulate the left in such political and ideological conditions? How to develop a critical stance in relation to the prevailing moral commonplace of the transition period, firmly in trance with neoliberalism, anticommunism and conservative nostalgia for the interwar period? How was a person that was just entering school in the 1990s able to resist socialization within this coordinates? We believe that precisely the generational experience of overlapping crises and the life lived in transitions enabled such a possibility. It thus offers a particular form of leftist subjectivation that so far has remained unnoticed—a fact that our work in general and this volume in particular seek to address.

The post-communist Romania left was not a political or ideological movement. Rather, it was the expression and mobilization of an existential reaction to the everyday life of transition. This affective, highly embodied, profoundly personal and biographical character fundamentally shaped the contours of the emerging leftist field and its inner dynamics, groups and preoccupations.

The Romanian left articulated not in relation to a local leftist tradition (which was feeble if not absent entirely) or to a body of texts but as a critical reflection on events in everyday life. Local left emerged as a critical commentary and thus as a form of resistance against brutal reality.

Thematically, the Romanian left concentrated on two key issues, which defined its emergence: the critique of anti-commuism and labor relations. It makes sense. Anticommunism was the hegemonic ideology of the transition and it does not seek to say something about the communist past. It is a dominant form of interpreting and fixing the past with a view to control the limits of the possible in the present. The leftist critique of anti-communism was only partially geared towards offering a new interpretation of the communist past (although it did that, a fact that is true not only in Romania, but across the post-communist region). Its main aim was to offer the possibility to understand everyday life of the transition beyond the monoglossia of anti-communism and the type of society imagined by it. It was an affirmation of the fact that the capitalist present has to be the object of criticism, just as much as the communist past was. By criticizing anti-communism the left opened the discoursive field for the articulation of a critical discourse in relation to the negative realities of the present, directly experienced by those articulating this critique.

At this point class is essential for the members of this generation that embarked upon the rearticulation of the left. Many come from families strongly linked with industrial production, in various capacities. As this sector was severely affected in postcommunism, the trajectory of these families was marked by severe turbulence. This enlarged the scope of criticism.

The concrete experience of labor, the pressures for earning a living in the capitalist context (with everything that reproduction entails, from wage to housing) solidified the criticism and became the second pillar of an emerging left. The experience of migration (direct or by family members) was also fundamental and strongly linked with labor issues. I refer here also to temporary migration for studying abroad which offered the possibility to connect to critical discourses and leftist experiences from other places which then became essential resources for rearticulating the local left.

The financial crisis deepened the critical stance and offered the image of a rotten capitalist system. This also tempered the triumphalism of anti-communism which ceased to be so powerful after 2010, at least compared to the early period of postsocialism. Between 2010 and 2014 there is an unprecedented opening which leads to the emergence of a genuine postcommunist leftist field populated by mushrooming small groups, in general animated by people born around 1980. It was their moment of affirmation, political subjection and generational clarification.

Conclusion

Keir Milburn (2019) analyzed the protest movement in Western Europe and the USA following the 2008 crisis and he concluded that we can talk of the affirmation of Generation Left. The mobilization against austerity imposed as a response to crisis and, more generally, against the structural conditions that caused it, it signaled the subjectivation moment of a part of a generation that was born in the West together with neoliberalism and that was betrayed by it. But Milburn's analysis is myopic in that he focuses solely on the West. He is not alone in identifying the left solely with the west. A similar situation occurred, perhaps more vividly, around the world, especially in South America, Middle East and Eastern Europe. The economic crisis offered the backdrop in which to articulate a leftist criticism of 40 years of neoliberalism.

In 2009, the twentieth anniversary of the fall of the socialist regimes overlapped with the Great Recession, perhaps the most formidable crisis since the 1970s. This junction enabled a double reconsideration: of socialism and its aftermath—the so-called transition—and of the capitalist system in its speculative and neoliberal guise. It was the moment when a whole generation was able to articulate the socialist experience, and what subsequently happened, as a global and universal history, not simply as a particularity of a certain region with its peculiarities and idiosyncrasies.

Moreover, this was simultaneously a political and intellectual movement. For the first time since the 1960s, perhaps, the East European region witnessed the appearance of groups that were explicitly trying to articulate a leftist, radical critique of both socialism and capitalism, with a view to also formulating radical politics in the present. Admittedly, these groups were small and loose, but bound by a common ethos, and were strongly linked across national and regional borders. They built on previously available political and intellectual resources, both local (scarce as they were) and global (often misunderstanding the eastern European experience as they do), to pierce the hegemonic anticommunism, and to invent a new language and sensibility in which every-day social issues could be addressed. The impact and significance of this political, ideological and theoretical work is yet to be properly grasped. Perhaps one of the reasons is due to the fact that while this work was successful, those who accomplished it failed to gain institutional stability and intellectual hegemony, and instead remained part of the global "proletariat of mental labor", which have to deal with all sorts of precarious life and work arrangements before being able to reflect upon its historical trajectory. It seems to us that this is the next challenge: the articulation of the political (auto)biography of our generation that recognizes its particular location in historical sequence—between the early 1980s and the present—as generation.

This is what we have suggested in this text. A careful reconstruction of the historical and sociological notion of generation can unlock new interpretative avenues that takes into account the dynamics of the post-communist space and the intricate nature of the changes that have unfolded in the past 30 years. It is also a more potent tool to understand the current malaise of the region, and especially the disenchantment of the citizens, beyond the catchy but ultimately hollow concepts such as illiberalism.

References

Arendt, H. (1973). *The origins of totalitarianism*. Harcourt Brace Jovanovich.

Arrighi, G. (2007). *Adam Smith in Beijing. Lineages of the 21st century*. Verso.

Arrighi, G. (2010). *The long twentieth century: Money, power, and the origins of our times*. Verso.

Ban, C. (2012). Sovereign debt, austerity, and regime change: The case of Nicolae Ceausescu's Romania, *East European. Politics and Society, 26*(4), 743–776.

Brenner, R. (2006). *The economics of global turbulence. The Advanced capitalist economies from long boom to long downturn*. Verso.

Brucan, S. (1990). *Pluralism and social conflict: A social analysis of the communist World*. Praeger.

Carchedi, G., & Roberts, M. (Eds.). (2018). *World in crisis. A global analysis of Marx's Law of Profitability*. Haymarket Books.

Chase-Dunn, C. K. (1982). *Socialist States in the World-System*. Sage.

Derluguian, G. M. (2005). *Bourdieu's secret admirer in the Caucasus: A World-System Biography*. University of Chicago Press.
Dunn, E. (2004). *Privatizing Poland: Baby Food, Big Business, and the Remaking of Labor*. Cornell.
Friedman, K., & Friedman, J. (2008). *Modernities, class, and the contradictions of globalization: The anthropology of Global systems*. AltaMira Press.
Harvey, D. (2005). *A Brief History of Neoliberalism*. Oxford University Press.
Hopkins, T, & Wallerstein I. (1996). *The age of transition: Trajectory of the World-System 1945–2025*. Zed Books.
Janos, C. A. (2000). *East Central Europe in the Modern World: The politics of the Borderlands from pre- to postcommunism*. Stanford University Press.
Kalb, D. (2005). From flows to violence: Politics and knowledge in the debates on globalization and empire. *Anthropological Theory*, 5(2), 176–204.
Krastev, I., & S. Holmes. (2019). *The light that failed. Why the West is losing the fight for democracy*. Pegasus Books. Epub format.
Lazarus, S. (2007). *Lenin and the Party, 1902 – November 1917 in Lenin Reloaded: Toward a politics of truth*. Duke University Press.
Mandel, R., & Humphrey. C. (2002.) *Markets and moralities: Ethnographies of postsocialism*. Berg.
Mannheim, K. (1952). *Essays on the sociology of knowledge*. Oxford University Press.
Milburn, K. (2019). *Generation left*. Polity Press. We return to this issue below.
Mills, W. C. (1959). *The sociological imagination*. Oxford University Press.
Streeck, W. (2014). *Buying time. The delayed crisis of democratic capitalism*. Verso.
Williams, R. (1977). *Marxism and literature*. Oxford University Press.
Yurchak, A. (2006). *Everything was forever until it was no more. The last soviet generation*. Princeton University Press.

When Did a Transition to Capitalism Start in Serbia?

Vladimir Simović and Tanja Vukša

Almost thirty years have passed from the moment the Socialist Federative Republic of Yugoslavia (SFRY) disappeared. These three decades are marked by wars and privatization. In fact, the radical change affected all social subsystems—political, economic and cultural. Capitalist relations fully permeated a society once identified as socialist.

Years have passed, but a specter of socialism still haunts the societies established on the ruins of SFRY. For the dominant classes socialism is to be blamed for all that is wrong today. Mainstream political and economic commentators often focus on the past in order to relativize the present crisis.

Economist Milojko Arsić defends the process of privatization and its consequences by emphasizing the already existing bad condition of the collapsed economy. For future economic policies, Arsić argues that:

"It is important to determine when large social enterprises failed and why 400,000 people lost their jobs. Did social enterprises fail because

V. Simović (✉) · T. Vukša
Center for Politics of Emancipation (CPE), Belgrade, Serbia
e-mail: vladimir@cpe.org.rs

T. Vukša
e-mail: tanja@cpe.org.rs

A. Gagyi and O. Slačálek (eds.), *The Political Economy of Eastern Europe 30 years into the 'Transition'*, International Political Economy Series,
https://doi.org/10.1007/978-3-030-78915-2_3

they were already weakened in a fundamentally defective self-management socialist system, and then hit by embargo and the world economic crisis, or did they fail due to the opening of the economy, liberalization and privatization after 2000?" (Milojko, 2019).

For Arsić the answer is obvious: the economy collapsed because of outdated technology and the lack of investment during the 1980s, along with excessive employment that was not "economically justified". Limited economic activity during the 1990s, due to the UN embargo, only further contributed to this collapse.[1]

While some authors try to show that the period of socialist Yugoslavia was problematic both politically and economically, for the many, the picture is not so clear. It is rather ambivalent, with widespread "Yugonostalgia" among "common people".[2] Sociologist Ivana Spasić states that "generally speaking, the image of socialist, 'Tito's' Yugoslavia is more positive (…) among common people than in official, 'state' views" (Spasić, 2012: 577). Unlike the hegemonic interpretation of the socialist period as authoritarian and repressive, no such reflections emerged during the research done by Spasić. Moreover, her results showed that the dominant feeling among "common people" is that "politics was better then and had less impact on people's lives than it is today, in an age of pluralism and democracy—which is then, not surprisingly, referred to as 'so-called democracy'" (Spasić, 2012: 584).

Debates develop even further, and some commentators, such as Miša Brkić, in a peculiar way erase the boundary between socialist past and

[1] Similarly, historian Nikola Samardžić argues that the root of the war crimes, which happened during the 1990s war in Bosnia and Herzegovina, can be traced straight to the national liberation struggle led by the Communist Party during the second world war. See: Samardžić, Nikola. 2007. *Putevi AVNOJ-a (The Paths of The Anti-Fascist Council for the National Liberation of Yugoslavia)* (https://pescanik.net/putevi-avnoj-a/).

[2] Sociologist Boris Jašović says in a commentary in the daily *Politika*: "From the point of view of the common people, Yugoslavia was a welfare state. Philosophers, sociologists and politicians can debate whether civil liberties were threatened in that country, but for most people Yugoslavia was synonymous with security and safety in all segments of life, and this is best illustrated by sentences such as: 'you could sleep in the park and feel safe'. We grew up with the feeling of living in a safe country—education and health care were free and accessible, and job security was guaranteed. Today we live with a painful feeling of general insecurity (…) that is why a large number of people have a nostalgic attitude towards the past". See more in: *Najbolje se živelo za vreme Tita (The best life was during Tito's time)*, (http://www.politika.rs/sr/clanak/283087/Najbolje-se-zivelo-za-vreme-Tita).

capitalist present. According to Brkić, the transition to capitalism never fully developed:

"no key determinant of the past (of the communist system) has been abolished and all of them together still dominate social consciousness today. The contamination by (virus) communism is deeply ingrained in the DNA of the citizens of Serbia, as well as its political, academic and cultural elite, and that is why a large group of the population has shown several times so far that it is against reforms and changes" (Brkić, 2015).

In another article he claims that transition is "a rapid shift from one social order (socialism) to another (capitalism), the exit of the state and the entry of private entrepreneurs into the ownership structure of companies, market formation, capital inflows and many new jobs" (Brkić, 2008). Brkić's main argument is that Serbian society is still stuck in collectivist ideology seasoned by authoritarianism, state interventionism and self-management.

The confusion that permeates debates about the current and past socio-economic system makes it difficult for us to understand social, political and economic processes, and to deliberate on the desired future.

Transition

In the last three decades, the term transition has been most commonly used to describe the social and economic context in Serbia. According to this approach, society is somewhere in between, it is neither socialist nor capitalist. The notion of transition comes from the field of modernization theories and represents the shift of society from socialism to capitalism, that is, the return from the socialist "aberration" to the "correct" path of the capitalist system. As Serbian sociologist Mladen Lazić states, "the 'socialist' episode is interpreted as a departure from the evolutionary line of historical development" (Lazić, 1995: 45). Socialism is understood as a negative phenomenon and is subjected to non-analytical terms such as totalitarianism or purely economistic characterizations such as inefficiency. Capitalism, on the other hand, has been interpreted as a democratic, dynamic and efficient system, and represents a normative ideal towards which society needs to reorient.

This transition is defined by strict instructions on how to switch from the "dead end" of socialism to "regular civilizational flows".[3] The proposed measures represent a totality that encompasses all spheres of society. One of the first interventions was the introduction of a multi-party system that would ensure "true" democracy. These changes are accompanied by the privatization of social[4] and state property along with market reforms that are supposed to ensure the smooth circulation of capital. But change doesn't stop there, it goes further at a structural level and aims to change value patterns and create the preconditions for transforming "people without initiative" into "entrepreneurs".[5] As Lazić notes, "the difficulty with this approach is that it has been applied many times over the past period in a number of 'Third World' countries, and as a rule it did not produce (theoretically) expected results" (Lazić, 1995: 46).

For proponents of the transition approach the argument is that the results are not satisfactory because a sufficient number of measures have not been implemented. Also, the argument is that those measures that have been implemented have not been adequately and thoroughly implemented. On the other hand, Paul Blokker urges the acknowledgement of "significant difference in the emerging societal orders" (Blokker, 2005:

[3] See for example: Đinđić, Zoran. 1991. *Komunizam van zakona (Outlawed communism).* (http://pescanik.net/komunizam-van-zakona/).

[4] After the split with USSR in 1948, SFRY departed from an etatist model of rigid centralized planning and gradually introduced a self-management model of the economy which was based on social ownership. We will discuss this further below. For now, it is important to note that social ownership meant that neither the state nor a particular enterprise had full ownership rights over the means of production. For further reading see example: Kardelj, Edvard. 1979. *Samoupravljanje i društvena svojina*. Belgrade: BIGZ.

[5] Philosopher Neven Cvetičanin states: "The postulate, which is at the root of the reconstruction of institutions, is the social popularization of work as a value, that is. constituting what we can call work morality, that is, business responsibility. The value system that has been imposed on us over the past half century through stories of self-management and workers' councils has popularized work evasion and virtual efficiency. The first point of the value system reform should be—work in order to make money" (Cvetićanin, 2002: 107). Also see: Resolution 1096 (1996) adopted by the Council of Europe. (http://assembly.coe.int/nw/xml/XRef/Xref-XML2HTML-en.asp?fileid=16507). Among other things, the resolution states that the goals of the transition process "must include a transformation of mentalities (a transformation of hearts and minds) whose main goal should be to eliminate the fear of responsibility". For additional reading see also: Makovicky, Nicolette (ed). 2014. *Neoliberalism, Personhood, and Postsocialism - Enterprising Selves in Changing Economies*. Farnham: Ashgate Publishing.

519). He argues that "theory should be both interpretative, in the sense that it should be able to recognize the construction of similarity without leaning on normative prescriptions, and hermeneutic, in the sense of being able to provide understanding from within the particularistic contexts in which projects of modernization arise, and which fundamentally shape the contours and substance of these projects" (Blokker, 2005: 519).

Some sociologists, such as Mladen Lazić, emphasized that instead of transition, it was more precise to talk about postsocialist transformation, given the fact that the outcome of social change was not clear.[6] Lazić elaborated on the concept of "blocked transformation" in the context of Serbia:

"It represented a process that initiated fundamental systemic changes such as the abolition of the planned economy as well as political and cultural 'monism' and the establishment of a market economy with legitimate private ownership and at least a formal presence of political and cultural pluralism. These initial changes were necessary to enable the mass conversion of public economic resources into the private ownership of nomenklatura members. Naturally, they were also necessary, at least formally, to bring the order closer to the externally imposed, unstoppable global surge to destroy socialism. However, immediately after the first wave, comprising the legalization and legitimation of private ownership and the introduction of a multiparty political system, the changes were frozen, in order to carry out the above-mentioned conversion based on the control that had thus been preserved over economic and political resources" (Lazić, 2015: 535).

In short, the slackening pace of socio-economic transformation is explained by the narrow interests of the dominant class in the political elite, close to the ruling Socialist Party of Serbia (SPS), and the new, emerging bourgeoisie. Although critical towards a unilinear transitional approach, which sees only one successful outcome of the postsocialist restructuring, Lazić seems to fall into similar logic—if the transition doesn't lead to the prescribed model of "Western market democracy" it must be because it is blocked. As Blokker noted in his critique of

[6] See for example: Lazić, Mladen (ed). 2000. *Račji hod (Crab-walk: Serbia in the Process of Transformation*. Belgrade: Filip Višnjić. See also: Sztompka, Piotr. 1994. *The Sociology of Social Change*. Oxford: Blackwell.

modernist transitology, "diversity becomes in this reading multiple pathways to a similar end destination while creative agency is confined to the invention of locally functioning, successful ways of reaching that goal" (Blokker, 2005: 513).

However, if we focus on the 1990s, we cannot ignore the context of the wars and UN sanctions that Serbia was exposed to at the time. The war economy always has a pronounced etatist character, and the inability to access the global market has further hampered the massive wave of privatization. Whatever the reason, it was obvious that capitalist restoration wasn't an unambiguous process. The questions that arise are when it actually began, and when it finishes?

Yet, for the transitional approach, entrenched in modernization theory, none of this really matters. A phantasm of a "better tomorrow", reproduced by the transient character of the society defined by the transition, enables the constant postponing and distancing of the present towards the supposedly better future. It turns out that the function of the transition concept, which was widely used in public discourse in the last three decades to describe the socio-economic context, is first and foremost a specific delay in any expected improvement.[7] Thus, the transition represents a suspension of democracy and labor rights, with the proclaimed better life being constantly postponed to an indeterminate future.

For the journalist and economic commentator Miša Brkić, the transition started in 1989 with Ante Marković, Yugoslav prime minister at the time and market-oriented reformist. Under Marković's government, a new law on enterprises was introduced which recognized the equal status of social, state and private ownership for the first time since the second world war (Music, 2012: 66). But the transition never came to an end. "These doors were only slightly, but never fully opened", Brkić

[7] It should be noted that since 2012 the usage of this concept largely fell away. The change of government in 2012 brought the Serbian Progressive Party (SNS) to power. The main political focus of SNS was the critique of political actors that were in government after the fall of Slobodan Milošević' regime, the actors which were in charge of the privatization process. "They stole and plundered and took everything they could from the people", said Aleksandar Vučić, current president of Serbia and the leader of SNS (see: *Vučić o 5. oktobru: Krali su i otimali od naroda, uništili su sve što je i Milošević ostavio u nasleđe*, *Blic*, 5 October 2018. [https://www.blic.rs/vesti/politika/vucic-o-5-oktobru-krali-su-i-otimali-od-naroda-unistili-su-sve-sto-je-i-milosevic/nyls2j0]). The distinction that SNS wants to make between them and their political opposition could explain why the current government doesn't utilize the term "transition".

states. Although he thinks that in 1989 "the 'spirit of entrepreneurship' was released from the bottle and managed to resist the socialist legacy" his point is that capitalism never came to be (Brkić, 2017: 128) Another breaking point for Brkić is the fall of Milošević's regime in 2000, but what happened after that also didn't meet Brkić's expectations. From today's perspective he declares:

"It will be almost two decades since Serbia officially, during the democratic changes in 2000, proclaimed that it had started building capitalism. It is not doing very well, capitalism is slowly being accepted in Serbia, socialism is alive in all pores of society and the appeal for that system is still great. Most people can hardly be surprised by the fact that they have to work for the capitalist and still believe that the state is their favorite boss (employer)" (Brkić, 2017: 136).

But can we establish a different approach to the analysis of this "postsocialist transformation"?

Socialism vs. Capitalism

History is an important legitimizing frame of existing political practices. The past is not an ordinary weapon, sociologist Todor Kuljić constantly reminds us.[8] It has been elaborated, revised and used in order to serve certain interests and as a basis for affirmation or defamation of political positions.[9]

In the context of Serbia, ideological struggle is in large part defined by the ideological struggle over Yugoslavia. The fact that there was not only one "Yugoslavia" makes the situation more complex. Altogether three communities with importantly different characters had been constituted under the toponym Yugoslavia. The dominant narrative in Serbia mostly refers to the first iteration—the Kingdom of Yugoslavia. The romanticized vision of the period between the two world wars, with luxurious lifestyles enjoyed by members of higher classes, is placed as a symbolic representation of the culmination of Serbian history.

[8] See for example: Kuljić, Todor. 2008. *Upotreba kvislinga (The use of quislings)*. (http://www.politika.rs/sr/clanak/47625/Upotreba-kvislinga).

[9] See for example: Kuljić, Todor. 2006. *Kultura sećanja (Memory culture)*. Belgrade: Čigoja; Kuljić, Todor. 2002. *Prevladavanje prošlosti (Mastering the past)*. Belgrade: Helsinški odbor za ljudska prava u Srbiji.

This period is contrasted to the second Yugoslavia—the Socialist Federative Republic of Yugoslavia—which emerged after the second world war.[10] In the dominant narrative, socialist Yugoslavia is a divergence in the capitalist continuum. But what is neglected in this narrative is the fact that both the Kingdom of Yugoslavia and the capitalist present are marked by a sharp economic polarization within the society, that has created a narrow circle of the rich and large tiers of impoverished and marginalized social groups.

Therefore, it is not a surprise that in the memory of the population the image of this historical development looks a bit different. Numerous pieces of research have shown that, despite systemic pressures to revise history, the nostalgia of "common people" is placed exactly in the period that the hegemonic narrative tries to discredit.[11] Socialist modernization brought accelerated progress, social security and previously unimaginable social mobility.

But what happened with socialism, and when did the restoration of capitalist relations begin? Socialism and capitalism, as socio-economic systems, can be analyzed at different levels of abstraction. At the highest level of abstraction, there is a specific reduction of complex phenomena. Such an interpretation suggests that capitalism exists in its pure form, and that socialism can also be understood as a uniform system. So we need to analyze these formations in more detail, in their historical forms. If we follow this path we will immediately face a huge challenge. Capitalism, as a system under constant transformation, has undergone tremendous changes during the twentieth century. Having gone through several crisis periods, this socio-economic order has gone full circle—from unregulated market competition and brutal exploitation of the workers, through a period of prosperity embodied in strong state interventionism and redistribution of wealth,[12] to the neoliberal incarnation based on the massive

[10] The "third Yugoslavia" was the Federal Republic of Yugoslavia, which consisted of only two republics—Serbia and Montenegro—and existed from 1992 until 2003.

[11] See for example: Vučković Juroš, Tanja. (2012). *Social changes and the generational differences in the formation of collective memories*, a dissertation submitted to the Department of Sociology, Indiana University; Velikonja, Mitja. (2010). *Titostalgija*. Belgrade: Biblioteka XX vek: Knjižara Krug.

[12] Of course, this excursion was not global, but mainly focused on old capitalist centers located in western Europe and North America. Nevertheless, it is important to notice that the period of the welfare state was induced by a strong workers movement, Communist and Social Democratic parties and competing socialist projects which emerged during the

privatization of public infrastructure and the concentration of the wealth in the hands of the richest one percent of the population. When it comes to socialism, the situation is not much different, and may be even more complex. If we take a look at various socialist societies we will see a whole series of qualitative differences. Not only between socialist societies, but also within each of these societies it is possible to trace specific changes that have taken place throughout history. Going deeper into the analysis, within each particular type of socialism, we can distinguish the whole series of stages. The period of an imminent revolution, as a period of a dramatic restructuring of society, is probably the most dynamic, but the subsequent events are no less stirring. In socialist Yugoslavia, for example, various political and economic reform programmes were implemented over the years—the introduction of self-management, gradual political and economic liberalization and decentralization, as well as the implementation of various forms of planning.[13]

So, what is the constant that allows us to define these socio-economic systems as capitalist or socialist? We could say that this is the logic of social reproduction, that is, the very foundations upon which society is based. "Ideally-typically", the logic of the capitalist mode of social reproduction is profit-led—all goods and services are produced in order to be exchanged on the market with the aim of obtaining a surplus. In socialism, the logic of social reproduction is not profit-led but oriented towards human needs. Thus, while in the capitalist mode of production there is the imperative of exchange value, in the socialist there is the imperative of use value.

Contested Reproduction

But can we easily separate actually existing systems? The socialist system in Yugoslavia emerged from a war conflict. It was established in a country ravaged by war, but it did not rise out of thin air. Actually, if we look at history, none of the new socio-economic formations developed by precisely separating itself from the previous one—feudalism from slavery,

twentieth century. See for example: Whal, Asbjorn. 2011. *The Rise and Fall of the Welfare State*. London: Pluto Press.

[13] See for example: Horvat, Branko. 1981. *Sistem samoupravnog društvenog planiranja*. Belgrade: Institut ekonomskih nauka. Also see: Lampe, John. 2000. *Yugoslavia as history*. Cambridge: Cambridge University Press.

capitalism from feudalism. The new society is "in every respect, economically, morally, and intellectually, still stamped with the birthmarks of the old society from whose womb it emerges" (Marks 1959: 16). In order to understand the full range of historical specifics of each socio-economic system, we need to understand the various contradictions that pervade and largely direct the development of these formations. It is, therefore, useful to take a look at the concept of contested reproduction developed by Canadian economist Michael A. Lebowitz (2012).

In his book "The Contradictions of 'Real Socialism': The Conductor and the Conducted", Lebowitz examines the experience of the Soviet Union and tries to grasp the underlying structure that generated this society. He identifies the main social groups in the system of social reproduction as the vanguard, managers of enterprises and workers. The vanguard was represented by the dominance of one party that presented itself as the only subject with the knowledge on how to develop and sustain the socialist mode of production. But because of the complexity of the given task, the vanguard couldn't do it on its own. So on the lower level, each enterprise had its own management which had a more narrow perspective and focused on the aims of the individual production unit of which they were in charge. While the vanguard approached the economic activities in their totality, managers had a particularistic approach. The atomization of economic subjects, with the subsequent introduction of market regulation, encouraged competitive relations and, as a consequence, the deterioration of solidarity principles. The success of the management was identified as the success of the enterprise, so the specific hierarchical structure conditioned the tendency that the managers act as de facto economic owners, even though formally and legally they were not. The third group were workers. Because of the specific division of labor, the working class still did not overcome its subordinate position. However, the position of workers was different than in capitalism. In the capitalist system, the working class is dispossessed of the means of production, and thus structurally forced to sell its own labor force. This economic coercion is based on the existential dependence of workers on capital. In capitalism, the labor force is unable to reproduce itself outside the market mechanism of regulation. In contrast, the vanguard and working class in societies of "actually existing socialisms" form a certain type of social contract that guarantees employment to the workers, rising income, high levels of labor rights and social benefits, as well as relative social equality. On the other hand, the working class renounces their political power in favor of the state and party (Lebowitz, 2012: 64).[14]

Lebowitz further develops his argument and states that an important part of production relations had the character of what he calls vanguard relations of production. The initial imperative of the vanguard, embodied in the vanguard party, is to develop the productive forces of existing society to the point where communism can be realized. The vanguard appears here as a guide, the only group to which the path to communism is known; it thus legitimizes its own position of those who "conduct" how society will develop. Lebowitz states that:

"control of managers through the administrative-directive plan and the existence of the social contract constitute a specifically vanguard mode of regulation that allowed both the reproduction of the vanguard as the owner of the means of production and the reproduction of workers in their existing relation to the means of production" (Lebowitz, 2012: 105).[15]

However, Lebowitz argues that the notion of vanguard relations of production is not enough if we want to understand the history of the "actually existing socialisms" and their collapse. He adds that "a successful mode of regulation is not automatic it is the terrain where contested reproduction occurs" (Lebowitz, 2012: 105). In order to understand this, it is necessary to note that in these societies there is another type of production that stands in contradiction to the vanguard relations of production. These are capitalist relations of production, embodied in the position of enterprise managers.

Individual enterprises weren't under the direct authority of the party. The role of the party was to orchestrate economic development from above through a predetermined plan. It was the role of managers of each enterprise to make sure that their particular production unit meets the goals set out in the plan. Lebowitz elaborates:

"The planners try in this respect to coordinate the activity of enterprises as part of a single integrated national economic unit. They want

[14] See also: Kagarlitsky, Boris. 1995. *Russia's New and Old System, interview*. (https://solidarity-us.org/atc/55/p2834/).

[15] Here we should note that Lebowitz in his analysis emhasises that it is not the plan as such which enables vanguard relations. Rather, "the plan is the way that enterprises are prevented from transforming their possession into property" (Lebowitz 2012: 104).

the enterprises to meet those targets because fulfilment by each enterprise of its output target is necessary if other firms are to get their input requirements and if adequate and planned supplies of consumer goods are to be available. In other words, the success of the annual plan as a whole depends upon the success of the individual enterprises" (Lebowitz, 2012: 40).

Lebowitz continues by noting that the managers were significantly rewarded if they managed to meet the goals set by the plan.[16] Although "actually existing socialisms" nominally insisted on egalitarian practises, they never became societies of absolute equality. Certain positions within the social structure brought with them various material benefits in the form of higher salaries, better housing units, the right to use a company car, etc. Finally, a higher position within the nomenklatura also created a greater opportunity for further ascension on the stratification ladder, the top of which was represented by the party leadership. So the managers, following their individual interests, engaged in the struggle to remove the constraints placed on them. In order to have more power within the enterprise, they required more autonomy and ability to dispose of the surplus in a way they find to be most productive. They also insisted on obtaining greater power over workers, that is, opportunities to fire or punish workers more easily. In this logic we can recognize the embryo of capitalist relations of production.

On the one hand, the vanguard promised to lead society towards a communist future, "to deliver not only the use-values necessary to satisfy its present and future obligations under the social contract but also the conditions necessary to approach the vanguard's promised society" (Lebowitz, 2012: 81). On the other hand, exploitation of the working class never ceased to exist. As Lebowitz notes:

"Despite the vanguard's view that the existence and extent of extracted surplus is simply a technical division on behalf of the working class between meeting their present and future needs, the workers themselves

[16] These bonuses were not a negligible part of the managers' income. For example, Lebovitz states that for the managers of Soviet companies in 1934, they accounted for about four percent of their total income. Already in 1940, this percentage rose to 11 percent, and during the second world war it jumped to as much as 33 percent. By 1960, the share of bonuses in salaries were gradually reduced and during Khrushchev's time (Nikita Sergeyevich Khrushchev) it was lowered to 7.7 percent, which was later interpreted as a mistake, so bonuses began to rise again, to 21.5 percent by 1966 and to 34.5 percent by 1970 (Lebowitz 2012: 41).

have no power to make this choice. Rather, it is made for them by 'those who know better.' Thus this surplus product is the result of (...) the 'political extraction of surplus labour.' And the ultimate destination of that surplus cannot change what it is. Even if workers were to be the sole recipients of this surplus product (that is, consume everything that was first extracted), the surplus would still be the result of the particular exploitation inherent in this vanguard relation" (Lebowitz, 2012: 82–83).

The result is a society that never overcame the division of labor based on thinking and doing. In such a context, the working class couldn't become a social protagonist which could more directly organize, or at least influence, the production process.

Yugoslav Socialism

Yugoslav socialism brings another dimension into the picture. Unlike the Soviet Union, Yugoslavia was developing self-management and introduced social ownership over the means of production. These institutions reduced the influence of the party and enabled workers to participate in the organization of production, although in a restricted manner. Briefly, in socialist Yugoslavia, we can locate the intersection of specific logics of the vanguard and capital, but also an alternative logic, the logic of the working class. These three logics were in the relation of interaction, they interpenetrated and deformed each other. "Precisely because there is contested reproduction between differing sets of productive relations, the interaction of the systems can generate crises, inefficiencies and irrationality that wouldn't be found in either system in its purity" (Lebowitz, 2010: 98).

At the very beginning, the system in Yugoslavia was constituted on the bases of vanguard relations of production. Unlike other Eastern European countries, in Yugoslavia socialism wasn't imposed through the military intervention of the Soviet Union. Rather it was constituted on the basis of an antifascist struggle led by the mass partisan movement which emerged as a winner in the second world war. Such a position enabled the Yugoslav political leadership to act relatively independently and reject the ultimatums and subordinated status within the USSR-dominated Eastern Bloc. The tension between Yugoslav and Soviet leaders culminated in the 1948 conflict. The break between Tito and Stalin led to a relative democratization of Yugoslav society and opened the space to the development of freedoms in the fields of culture, art, science, and to a certain extent politics. However, the biggest change was the introduction of self-management, that is, structural changes in the organization of the economy.

The institution of workers' councils[17] was a new instrument and an initial prerequisite for the realization of working class logic—the organization and control of the work process by workers themselves. An important aspect was the introduction of social ownership as a material basis for self-management. In fact, "the politics of self-management (…) dispossess the state itself and declares ownership to be social. Formally there are no more owners; ownership belongs to everyone, everything is social" (Kirn, 2010: 215).

Along with the elements of self-management, the decentralization of social life was implemented. The power was gradually transferred from the highest federal levels to the levels of republics and provinces. As central planning faded, the economy was losing an integrating factor. In this context, managers "immanently seek to increase the autonomy of the enterprise" and therefore to establish the logic of the market-type economy (Lazić, 1994: 117). The effect of this process was the intensification of competitive relations and, consequently, unequal redistribution between particular production units and the entire production branches. Workers' councils remained on the sidelines of the production system as a whole. Their role was maintained at the protocol level: workers "can express their opinions and suggestions that management may or may not accept" (Bolčić, 2003: 258). Although the system proclaimed the governance of the working class, the hierarchical distribution of power remains dominant with the professional management keeping the upper hand in relation to the workers and their elected representatives. The full emancipation of the working class, in the sense that workers themselves can

[17] "Workers' councils had between 15 and 120 members, and in companies with fewer than 30 employees the entire collective was in the workers' council. Workers elected and recalled members of workers' councils by universal, direct and secret vote. The election term lasted one year but was later extended to two years. The workers' council decided as a collective body. It adopted the most important acts of the company (rules, production and financial plans, tariff regulations), conclusions on business, selected and recalled members of the legal board, and decided on the distribution of the part of the accumulation that the company had at its disposal" (Petranović 1988: 296). However, it should be noted that their legal powers changed over time through different reforms of the Yugoslav economic system. Also, in practice, workers' councils did not always function with the same qualitative characteristics.

fully control the whole process of production, never happened. It must be noted that socialist Yugoslavia achieved high levels of social mobility. But still, the working class did not dominate either in economical or in the political sphere—control of these spheres remained in the realm of the struggle between the two factions, vanguard and managers.

Market Reforms

During 1950 and 1951, the jurisdiction over the entire economy of Yugoslavia was transferred to the level of republics, which made the administration of the republics the most important factor for managing the economy. Further reforms strengthened the independence of individual enterprises in 1958. This meant that a particular enterprise could decide how to distribute revenues that are left after all obligations had been settled (Bilandžić, 1985: 176–238). Such a trend would lead to the decentralization of the party itself, and to the de facto "multiparty system" that was generated during the 1970s, with each republican party established as an entity for itself (Centrih, 2014: 16).

Major market reform happened in 1965. Until 1965, the state set the price level for almost all products. In order to meet the needs of the internal market, its aim was to provide cheap raw materials for manufacturing industries. The disproportionately low cost of raw materials compared to final consumer goods had led to instability in the economy. As there was an incentive to increase income, the enterprises, republics and other entities increasingly oriented towards manufacturing industries at the expense of developing the raw material base of industry (Bilandžić, 1985: 306). The consequences were "highly pronounced differences in the ability of some branches to perform extended reproduction, either on the basis of their own accumulation or on the basis of their creditworthiness" (Bilandžić, 1985: 307–308). It is also important to underline that cheap raw materials were produced in the parts of the federation which were less developed. The low prices of products they produced made it difficult for these parts of the country to "catch up" with more developed regions.

One of the main arguments for the 1965 reform was that many industrial production units were "inefficient", "technically backward" and had to be financially subsidized. It was also argued that protectionism and a monopolistic position in the market did not encourage enterprises to change. The imperative was to foster "intensive" economic growth and to continue the rise of workers incomes. Both of these proved impossible: first, because of competition among republics, and second, because workers' councils persisted and unanimously refused to fire people (Suvin, 2014: 238).

The elimination of taxes on high productivity further stimulated competition relations in the economy. Accumulation was transferred from the state level to the level of enterprises. However, capital from the enterprise investment funds was handed over to the federal, republic and communal banks, which enabled the rise of the financial sector (Bilandžić, 1985: 310). The republics, led by separate factions of the party, kept gaining power equivalent to the central state administration and tilted the economy more towards classical capitalist relations (Suvin, 2014: 193). The idea was that the introduction and expansion of market relations would enable the self-regulation of the economy. On the other hand, the major problem was that enterprises, as well as regions, were not in the same position and that market relations further invigorated uneven development. In addition to the increased competition between enterprises, competitive relations between the republics intensified. A newly adopted legal framework

> "introduced the economic principle in the relations between the political territorial communities, and according to this principle the citizens of each community themselves bear the expenses for the operation of all kinds of social services such as health, education, culture, state administration, economic interventions, etc. Based on these measures, already in 1964, the process of redistribution developed in favor of some socio-political communities" (Bilandžić, 1985: 311).[18]

The federation increasingly oriented towards the international market. The dinar was devalued in order to encourage exports. Prices, on the other hand, increased and income became tightly linked with productivity. The consequence of these measures was the rise in the cost of living which didn't hit the entire population equally. The whole constellation hindered product placement and sustainability of enterprises which were exposed to

[18] According to Bilandžić, in the beginning of the 1970s the differences in the level of economic development were very large: "the national income per capita between Slovenia and Kosovo is 6:1, and between the most developed and least developed communes 20:1. Three republics (B&H, Montenegro and Macedonia) and one province (Kosovo) have the status of underdeveloped members of the federation" (Bilandžić 1985: 353).

market instability. "In order to avoid a reduction of personal incomes, the first reaction of working collectives (...) was to almost completely suspend the hiring of new workers, after which the firing of employed workers started" (Bilandžić, 1985: 314). Despite these interventions, income did not continue its upward trend from the previous period. The solution to the problem was sought in the export of unemployed labor[19] and its retention in the countryside, which produced only short-term positive effects. The aggravation of the crisis in capitalist countries during the 1970s forced a large number of emigrants to return home (Suvin, 2014: 194).

Economic growth had stopped, while industrial and agricultural production stagnated. Nevertheless, the economy continued to be directed towards the international market which increasingly dragged it into the vortex of international competition. Historian Dušan Bilandžić noted:

"The moment when Yugoslavia opened its borders widely to competition from foreign production, other countries put more restraints on their internal market, especially those of the European Economic Community. Yugoslav countermeasures were absent. The state has shied away from a series of necessary actions to direct and organize the economy, and a self-management structure hasn't yet been developed to adequately replace some of the state functions" (Bilandžić, 1985: 317).

As the crisis hit the countries of the capitalist center in the 1970s, the possibility of cheaper loans was diminishing. Also, the return of workers who could no longer easily find employment in Western countries reduced the inflow of foreign currency remittances to Yugoslavia.

The end of 1960s and the beginning of 1970s were marked by political turmoil. In 1968 students occupied the university in Belgrade and demanded a more egalitarian and democratic society. They wondered why their parents settled for partial success; "The revolution is not complete!", was one of slogans of the student protests. The party was faced with the problem that the unrest was escalating beyond its ranks—engaging

[19] As Susan Woodward wrote: "Periods of emigration always lowered the unemployment rate. For example, its sharp drop in 1955–1957 can be attributed almost entirely to the permanent exodus of ethnic minorities and political malcontents when borders opened, and the fall in unemployment in 1961 corresponded to the federal government's organization of temporary labor migration abroad. The number of workers who left in 1969–1973, about 500.000, was almost equal to the increase in social-sector employment during the same period" (Woodward 1995: 198–199).

in polemics was acceptable, but in a controlled environment. As soon as it was carried out in the street, things take a serious turn. After all, how was it possible that citizens of a successful socialist country rebel by demanding more socialism?

Nationalism was also on rise. In the early 1970s, dominant position in the Croatian wing of the party opposed the centralization of the federal state. Although the nationalist tendencies were quickly tackled, and the main protagonists were removed from office and arrested, nationalism started to develop all around the federation. The main force beyond interethnic disputes was the economic interest of particular republics. As Bilandžić states: "the most developed republics, Slovenia and Croatia, were the most dissatisfied" (Bilandžić, 1985: 357). It should be noted that until 1965 only a third of the investment funds was in the hands of the federation, which was a significant reduction, since before 1952 100 percent of these funds were in the jurisdiction of the federal administration (Bilandžić, 1985: 357). In the face of market reforms and further decentralization of the state, each republic fought to secure as much funding as possible from the federal level. Bilandžić also notes that the intensity of confrontations intensified

> by the nature of the self-management system, because in it the workers 'share the fate' of the income of 'their' company. Their income also depends on better or worse business conditions, and they were determined by the federal state. In other words, each worker feels these conditions in his own pocket. That is why it was not difficult to move people into confrontations to change, that is, to maintain the existing socio-economic relations. (Bilandžić 1985: 357)

Although politically, the party induced more authoritarian tendencies, further decentralization of the state was prompted by the 1974 constitutional reform. In economic terms, Yugoslavia was further oriented towards foreign markets and heavily dependent on imports of "machinery, semi-finished products and spare parts for domestic production; by the early 1980s, 99.6 percent of imports were essential to the production process" (Woodward, 1995: 226). Foreign debt rapidly increased from \$1.2 billion in 1965 to \$11.8 billion in 1978. This trend continued, and in 1981 it amounted \$21 billion (Čolanović, 1985: 9, 12, 19; Cemović, 1985: 106).

The constant need to adapt to external conditions led to a high level of unpredictability. Planning and the general level of administering the economy and wider society were very difficult in the given situation (Woodward, 2003: 77). The state continued to strive to consolidate within its own borders on socialist principles, although they were increasingly subject to the imperatives of capitalist efficiency and growth. Consequently, product placement became more important than the producers themselves. The effects of this policy have caused constant upheavals and turmoil in society. This intensified in the 1980s and escalated in the early 1990s.

Market relations further disintegrated the working class which couldn't appear as a unified social actor. "The freedom of each company to pursue its own interests in the market created conditions for workers to identify their well-being with the company management against the state or rival companies" (Musić, 2014: 13). This is understandable given the fact that their income depended on the market performance of their production unit:

"Inversely, once companies fell into financial problems, or the gap between the incomes of different occupational groups became too wide for socialist norms of the income distribution, the workers could form an alliance with parts of the political bureaucracy and demand a roll-back of market reforms and the powers of management. The system thus oscillated between market and political control over the economy" (Musić, 2014: 13).

The spiral of the logic of market-type economy further dragged the society away from socialist principles. By the time the foreign debt reached its historical peak, the party nomenklatura didn't hold all the threads of power in its hands, and the working class didn't have the necessary infrastructure that would enable it to act as a coherent actor.

From the end of the 1970s till the end of the 1980s, Yugoslavia signed six stand-by agreements with International Monetary Fund (IMF). From the perspective of the federal government, this was necessary to ensure the continued inflow of foreign capital (Lowinger, 2009: 55). The loans were tied to the imperative implementation of IMF instructions, which included a restrictive monetary policy, a reduction in the trade deficit, debt payment, fluctuating exchange rates, price liberalization in the domestic market, cuts in domestic consumption and stimulation of exports. The enterprises were instructed to reduce costs (that is, to fire workers) and use their own savings for investment purposes. The consequences of these measures were immediately felt in the form of recession (Woodward, 1995: 229). The "need" for IMF credit had forced the Yugoslav leadership to agree to such a policy, which was imposed as a necessary condition in order to secure international support. At the same time, the leadership was assuring the workers that these reforms would make socialist self-management competitive and sustainable. As a matter of fact, "more market influence was introduced under the slogan of expanding workers' self-management and increasing the autonomy of labor in relation to the state" (Music, 2014: 16).

But the reforms undertaken, which we can understand as austerity measures, triggered the reaction of workers. In 1985, 61 percent of households stated that their incomes were not sufficient, while costs of living exceeded incomes in more than half of households (Lowinger, 2009: 57–58). As a result of efforts to implement the IMF instructions and introduce austerity measures, Yugoslav workers launched 625 strikes between 1980 and 1982. Pressures on workers' wages were the primary cause of the strike decisions. Facing the pressure of creditors on the one hand, and labor on the other hand, the government was forced to pursue inflationary policies that were ultimately neither in line with the IMF directives nor in the interests of the workers (Lowinger, 2009: 55–56). Although the most extreme measures were not implemented due to fear of broader social discontent, the number of strikes increased to 696 in 1985. The characteristic of strikes between 1983 and 1985 is that they were extremely defensive and represented a reaction to a decline in purchasing power, a deterioration in living standards, and a limitation on decision-making processes at the workplace.

With the adoption of the Labor Relations Act in 1988, the restoration of capitalism in Yugoslavia came to its final stage. A clear signal was given that social ownership was not the dominant form of ownership, that is, legitimacy was given to private, cooperative and "mixed" ownership (Novaković, 2013: 31). Even before this period we had the effective atomization of economic entities, but by the end of 1980s it was openly advocated by government officials. The influence of market elements, which had been present within the framework of the Yugoslav socialist society for decades, directed production units to act in accordance with their own particular interests in order to maximize profit. The imperative of organized fulfilment of social needs faded. The institution of social property remained the last obstacle to the enthronement of capitalism, but this was swiftly fixed through the privatization process. In 1989, the Law on Social Capital was adopted, and the process of privatization of self-managing enterprises began on the Federal level. By 1991, each of the republican bureaucracies introduced their own laws on property transformation (Musić, 2012: 66).

Conclusion

What followed was the full restoration of capitalist relations of production. As history has so often shown, the initiation of this system was violent in every aspect. Also, the abolition of the social and economic rights which socialism developed couldn't be carried out without resistance. This is so clearly visible when we take a look at the number of workers' strikes during the 1980s. However, these mobilizations were soon restrained and rearticulated from social into nationalist frameworks. Of course, one should not assume here that nationalist rearticulation of social struggles was the result of the mere ideological change—it is actually a logical product of the dynamics of the material base, development and eclectic nature of Yugoslav society, which developed on the basis of the contested reproduction of vanguard, capital and working class logics. Such a structure of socialist Yugoslavia continually encouraged fragmentation and competitive relations of political and economic entities, which made it impossible to establish a ground for unified actions of workers. The dissolution of the federation took place on the basis of the insistence of the particular republics for even greater autonomy, which escalated to the demand for national homogenization.

Socialism in Yugoslavia, in its actually existing form, lasted less than five decades. The system didn't manage to develop as a particular organic system of production, distribution and consumption. Instead, it was ridden by contested reproduction of different logics which created inconsistencies and permanent crisis. And this is something we have to take into consideration when we talk about the restoration of capitalism. But what was the point in time when the restoration started? Can we locate it in 1979, the year when the SFRY signed the first stand-by arrangement with IMF? Or is it 1965, the year in which major market reform was introduced? Or maybe it was 1948 and split with USSR? In this regard, it may be more insightful to analyze socialism through the distinction between the "becoming" and "being" of an organic system. Following the argumentation laid out by Michael Lebowitz, we can detect contradictions that are not visible if we stay on a higher level of abstraction. Actually existing socialism never managed to develop to the level of an organic system. In fact, it was a battlefield on which capitalist logic managed to emerge victorious.

In 1989 the restoration process started to accelerate. The vanguard relations deteriorated as the Communist party lost its monopoly over the political and economic spheres. A multi-party system was introduced, and the privatization process started. Capitalism took its full form, although the wars and UN embargo did slow down the process of privatization. After the fall of Slobodan Milošević's regime, a new acceleration took place. Shock therapy was introduced with widespread privatization and further deterioration of social and labor rights. Rather than posing the question "have we reached capitalism yet", it would be beneficial to understand what capitalism on the periphery of the world system looks like.

References

Bilandžić, D. (1985). *Historija Socijalističke Federativne Republike Jugoslavije: glavni procesi 1918–1985*. Školska knjiga.

Blokker, P. (2005). Post-communist modernization, transition studies, and diversity in Europe. *European Journal of Social Theory, 8*(4), 503–525.

Bolčić, S. (2003). *Svet rada u transformaciji*. Belgrade: Plato.

Brkić, M. (2008). Žrtve zaustavljene tranzicije. *Peščanik*, 11 February 2008. https://pescanik.net/zrtve-zaustavljene-tranzicije/. Accessed 10 February 2021.

Brkić, M. (2015). Živahna deca komunizma. *Peščanik*, 19 April 2015. https://pescanik.net/zivahna-deca-komunizma/. Accessed 2 February 2021.

Brkić, M. (2017). Deca Antinih reformi – teško porađanjenove poslovne elite u Srbiji. *Hereticus, 15*(1–2), 127–140.

Cemović, M. (1985). *Zašto, kako i koliko smo se zadužili*. Institut za unapređenje robnog prometa.

Centrih, L. (2014). *The road to collapse: The demise of the League of Communists of Yugoslavia*. Rosa Luxemburg Stiftung.

Cvetićanin, N. (2002). Rekonstrukcija Sistema vrednosti srpskog i jugoslovensog društva. In Cvetković, Vladimir (Ed.), *(Re)konstrukcija institucija – godinu dana tranzicije u Srbiji*. Institut za filozofiju i društvenu teoriju.

Čolanović, B. (1985). *Dugovi Jugoslavije*. Dnevnik.

Đinđić, Z. (1991). Komunizam van zakona. *Peščanik*, 31 July 1991. http://pescanik.net/komunizam-van-zakona/. Accessed 3 February 2021.

Horvat, B. (1981). *Sistem samoupravnog društvenog planiranja*. Institut ekonomskih nauka.

Kagarlitsky, B. (1995). Russia's new and old system. *Against the Current*, 3 March 1995. https://solidarity-us.org/site/node/2834. Accessed 3 February 2021.

Kardelj, E. (1979). *Samoupravljanje i društvena svojina*. BIGZ.

Kirn, G. (2010). Jugoslavija: Od partizanske politike do postfordističke tendencije. *Up & Underground, 17*, 208–229.

Kuljić, T. (2002). *Prevladavanje prošlosti*. Belgrade: Helsinški odbor za ljudska prava u Srbiji.

Kuljić, T. (2006). *Kultura sećanja*. Belgrade: Čigoja.

Kuljić, T. (2008). Upotreba kvislinga. *Politika*, 3 July 2008. http://www.politika.rs/sr/clanak/47625/Upotreba-kvislinga. Accessed 3 February 2021.

Lampe, J. (2000). *Yugoslavia as history*. Cambridge University Press.

Lazić, M. (1994). *Sistem i slom*. Filip Višnjić.

Lazić, M. (1995). Pristup kritičkoj analizi pojma tranzicije. Centar za informativnu djelatnost – SIZ za kulturu i naučne djelatnosti.

Lazić, M. (Ed.). (2000). *Račji hod*. Filip Višnjić .

Lazić, M. (2015). The making of a new economic elite in Serbia. *Südosteuropa, 63*(4), 531–548.

Lebowitz, M. (2010). *The socialist alternative: Real human development*. Monthy Review Press.

Lebowitz, M. (2012). *The contradictions of "Real Socialism": The conductor and the conducted*. Monthly Review Press.

Lowinger, J. (2009). Economic reform and the „Double Movement" in Yugoslavia. An analysis of labor unrest and ethno-nationalism in the 1980s. Doctoral dissertation, Johns Hopkins University..

Makovicky, N. (Ed.). (2014). *Neoliberalism, personhood, and postsocialism - Enterprising selves in changing economies*. Ashgate.

Marks, K. (1959). *Kritika Gotskog programa*. Kultura.

Milojko, A. (2019). I Koštunica i Cvetković su bili bolji. *NIN*, no. 3579, 1 August 2019.

Musić, G. (2012). Od „svačije-ničije" do nečije, samo čije? Društvena svojina i javno dobro u srpskoj tranziciji. *U borbi za javno dobro*, 4 January 2013. https://cpe.org.rs/publikacije/zbornik-u-borbi-za-javno-dobro-analize-strategije-i-perspektive-pdf/. Accessed 3 February 2021.

Musić, G. (2014). *Radnička klasa Srbije u tranziciji 1988–2013*. Rosa Luxemburg Stiftung.

Najbolje se živelo za vreme Tita. (2014). *Politika*, 1 February 2014. http://www.politika.rs/sr/clanak/283087/Najbolje-se-zivelo-za-vreme-Tita. Accessed 3 February 2021.

Novaković, N. (2013). Štrajkovi, sindikati i privatizacija u Srbiji. *Sociološki Pregled, 67*(1), 23–52.

Petranović, B. (1988). *Istorija Jugoslavije 1918–1988. Treća knjiga: Socijalističja Jugoslavija 1945–1988*. Nolit.

Samardžić, N. (2007). Putevi AVNOJ-a. https://pescanik.net/putevi-avnoj-a/. Accessed 3 February 2021.

Spasić, I. (2012). Jugoslavija kao mesto normalnog života – sećanja običnih ljudi u Srbiji. *Sociologija, 54*(4), 577–594.

Sztompka, P. (1994). *The sociology of social change*. Blackwell.

Suvin, D. (2014). *Samo jednom se ljubi: radiografija SFR Jugoslavije 1945.-72; uz hipoteze o početku, kraju i suštini*. Rosa Luxemburg Stiftung.

Velikonja, M. (2010). *Titostalgija*. Biblioteka XX vek: Knjižara Krug.

Vučić o 5. oktobru (2018). Vučić o 5. oktobru: Krali su i otimali od naroda, uništili su sve što je i Milošević ostavio u nasleđe. *Blic*, 5 October 2018. https://www.blic.rs/vesti/politika/vucic-o-5-oktobru-krali-su-i-otimali-od-naroda-unistili-su-sve-sto-je-i-milosevic/nyls2j0. Accessed 3 February 2021.

Vučković Juroš, T. (2012). Social changes and the generational differences in the formation of collective memories. Doctoral dissertation, Indiana University.

Woodward, S. (1995). *Socialist unemployment: The political economy of Yugoslavia, 1945–1990*. Princeton University Press.

Woodward, S. (2003). The political economy of ethno-nationalism in Yugoslavia. *Socialist Register, 39*, 73–92.

The Restoration of Capitalism in Slovenia and Croatia

Marko Kržan and Dimitrije Birač

The Formation and Demise of "really Existing Socialism" in Yugoslavia

From the broadest perspective, the modern history of the world periphery in general, and eastern Europe in particular, consists of three processes (Amin, 2019).

First, the tendency of the ruling classes to enlarge their space for manoeuvre internationally, that is, to achieve and/or enhance state independence. In eastern Europe, this tendency has materialized in the (re)creation of nation-states after the collapse of the German, Austrian and Russian empires following the first world war. One of those states was Yugoslavia.

Second, the striving of nations for modernization, that is, the development of industrialized economies and "civil society" freed from the domination of traditionalist—especially religious—institutions. In Yugoslavia, the transition from agrarian to industrial society was only achieved after the second world war, but very rapidly: a process that took more

M. Kržan
Ljubljana, Slovenia

D. Birač (✉)
Faculty of Political Science, Zagreb, Croatia

A. Gagyi and O. Slačálek (eds.), *The Political Economy of Eastern Europe 30 years into the 'Transition'*, International Political Economy Series,
https://doi.org/10.1007/978-3-030-78915-2_4

than a century in the first capitalist countries was achieved in 15 years (1945–1960).

Third, this was not capitalist modernization, however, which would amount to the creation of a capitalist economy, plus a bourgeois "civil society". Modernization was part of a wider struggle of the working people for socialism, a society without class exploitation and oppression.

By modernization, we mean the development of productive forces (industrialization in the broadest sense, not limited to manufacturing) with the concomitant development of human needs and the means to satisfy them (resulting, for example, in a drop in mortality rates, higher consumption etc.). It also means rationalization of the juridical-political superstructure, forms of social consciousness and of everyday life (that is, secularization of the state and civil society) and the subsequent reduction of extra economic inequalities of gender, race, etc. One cannot entirely separate modernization from political-economic relations, in which it is situated, nor separate its Eurocentric features from universal properties of human progress. However, history confirmed it is a relatively autonomous phenomenon: On the one hand, capitalist development obstructs the modernization of peripheral countries even by its own standards (underdevelopment). On the other hand, "real existing socialism" was able to take modernization much further, and even core capitalist countries relied on statist methods to modernize and develop. The main difference between "capitalist" and "socialist" modernization would thus be that the capitalist class does not dominate the social bloc that carries out modernization and that modernization does not enforce capitalist social relations.

In such a case, the scope and form of modernization depend on the progress of socialist transformation. Although the Yugoslav masses did not achieve socialism, they did accomplish the basic conditions for it: they expropriated the propertied classes, nationalized enterprises and infrastructure, and liquidated bourgeois political institutions. This was achieved by a genuine revolution rather than by Soviet intervention, and gave Yugoslavia an unseen degree of independence in relation to both its prewar masters (imperialist countries) and the Soviet Union (after Tito's split with Stalin in 1948).

Indeed, after a short period of imitating the Soviet system after the second world war, Yugoslavia came quite close to establishing a socialist mode of production instead of only a form of "state capitalism". The introduction of social property as opposed to state property, and workers' self-management of enterprises as opposed to bureaucratic management, gave workers' collectives much power in enterprises; further, allocation of capital (investment) was determined by indicative planning, rather than detailed administrative planning of the Soviet type. Indicative planning weakened the power of the state bureaucracy, while self-management limited the influence of the managerial groups (dubbed "technocracy") that increased when enterprises became more autonomous. The founder of this system, Boris Kidrič, envisioned further improvements especially with regard to perfection of and workers' control over planning (Suvin, 2016: 86–98). The system was also quite effective, as witnessed by the fact that economic growth in the first post-war period (until 1965) was much higher, development more even, and the economy more stable than in subsequent periods, as witnessed by GDP and employment growth, efficiency of investment, external trade balance and inflation rates (Kržan, 2019). Therefore, the Yugoslav economic system strengthened the control of the working people over the means of production (it enabled socialist transformation) in a way that was economically "efficient" (it enabled modernization).

However, during the market reforms of the 1960s, workers' self-management became increasingly connected to market relations. Workers' autonomy was conceived as the autonomy of their firms, and the autonomy of the firms was to be achieved through re-establishing market relations. It is important to note that reforms established not only market relations among the firms, and between firms and consumers, but also market control of credit (investment) and labor. Banks, rather than state funds, were made the effective owners of capital, and investment (and income) became guided by the return on capital, rather than the rate of accumulation determined by the plan. Managers and professionals in charge of market transactions and technical organization ("technocrats") were gaining the upper hand in self-managing bodies, especially in enterprises, but also in the political sphere. Immediate consequences of market reforms were the escalation of living costs and income inequalities, accompanied by the reduction of employment, which marked the beginning of "socialist unemployment" in south–eastern parts of Yugoslavia, exceptional among post-capitalist societies and important for nationalist mobilizations (Woodward, 1995).

The "opening" to the world market (for example, GATT agreements) strengthened internal capitalist tendencies. Instead of a strictly regulated relationship with the world capitalist system (what Amin termed "de-linking"), there was a tendency to abolish import tariffs and adopt world prices for domestic products. In the late 1960s, the first trade agreements were signed with the EEC in what can be called the "first cycle of EU integration" (Živković, 2013). Thus, the world market began to determine the structure of the economy, entrenching the already peripheral features of the Yugoslav economy (unequal development).

Therefore, in the 1960s, modernization was tied to capitalist tendencies. It happened not only in the sphere of economy (industrial society), but also in the sphere of "civil society". It amounted to the "liberalization" of ideological apparatuses, such as cultural institutions and academia, and the spread of consumerism. The process was so thorough that, like in the West, anti-systemic movements emerged, especially in the student movement. Although they criticized the negative effects of the emerging capitalist tendencies on the working people, they did not align themselves with the working class against the "technocracy", but focused on the struggle for civil liberties against bureaucracy (Močnik, 2021).

Unsurprisingly, nationalism emerged as well, based on the diverging economic interests of managerial and bureaucratic groups in different federal republics, which gained much more power through the decentralization of the economic and political system, parallel to market reforms. The nationalist tendencies that gained ground in mass movements, especially in Croatia between 1969 and 1971, seriously threatened the unity of the country. It is hard to say what would have happened, if nationalist and capitalist tendencies had gone unchecked. However, when they reappeared in the late 1980s, they led to the restoration of capitalism, the dismemberment of the country, and a descent into war.

In the early 1970s, however, Party and state bureaucracies blocked the capitalist tendencies and regained control. The crisis was solved "dialectically": nationalist republican leaderships were removed in 1971, but a new—confederate—constitution was adopted in 1974, which paradoxically reinforced rather than tempered nationalist tendencies. This constitution also reaffirmed self-management rights, but in a way that failed to involve the working classes in the management of the economy. Reforms limited market coordination of investment, but did not restore planning. Administrative measures, increasingly taken by republican authorities and enforced by large enterprises, progressively replaced macroeconomic coordination. In both cases, the result was fragmentation of the economy, and society as a whole, along republican—ethnic—lines.

This was a compromise between the two fractions of the ruling group at the expense of the working class. It was a sort of Thermidor, because it blocked progress towards socialism (since it reinforced the economic and political monopoly of the ruling groups), without restoring capitalism (bureaucracy controlled technocracy). History of "really existing socialism" shows that this constellation was "viable", as long as it could ensure modernization crucial for maintaining hegemony over the working class.[1] This was no longer the case in Yugoslavia: large investments, based on foreign credits, failed to produce long-term growth in the 1970s. Moreover, external circumstances—neoliberal turn in core capitalist countries and international relations—precluded "peaceful coexistence" of "really existing socialism" with the capitalist world system. Thus, in the 1980s, the ruling groups in Yugoslavia and other post-capitalist countries had to establish another basis for their reproduction: capitalism, more specifically, peripheral capitalism. As Amin (2012) put it, eastern Europe is (again) western Europe's "backyard", just like Latin America is the "backyard" of the US/Canada.

One cannot but wonder, whether Thermidor and restoration were inevitable from the start. We think there was a third possibility, socialist path enforced by the working class. The reason it did not materialize was the lack of the ideological and organizational autonomy of the working class, which in turn prevented it from becoming a hegemonic force. When the system was at the crossroads, like in late 1950s and early 1970s in Yugoslavia, either technocracy or bureaucracy imposed its partial interest as a common cause. The question of working class autonomy is, therefore, crucial to understanding of "really existing socialism" and the labor movement in general, as can be seen by the analysis of restoration, to which we now turn.

Restoration of Capitalism in Slovenia and the Consequent Prevalence of "Comprador" Tendencies over "National" Ones.

The restoration of capitalism was dependent on the initial conditions, which limited the choices of the ruling social groups. Northern Yugoslav republics, particularly Slovenia, enjoyed full employment and rising living standards up to the terminal crisis of the late 1980s, whereas southern republics have long witnessed unemployment, mass emigration and stalled modernization. Although the ruling groups in all federal

[1] According to Amin (2013), this is still the case in China.

republics adopted "liberalism"—in the broadest sense of ideology of capitalism—this resulted in differing political and economic strategies (Živković, 2013).

In Slovenia, where a strong export sector was relatively competitive, immediate integration into the EU seemed a natural choice. Since other Yugoslav republics were seen as unfit for that, Slovenian liberalism was separatist. On the other hand, Serbian ruling groups depended on basic and arms industries so that direct alignment with the capitalist class in the center was neither possible nor desirable. Contrary to other countries in the region, the Serbian ruling groups reasserted independence and sought the support of the masses by what would now be called populism. In combination with the restoration of capitalism, the reassertion of national independence in defiance of NATO, the EU etc. precluded modernization, not to mention the cost of wars. This blockage—along with foreign intervention—finally made the regime collapse and cleared the way for dependent peripheral capitalism. Still, the presently ruling class wants to retain some space of manoeuvre by relying on populist mobilization of the masses rather than total subordination to core states (the EU). In fact, it is a wider tendency, manifested in populist regimes in Hungary and Poland as well, which might be described as "emerging conservative national capitalism" as opposed to completely "comprador capitalism".

However, a sort of "liberal national capitalism" was also possible that did not compromise modernization. It emerged in Slovenia in contrast to more comprador varieties in other post-socialist countries. It was based on four pillars (Kržan, 2014):

First, a privatization process that favored managers, workers and the state instead of foreign capital. It facilitated internal accumulation (investment of retained profits) and enabled "voluntary" intensification of labor productivity needed for retaining cost competitiveness.

Second, a monetary policy of a slightly depreciated currency instead of fixed-exchange rates. This too forced the management to rely on internal accumulation rather than direct foreign investment or loans, and partially offset the effects of relatively high wages on cost competitiveness.

Third, collective bargaining with agreements covering the labor in both private and public sectors ("neo-corporatist capitalism"), rather than company-based unionism. Centralized efforts secured relatively high wages, and gave trade unions influence on the legislature and government policies.

Four, an expanding, rather than shrinking, welfare state. This secured the relatively high living standards of working people beyond the purchasing power of wages, which was especially important for the retired and the unemployed. It also contributed to internal consumption and savings, important for this regime of accumulation.

In short, Slovenia behaved like central European capitalist countries behaved before neoliberalism prevailed. It was not only the consequence of the emerging capitalist class' self-interest (as effective owners who wanted the economy to develop). It was also an outcome of other processes: secession from Yugoslavia, the ideological hegemony of national over comprador fractions of the emerging ruling class, and the class struggle of the working class. The IMF's stabilization programme of privatization and deregulation relied on the Yugoslav federal authorities, whereas the focus of the separatist Slovenian bureaucracy was to obtain monetary and fiscal sovereignty (Podvršič, 2018: 30). Furthermore, the country lacked the financial means to uphold a fixed exchange rate, having introduced its currency before becoming a member of the IMF. Monetary policy was based on the deliberate decisions of the leading economists, who were Keynesians. This, in turn, reflected a wider hegemony of the emerging national bourgeoisie and its political and ideological representatives, who certainly opted for capitalism, but not neoliberalism.

Trade unions quickly transformed from organizations for pacifying labor into militant opposition to the managerial groups and the state (Breznik & Mence, 2020). The process began in the late 1980s, with the wave of wildcat strikes and culminated with the general strike in 1992, which forced the government to abandon an anti-inflationary wage policy and increase welfare benefits. This in turn helped to end the transition depression in 1993, sooner than in other post-socialist countries.

One should not idealize this regime of accumulation. It was restoring a system of exploitation with a rate of exploitation higher than in core countries. The working people were no longer formal owners of all social capital, but wage laborers with small and diminishing shares of private ownership. Workers' self-management rights were reduced to co-determination (Mitbestimmung). The establishment of a full-fledged capital market exposed enterprises to profit logic and unhindered foreign competition. This brought down entire industrial branches, and created a massive industrial reserve army of unemployed or early-retired workers after almost 40 years of full employment. Managerial and bureaucratic groups transformed into a capitalist class, the classical petit-bourgeoisie (large and medium farmers, small business owners) multiplied and gained influence. Land was re-commodified; the land ownership of the Catholic Church and pre-war propertied classes was restored, often in situ. It was still restoration of capitalism on the ruins of a society that came far in abolishing it. However, it enabled a decade and half of modernization, benefiting not only the middle strata but a large part of the population, without amassing a balance of payments deficits or external/public debts characteristic of developmental strategies in the peripheries (Kržan, 2014).

By the early 2000s, intensified competition eroded the power of trade unions and the solidarity of the working class by destroying uncompetitive sectors and fragmenting both the economy and labor. The share of employment in small enterprises with low unionization kept rising. Outsourcing created a large low-technology (service) sector with much higher rates of exploitation than in exporting or public sectors (Bembič, 2017: 376). This, in turn, differentiated the interests of various segments of labor and weakened their solidarity.

However, the decisive blow to "emerging national capitalism" was institutional (Kržan, 2014). Accession to the EU and Eurozone after 2004 brought down two pillars of the "emerging national capitalism", "Keynesian" monetary and fiscal policies. It is self-evident that the Euro means a fixed-exchange rate and ever more appreciated currency, plus a central bank not willing to support government spending or debt servicing. The EU's fiscal rules—included into the Slovenian constitution in 2017—preclude fiscal intervention and developmental measures, whereas the European common market precludes economic autonomy, especially the control of capital flows.

Right-wing governments and the crisis of the Eurozone have done away with the third pillar, state ownership of the banking sector and much of the domestic (private) ownership in other sectors. This process was quite abrupt and was due to a combination of an influx of cheap credit after the alignment with the Eurozone in 2004, and a new wave of privatization of the remaining state shares, mostly attempted in a form of management buyouts (MBOs). The severe drop in economic activity in 2009 (–7.8%) coupled with a protracted recession in 2012 and 2013, caused by austerity policies and the Eurozone debt crisis, was reflected in a rise of non-performing loans. The government recapitalized and later privatized state-owned or nationalized banks. Many attempts at MBOs failed, leading to bankruptcies—especially in the construction sector—or foreign takeovers.

This reduced the basis of the "emerging national bourgeoisie" especially in the construction and trade sectors, but also in manufacturing. It also eroded the fourth "pillar", collective bargaining. Parallel to integration into the EU, governments deregulated not only labor (by legalizing agency work and other atypical forms of employment), but also business organizations, especially by abolishing compulsory membership. This further reduced the scope of collective bargaining and established competition among employers' organizations, which strengthened the influence of employers in low-wage sectors and caused a general radicalization (Bembič, 2017: 377–378).

Although the Great Recession did not initiate a new period, it strengthened the comprador tendencies that became dominant with the accession to the EU. Moreover, pressures that enhance comprador tendencies will probably increase: with western Europe's capacity to sustain global competition falling, taking advantage of "internal peripheries" will become more important (Močnik, 2019: 30). Although Slovenian labor still enjoys the highest living standards and level of social and participatory rights among "post-socialist" countries and although the welfare state has not yet been dismantled, the achieved standard is far from secured.

If our analysis is correct, "emerging national capitalism" in Slovenia turned into a comprador system not because it was economically unsustainable, but because both the "emerging national bourgeoisie" (including its political and ideological representatives) and the trade unions (as the sole representatives of the working classes) renounced independence—the basis of their relative success—for the sake of "joining Europe" and "adopting the Euro". This decision depended on a broader "orientalist" ideology, according to which accession to the EU and NATO meant "getting away from the Balkans" and becoming a "normal state". This ideology neglected opposition between the center and periphery, and ignored the lagging behind of the southern European countries that was already evident (cf. the crisis in Portugal after it joined the Eurozone). For the capitalist class, giving up autonomy seemed to be an acceptable price for tighter integration into European production chains and expanding exports, even though it also meant losing much of their ownership of the means of production.

It is harder to understand why trade unions not only did not oppose this, but were even willing to sacrifice basic workers' rights in order to achieve it. This leads us back to the question of working class autonomy. In the early 1990s, trade unions formulated an authentic working class position (in a capitalist horizon, but still) and had the power to enforce it. At the height of the transition depression in 1992, they derailed the government's anti-inflation program by enforcing higher wages and benefits, whereas in 2004, they did the opposite for the sake of "adopting the Euro". After only ten years of capitalism, they were unable to form an alternative worldview thus becoming ever more reliant on the ruling ideology. This eroded their influence among the working class and increasingly limited their scope of action in the class struggles. In 2014, first substantial anticapitalistic political party—the Left—emerged and entered the parliament. It remains to be seen, though, whether it will become a force to re-establish an authentic working class position or just one of the facets of the parliamentary state apparatus.

The Restoration of Capitalism in Croatia: The Transformation of "technocracy" into a National Capital Class Blocked by Bureaucracy

The restoration of capitalism in eastern Europe was realized through the political mechanism of the nation state (Močnik, 2021). Former ruling groups used the political superstructure to introduce capitalist social relations and not vice versa, as happened in western Europe, where the capitalist class was able to expand, directly or indirectly, capitalist relations from economy to superstructure. However, in the case of Yugoslavia, restoration was not enforced so much by the central power (federation), but by its constituent federal republics. Each restored capitalism in a complicated socio-political environment, often acting against other republics as well as against the federal institutions.

The federal government of Ante Markovic was following IMF instructions that initiated the process formally by enabling privatization of social ownership in 1988/1989 (Bicanic & Franicevic, 2003; Bicanic, 1993). However, it was only after the Croatian Democratic Union (HDZ) took power in May 1990 that actual change began to take place. This was because the HDZ diverted all resources into establishing a bourgeois-democratic republic, which acquired legitimacy with the so-called "referendum for independence" in May 1991.

The privatization processes that started in Markovic's time aimed to transform social ownership into private ownership (and joint stock companies), with employees as the main shareholders. At that time, it seemed that the problems were predominantly in the economic sphere. But the form was political—Markovic strove to gain legitimacy at the federal level by redirecting the political crisis (the national question in Slovenia and Serbia, with the real possibility of it spreading to Croatia) towards economic solutions, although some authors claim that he devoted his energy towards political initiatives (Sasso, 2020). However, the complexity of the problem was in the fact that this was indeed an economic crisis, but one of political economy. Attempts in the late 1980s to gradually transform one part of ownership from social to private, to further liberate market tendencies, meant one thing—capitalist tendencies started to overcome socialist tendencies. So it seemed the stage was set for a final political clash where socialist tendencies would be liquidated. One could see the full complexity in the case of the Borovo workers in Vukovar. Current analysis of their struggle in 1987–1991 corrects the traditional nationalistic and pessimistic approach (see Cvek et al., 2019). An important part of this was expressed through the struggle between the various opposition parties that emerged in the 1989/90, on one side, and the reformed Croatian Communists, on the other. So it was not by chance that some of the trade union leaders eventually became functionaries of the HDZ and vice versa. In that way, the HDZ intervened in their economic struggles and installed the political (nationalistic) platform.

Economic issues in a broader sense took the form of a struggle for the national question as well as a political struggle for the Confederation of Yugoslavia. It could even be said that Slobodan Milosevic, then president of Socialist Republic of Serbia, had a considerable influence on the election outcome in Croatia. Milosevic's policy of overthrowing the leadership in Vojvodina, Montenegro and Kosovo, with indications of similar moves in the Croatian political scene antagonized Croats and Serbs in Croatia even more, thus giving the HDZ impetus for political action. In that context, the party that would advocate the most consistent political solution of the national problem, that would resist Milosevic, and that would fight for redefinition of the Serbian question in Croatia, had the best chance of winning power. Especially because the League of Communists (LC) did not manage to accommodate to the new situation (Marijan,

2016; Pauković, 2008). In addition, as the LC called parliamentary elections, they decided not to go with proportional representation but with a majority first-past-the-post system. So the HDZ, with a narrow win in the elections, actually won a big majority in the parliament.

All this created a situation in which the ruling party didn't have any serious opposition. Critics often said that the HDZ did not present its economic program during the election campaign, that is, that the HDZ was carefully hiding it. The explanation for this is simple—nominally they didn't have a real economic program at all. In reality, however, they had an elaborated economic program based on two pillars (Tuđman, 1995): the abolition of social ownership, and the right of Croatia to choose a different political, cultural and economic system, that is, the right to choose capitalism. With these demands, the HDZ was far more consistent than other parties. They had economic programs based on capitalist relations, but failed to recognize that the road to power was through the national question, and that the most effective road to introducing capitalism was through the immediate abolition of social ownership. Thus began a process of transformation and privatization that had two main features.

"Irregularities" and corruption were not the essence of restoration. Rather, it was the expropriation of the working class, that is, its separation, as immediate producers, from the means of production they owned and created—enlarged 12-fold in the previous four decades (Horvat, 2007). The historical process of separation was carried out by the state, abolishing social ownership, through privatization as well as nationalization. Therefore, the real issue for us is to underscore this historical fact, and to include those seemingly specific features (such as privatization irregularities and financial corruption) in the total context of expropriation. Most Croatian economists had a problem with this kind of analysis, because they believed that the capitalist system would be more efficient, thus bringing more welfare (Vojnić, 2003). In addition, they were immersed in the ideology of neoliberalism (Babić, 1993), even though the actual policies of the HDZ governments often diverged from neoliberal recipes (Šonje & Vujčić, in Meštrović, 2001).

The potential national bourgeoisie in Croatia got off to a bad start because the bureaucrats had political supremacy over the technocrats. Many former managers were removed and their political representative, federal Prime Minister Markovic, sidelined. Bureaucrats took complete control of the economy, as witnessed by the fact that Josip Manolic, a 70-year-old apparatchik and the representative of the former administrative (and secret service) regime, was made the first prime minister (Krušelj, 1990:14–15). During his brief mandate (24 August 1990–17 July 1991) he sanctioned the removal of all economic representatives of the technocracy and of the privatization view, that is, the removal of proponents of minimal state involvement.

The process of restoration was, of course, also influenced by the war. First of all, the economy was still shaken by the wave of strikes in the late 1980s. So, when the nationalist HDZ took power—sparking the rebellion of Serbs in Croatia in August 1990, attacks on the labor movement intensified. A narrative was then constructed that strikes were not only a destabilizing factor during wartime, but also an attempt to align with the Serbian enemy (especially if the workers' leaders were Serbs). Political pressures resulted in the "Agreement on cooperation and action during a state of war or imminent threat to the independence and unity of the Republic of Croatia", signed in September 1991. The Agreement guaranteed the Croatian government breathing space from strikes. However, because of the Government's political manoeuvres, the Agreement lasted only six months (Rul, 2016). Shortly thereafter, a leader of the railway trade union—which was the first union founded in Croatia—was killed on his doorstep. In the following months and years, there were dozens of attacks on union leaders.

In 1998, another protest was organized in Zagreb, which brought together around 10,000 workers from all over the country. The protest was supposed to take place on Zagreb's main square, but this was prevented by the police who had deployed 12,000 highly armed and equipped members of the regular and special police forces, members of the military police, firemen and elite army combat units from all over the country (Ivandić & Livada, 2015: 51–52). All of the above points to the modus operandi by which the initial accumulation of capital took place in Croatia.

In its next phase, "Croatian" capitalism was becoming capable of reproducing itself more through economic mechanisms. Besides the war, Tudjman's ruling model (autocratic tendencies, orientation towards autarchy, Euroscepticism) turned out to be a major obstacle for foreign capital. For its political representatives there was no dilemma in supporting an anti-HDZ coalition in the following parliamentary elections. This led to an election win in 2000 by the coalition of opposition parties, under the leadership of reformed Communists. Foreign capital now had more room for action. In the 1993–1999 period, Croatia realized €3.347 million of FDI, but in the following fourteen years until EU accession (2013) this had increased seven times –€23.517 million (Proposal of Investment Promotion Strategy in the Republic of Croatia: 14).

In the meantime, conflict was developing on two fronts, especially after the 2008 financial crisis, which in Croatia lasted until 2014/2015. On the one side, industrial capital, mainly represented through exports and domestic production, that is basically the weaker faction. On the other side, commercial and financial capital, predominantly foreign-owned. Situation is complicated by SMEs, both domestic and international with their own dynamics that incorporates parts of both factions. However, they are direct result of the capitalist reproduction and not primary accumulation. Present epidemiological crisis only highlights the main demand of SMEs—limiting the state influence in the economy (Šonje, 2020). Their appeal for a lesser role of the state is thus primarily confirmation and expression of objective level of development where the state, along with its administration, has become a constraint for their further economic expansion. Since 2015, SME's have gained a larger share in the country's total exports than big enterprises, and realized rapid rise in the share of the total income. That's why it could be said that the relationship towards the state and its role in the economy is going to be very good indicator of the class conflict dynamics between factions of capital—old and new—which have developed in the last 15 years. Further strengthening of the state will mean maintaining the status quo. Conversely, its weakening, along with a simultaneous restructuring of the public sector, cutting the price of labor and removing entry barriers for new financiers, suggests that the conflict is resolving in the direction of the rising power of the new class. However, because the battleground is peripheral capitalism, the weaker faction, that is industrial capital and SMEs, will very likely fail in their intention. Whatever the outcome, Croatian capitalism will continue to be a comprador one first and foremost (Birač, 2020).

Part of the dynamics of the class struggle described above found its expression in 2020 parliamentary elections. Almost two-thirds of parliament consists of the right-wing parties that are connected with both factions of capital, who is, for now, looking for representatives among conservative rather than liberal parties. On the other hand, a new left-green coalition that developed out of various social and civil movements in the last fifteen years, won seven seats in parliament. This implies that the recent convergence of the regime of accumulation in Croatia and Slovenia has produced similar political effects, at least on the left.

References

Amin, S. (2012). Implosion of the European system. *Monthly Review, 64*(4), 89–104.

Amin, S. (2013). China 2013. *Monthly Review, 64*(10), 14–33.

Amin, S. (2019). The new imperialist structure. *Monthly Review, 71*(3), 32–45.

Babić, M. (1993). The problems of transition from a socialist to a market economy in Yugoslavia. In M. Baldassarri & R. Mundell (Eds.), *Building the New Europe. Volume 2: Eastern Europe's transition to a market economy*. Palgrave Macmillan.

Bembič, B. (2017). From victory to victory to the final defeat. *Tiempo Devorado, 4*(2), 363–398.

Bićanić, I. (1993). Privatization in Croatia. *East European Politics and Societies and Cultures, 7*(3), 422–439.

Bicanic, I., & Franicevic, V. (2003). Understanding reform: The case of Croatia. *Balkan Observatory Working Papers 33*, The Vienna Institute for International Economic Studies, wiiw.

Birač, D. (2020). *Pandemijska kriza i njene posljedice za ekonomske i klasne odnose u Hrvatskoj*. http://politickamisao.com/pandemijska-kriza-i-njene-posljedice-za-ekonomske-i-klasne-odnose-u-hrvatskoj/. Accessed 6 July 2020.

Breznik, M., & M. Mence (2020). Workplace struggles in the background of trade unions collective actions in the post-socialist Slovenia. *Balkanologie, 15*(2). https://doi.org/10.4000/balkanologie.2592

Cvek, S., Račić, J., & Ivčić S. (2019). *Borovo u štrajku: rad u tranziciji 1987–1991*. Zagreb: Baza za radničku inicijativu i demokratizaciju.

Horvat, B. (2007). *Dinamični gospodarski razvoj*. Dom i svijet.

Ivandić, M., & Livada, I. (2015). *Lines of (Dis)Continuity: Forms and methods of labour struggle in Croatia 1990–2014*. Rosa Luxemburg Stiftung.

Krušelj, Ž. (1990, November 13). *Premijer za predah*. Danas (pp. 14–15).

Kržan, M. (2014). Crisis in Slovenia: Roots, effects, prospects. *Studies in Development (Middle East Technical University, Ankara), 41*(3), 323–348.

Kržan, M. (2019). Razvoj in nauki jugoslovanskega samoupravljanja. In I. Erdei, B. Dimitrijević, & T. Toroman (Eds.), *Jugoslavija: zašto i kako?* (pp. 126–148). Muzej Jugoslavije.

Marijan, D. (2016). Događanja naroda u Kninu 1989. Godine—slom jugoslavenske ustavne konstrukcije u Hrvatskoj. *Radovi Zavoda Za Povijesne Znanosti HAZU u Zadru, 58*, 439–467.

Močnik, R. (2019). What is new in new forms of nationalism. In V. Milisavljević & N. Mićunović (Eds.), *Xenophobia, identity and new forms of nationalism* (pp. 23–41). Institute of Social Sciences.

Močnik, R. (2021). 1968 in Yugoslavia, *Interventions. International Journal of Postcolonial Studies, 23*(3). https://doi.org/10.1080/1369801X.2020.1762694

Pauković, D. (2008). Posljednji kongres Saveza komunista Jugoslavije: Uzroci, tijek i posljedice raspada. *Suvremene Teme, 1*(1), 21–33.

Podvršič, A., & L. Schmidt (2018). From crisis to crisis. Behind the Scenes of peripherisation and europeanisation of Slovenia. *Revue de la regulation*, *24*(1). doi.org/https://doi.org/10.4000/regulation.13378

'Proposal of Investment Promotion Strategy in the Republic of Croatia'. 2014. *Ministry of economy and sustainable development*. Croatia.

Rul, M. (2016). *Uspon i pad sindikalnog pokreta u HŽ-u 1990-ih godina*. http://radnickaprava.org/tekstovi/clanci/mirna-rul-uspon-i-pad-sindikalnog-pokreta-u-hz-u-1990-ih-godina?fbclid=IwAR0To5QEFRiXcXnxnajhk0DifPFtWQqdgrm8-uEx0D_-s_wjzgAzUJ5uwCE. Accessed 11 July 2020.

Sasso, A. (2020). The political dimension of Ante Marković's reform project. *Contemporary Southeastern Europe, 7*(1), 25–48.

Suvin, D. (2016). *Splendour, misery, and possibilities. An x-ray of socialist Yugoslavia*. Brill.

Šonje, V., & Vujčić, B. (2001). 'Liberalizam' u vođenju ekonomske politike. In M. Meštrović (Ed.), *Globalizacija i njene refleksije u Hrvatskoj* (pp. 149–164). Ekonomski institut.

Šonje, V. (2020). *Hrvatska stagnira jer smo 100 godina zarobljeni u romantičnu ideju da će nam država sve riješiti*. https://www.telegram.hr/price/sonje-hrvatska-stagnira-jer-smo-100-godina-zarobljeni-u-romanticnu-ideju-da-ce-nam-drzava-sve-rijesiti/. Accessed 22 February 2020.

Tuđman, F. (1995). *Usudbene povijestice*. Hrvatska sveučilišna naklada.

Vojnić, D. (2003). Ekonomija i politika tranzicije u praksi—Gdje je Hrvatska? *Ekonomski Pregled, 54*(7–8), 621–650.

Woodward, S. (1995). *Socialist unemployment: The political economy of Yugoslavia, 1945–1990*. Princeton University Press.

Živković, A. (2013). *The future lasts a long time: A short history of European integration in the ex-Yugoslavia*. https://www.criticatac.ro/lefteast/the-future-lasts-a-long-time-a-short-history-of-european-integration-in-the-ex-yugoslavia-2/. Accessed 17 February 2020.

Bosnia and Herzegovina After the Transition: Forever Postwar, Postsocialist and Peripheral?

Danijela Majstorović and Zoran Vučkovac

This article brings together several strands of research which we as authors conducted or participated in over the course of almost a decade, conjoined with our experience as activists involved in numerous direct actions in Bosnia and Herzegovina (BiH or Bosnia). This chapter is mostly an overview covering our previous research and thinking about BiH's colonial, postwar and postsocialist condition, and attempted productive theoretical readings of such spaces and subjectivities with respect to the economic and socio-political basis for postcoloniality, peripherality and marginality (see Majstorović & Vučkovac, 2016; Majstorović, 2019b). It further examines political and market reforms since the 1992–1995 wars, and forms of resistance to shady privatizations (Majstorović et al., 2015), epistemes of nationhood and genocide denial (Majstorović in Salamurović & Berocal 2019), as well as grassroots commemorative struggles (Vučkovac in Milošević & Trošt, 2020) and migration as resistance (Majtorović, 2020). We have also been involved

D. Majstorović (✉)
University of Banja Luka, Banja Luka, Bosnia and Herzegovina

Z. Vučkovac
Justus Liebig University, Giessen, Germany
e-mail: zoran.vuckovac@gcsc.uni-giessen.de

A. Gagyi and O. Slačálek (eds.), *The Political Economy of Eastern Europe 30 years into the 'Transition'*, International Political Economy Series,
https://doi.org/10.1007/978-3-030-78915-2_5

in activist struggles through various initiatives in BiH and other post-Yugoslav countries, most recently with the "Justice for David" movement, which arose after a 21-year-old's body was found on the riverbank in Banja Luka and subsequent state-sanctioned violence against the protesters who occupied the main square for almost two years.

The chapter first discusses issues of marginality and peripherality in BiH as a postwar and postsocialist country, trying to shift the term away from the economic reasoning present in much of world-systems theory to regimes of biopolitical governance that actively produce internal peripheries through clientelism, the salariat (Standing, 2011), police brutality and undemocratic ethnonationalist rule. Even though the European Union (EU) and United Nations (UN) have had protocolonial mechanisms of control built into the constitution of BiH, most notably in the Office of High Representative (OHR), they have been complicit in maintaining ethnonationalists in power, supported multiple waves of privatization and have condoned violence against migrants via the International Organization for Migration (IOM) and other international organizations. We further trace the economic and political restructuring that has occurred after the war, as well as acts of resistance through the examples of the February 2014 protests, Dita workers' resistance to shady privatizations and the "Justice for David" movement, as well as economic migrations and political asylum seeking.

On Being Peripheral

The two wars and their aftermath mark most notably the statehood of contemporary BiH: the Second World War (WWII) and the 1992–1995 war. It was during the WWII that the Socialist Republic of BiH (SRBiH) was founded within the Socialist Federal Republic of Yugoslavia (SFRY), propelling the formerly poorest parts of the Ottoman and Austro-Hungarian empires, and later the first Yugoslavia (1918–1941) into the socialist modernity. It must be noted that even within this constellation Bosnia still ended up on the flip side of Yugoslav uneven regional development despite attempts to alleviate the discrepancies (see for example Bombelles, 1991). Furthermore, the project was abandoned altogether during the 1992–1995 war resulting in close to 100 000 war casualties (Tokača, 2012).[1] After the 1992–1995 war, the contemporary BiH state came about as a result of the peace talks in Dayton, Ohio[2] as a federation of two entities: the Republika Srpska (RS), and the Federation of BiH (FBiH) along with the Brčko district. The Dayton Peace Agreement (DPA) thus legitimized the ethnonationalist division of the country ushered in by ethnic cleansing and genocide, and on top of that it marked the rule of the OHR—the single most powerful authority with powers to oust democratically elected individuals, introduce and revoke laws etc.[3]

In world-systems scholarship, SFRY, as a Second World, socialist, eastern European country, was first classified as semi-peripheral in the 1960s and 1980s (Wallerstein, 1974) and some thirty years later as a "periphery" (Dunaway & Clelland, 2017: 415). Though the socialist BiH has been underdeveloped and substantially marginalized, in the postwar years the country has been referred to as a "semi-periphery" (Bonfiglioli, 2015; Blagojević, 2009) and, more recently, as a "super-periphery" (Bartlett, 2009), or "periphery of the periphery" (Bechev, 2012). The reason for this "escalating" peripherality is not just the terrible devastation of the early 1990s, but also the exceptionally high unemployment[4] and low growth rates during the country's postsocialist phase, marked by incompetent, corrupt governments, migration processes and the crises spilling over from the EU (see Majstorović, 2019b: 134). In other words, we are further "complicating" the world-systems arguments of peripheralization by taking into account political and social factors like the BiH's protocolonial condition, privatization processes, protests and uprisings as well as the silencing of opposing voices that result in economic migration and political asylums.

In addition to the 1990s war, the switch to a market economy or what Jansen calls "forced transition" (2006: 186) endorsed by the international

[1] The estimated death toll is 95,940 of whom more than 38,239 were civilians, out of whom 31,107 Bosniaks, 4178 Serbs, 2484 Croats and 470 others.

[2] The General Framework Agreement for Peace in BiH or the Dayton Agreement is the peace agreement reached at Wright-Patterson Air Force Base near Dayton, Ohio, United States, on 1 November 1995, and was formally signed in Paris, France, on 14 December 1995. These accords put an end to the three and a half year-long war in BiH.

[3] The High Representatives heading the OHR have since 2006 mostly given up on their use of Bonn powers to impose laws, but the institution of OHR as the final interpreter of BiH constitution which is the Dayton agreement.

[4] According to the most recent statistics, unemployment rate in Bosnia and Herzegovina (BiH) averages around 42.39% (2017–2018).

community (most notably the OHR), and the ethnonationalist power over postwar privatizations, peripherality in BiH has also been the consequence of the quasi-democratic rule of these elites personified by the three strongest political parties SNSD, HDZ, SDA.[5] They have secured the continuation of warlike logic in holding sway of power and assets obtained through the war, often by heavy policing, securitization and even retribution against its most outspoken critics.[6] While during the 1992–1995 ethnic exclusionism resulted in mass killings of those belonging to other ethnic groups,[7] twenty years after Dayton different biopolitical regimes continued marginalizing the disobedient members of their own ethnic group—very often when talking about why they immigrated in the post-2015 wave, Bosnian and Herzegovinians would bring up these examples (Majstorović, 2020).

The socio-economic origins of peripherality can be looked at from the position of a politico-economic restructuring and its three phases (Majstorović et al., 2015). The early political restructuring includes the neocolonial-style Europeanization and democratization between 1996 and 2006. The second phase is the one of the late political restructuring (2006–2014) marked by the rise of the new ethnonationalist elites whose members privatized strategic companies thus solidifying their position of power. The third phase, involving the period after 2014, was marked by the civic and workers' protests and plenums in major Bosnian

[5] These are the three ruling parties in BiH at the moment. SNSD stands for the Alliance of Independent Social Democrats- the major Bosnian Serb party; SDA stands for the Party of Democratic Action—the major Bosniak party; HDZ stands for Croatian Democratic Community—the major party of Bosnian Croats. Due to complex constitutional framework it was impossible to avoid coalitions that exclude any or all of them from state, entity or cantonal government.

[6] Damir Arsenijević writes that the logic of privatization bears the same marks as the wartime creation of mass graves, "from the negligence of the toxic materials for profit, all the way to denying existence of any potential harm." From Arsenijević, D. (2020, June 16). Ekološko nasilje ima istu logiku kao ratno. *Bilten- Regonalni portal*. Retrieved from: https://www.bilten.org/?p=33766.

[7] Both BiH entities continue to exist as territories where ethnic cleansing was successful with 3.6% of Serbs in the Federation of BiH and 13.99% of Bosniaks in RepublikaS-rpska according to the results of the 2013 census. The 2013 census did not pass without conflicts on both methodology and final results. See Arnautović, M. (2016, June 30). Rezultati popisa: Bošnjaci polovina bh stanovništva, entiteti etnički homogeni. *Radio Slobodna Evropa*. Retrieved from: https://www.slobodnaevropa.org/a/popisni-rezultati-nakon-25-godina-u-federaciji-vecina-bosnjaci-u-rs-srbi/27830387.html.

cities including Sarajevo and Tuzla against shady privatizations that have resulted in the burning of several cantonal government buildings; the most radical experiment in non-institutional politics since the collapse of Yugoslavia (albeit short lived). Protesters stated they "were hungry in all three languages," and through acts of rebellion marked by significant "cross-entity" relations of cooperation, bypassed Dayton-embedded ethnic divisions. They have paved the way for common citizenship and class solidarity, more social justice and a redefinition of left politics in BiH (see Arsenijević, 2014). This phase has had its continuation on the main square of Banja Luka four years later reacting to the political refusal to find out who killed David Dragičević. This case was first characterized by the police as an accident, then as a homicide, and led nine months later to the police violently expelling and chasing the protesters. The protests started when the father of the murdered David Dragičević—a student whose death the authorities refused to investigate—held a 900-day plenary session (since 24 March 2018, continuing to this day but in much smaller numbers) naming the Republika Srpska entity, as part of the new Dayton state, as culpable of David's death.

Police brutality against the "Justice for David" supporters escalated during the days between 25 and 31 December 2018 followed by the police officially banning the protests[8] several protesters ending up in prison and David's father Davor Dragičević seeking political asylum in Austria, followed by public intellectuals like Srđan Šušnica, and also some prominent "Justice for David" members like Sofija Grmuša and Daniela Ratešić, leaving BiH.[9] In a nutshell, BiH is not just an economic periphery in relation to the rest of the EU, but it has peripheralized

[8] See for example Filipović, G. (2018, December 31). Bosnian-Serb Police Ban Anti-Government Rallies, Target Activist. *Bloomberg*. Retrieved from: https://www.bloomberg.com/news/articles/2018-12-31/protests-in-banja-luka-pose-dilemma-for-bosnian-serb-government.

[9] For more background information on the asylum seekers see: *Trajno preseljenje: Danijela Ratešić iz "Pravde za Davida" napušta RS?*. (2019, January 18). Opcija.net. Retrieved from https://tv1.ba/istaknuto/ratesic-dosen-za-tv1-ba-zasto-sam-morala-napustiti-svoju-zemlju/ and *Ubiti Šušnicu: nastavlja se Dodikov progon protivnika režima*. (2019, February 7). Tačno.net. Retrieved from: https://www.tacno.net/novosti/ubiti-susnicu-nastavlja-se-dodikov-progon-protivnika-rezima/?fbclid=IwAR1CmL7-6RJ-sc596YcoBhe5KEi_r3QsA2Wcrm0uEjelziL71Sj1gQcsMbE.

from within by the ruling oligarchs while leaving most people at the socio-economic margins[10] (Majstorović, 2019b: 135).

Approach and Methodological Notes

Our role in writing this has been twofold: we approach it both as academic researchers and engaged activists who either participated in the protests or their aftermath, trying to connect with all those demanding social justice as a radical shift from the previously known ethnopolitics. Coming from Banja Luka, we had been a part of the protest for "Picin park," against selling off a central park to a shady investor back in 2012.[11] After the February 2014 protests that were mostly occurring in the Federation of BiH, we actively participated in an attempt to create a political platform for workers and civic protesters. In 2015 we were a part of a collective from Banja Luka that established a social center (BASOC) that sought to spark debates and initiate actions dealing with historical revisionism, feminist struggles and social justice. This meant countering the ongoing erasure of progressive Yugoslav heritage and genocide denial, as well as supporting commemorative struggles regarding the latest war throughout BiH. Work here revolved around public debates on historical revisionism,[12] interventions in public events[13] and commemorative

[10] One could rightly raise the issue of popular will in voting for Dodik and the SNSD at the October 2018 election including his skill in completely ruining the opposition. There are no voting behavior studies in BiH for the 2018 elections, but our assumption is that people voted for him not only for ethnonational security and political clientelistic reasons, but also because they were told to do so. In any event, after October 2018, there is no opposition whatsoever in the RS and police violence can be directed, as was shown in December 2018, to silence anyone who thinks differently; so marginalization can be seen in the self-censorship of many public figures for fear of life and security.

[11] See Picin Park: Its defenders earned hardline retribution (n.d.). Retrieved from https://stop-persecution.org/bih-banja-luka-picin-park-zeljko-vulic.

[12] Public debate about historical revisionism in RepublikaSrpska entity. For a description in Serbo-Croat see M.I.D. (2017, October 17) Preispitivanje nacije i istine: Kakva je to (nova) *Istorija Republike Srpske*.Buka magazin. Retrieved from:https://www.6yka.com/novosti/preispitivanje-nacije-i-istine-kakva-je-to-je-nova-istorija-republike-srpske.

[13] Intervention in official commemorative process of the Battle of Kozara from the second world war. See in Serbo-Croatian: Obrenović, M. (2015, July 5). Kozara: Legitimisani zbog partizanskih pjesama tokom himne RS-a. Al Jazeera. Retrieved from: http://balkans.aljazeera.net/vijesti/kozara-legitimisani-zbog-partizanskih-pjesama-tokom-himne-rs.

landscapes.[14] We further worked with independent workers' unions on various issues, from changes to the labor law to economic restructuring, and supported feminist struggles throughout BiH and the region, both as academics and activists.[15] Our academic work for the past five years has also revolved around similar issues, and the text presented here is a recapitulation of sorts, bringing together our research on history and memory, gender and class struggles that was either previously published (Majstorović, 2019a, b, 2016a, b; Majstorović & Vučkovac, 2016; Vučkovac, 2020), or is ongoing.[16]

Demanding social justice above ethnic justice, as a discourse that rested on people's fear while political elites grew stronger, is at times what Denzin and Giardina (2009: 200) calls "a militant utopianism, a provisional Marxism without guarantees, a cultural studies (sic) that is anticipatory, interventionist, and provisional." Our politics are unambiguous here, by engaging simultaneously in "doing research" and "performing resistance" by engaging in a wider resistance front in BiH, and actively creating space to nurture this front, we seek to provide the grounds for liberation practice and a pedagogy of freedom, against

[14] Initiative *Jer me se tiče* has set up a number of so-called guerrilla monuments, one such commemorates the Sarajevo Serbs executed at the location of Kazani. For more, see Sarajevo: Postavljena spomen-ploča za žrtve zločina na Kazanima, traže procesuiranje zločina u opkoljenom Sarajevu.(2015, December 7). Buka magazin. Retrieved from: https://www.6yka.com/novosti/sarajevo-postavljena-spomen-ploca-za-zrtve-zlocina-na-kazanima-traze-procesuiranje-zlocina-u-opkoljenom sarajevu.

[15] Both entities have been tailoring their labor codes according to IMS's guidelines which sparked a lot of discussion and protests (see for example this protest from the end of 2015: Veselinović, G., Milojević, M. and Katana, E. (2015, Decemebr 28). Banja Luka: Vladajuća većina usvojila novi Zakon o radu. Radio Slobodna Evropa. Retrieved from:https://www.slobodnaevropa.org/a/sindikalni-protest-u-banjaluci-ne-damo-da-nam-umanje-prava/27453021.html.). Since the protests of February 2014, BiH saw a number of initiatives and protests against disinvestment in public infrastructure and services, as well as privatizations and public policies that threaten the environment or are a cause of major health concerns. Examples are the protest against mini dams by women of Kruščica, workers of Fortuna and Dita fighting for their factories, as well as struggles for clean air and public water infrastructure in Sarajevo.

[16] Majstorović is currently researching the economic migrations from BiH with the support of a Humboldt scholarship at the University of Giessen where Vučkovac is currently working on a dissertation regarding the lived experience of class in postsocialist transition and privatization as well as attempts to commemorate victims from the latest war at now privatized localities.

the systematic production of poverty and inequality insisting on reflective memory politics. In this way, we enact what Denzin and Giardina (2009: 47) calls "pedagogies of hope...(which) offer ways of holding fraudulent political regimes accountable for their actions." Lastly, we are concerned with a performative social science that is multidisciplinary and oriented to mixed-method data collection, while exposing the complexities and contradictions that exist under official history (Trouillot, 1995; Mutua & Swadener, 2004: 16) and showing the critical potential of the aforementioned struggles.

In this respect we trace a short history of the systemic destruction of the organized resistance and side-lining of working class issues in Bosnia through war and genocide, the dismantling of social property and self-management, an irredentist nationalism inscribed in the constitution that has cemented ethnic over social justice. The resistance strategies we showcase here range from occupation and grassroots actions, to economic migration and abandonment.

From Socialist Yugoslavia to Privat(Ized) Bosnia

Whereas the SFRY had a privileged international role after the second world war being "between the East and the West," after its breakup, the newly formed states were removed from this former Second World centrality. While new "ethnopolitical entrepreneurs" (Brubaker, 2002: 166) benefited from ethnic nationalism and ethnic cleansing, for others—those who still see the socialist Yugoslav period as a period of modernity both in the sense of emancipation (Majstorović in Dugandžić & Okić, 2016b: 84–115) and also development (Kirn 2019)—Yugoslavia as a lived experience and a figure of thought has remained an open wound (Majstorović, 2019b). The 1992–1995 war was the rupture in which the Yugoslav socialist legacy died—ethnonationalist and capitalist hegemony won out as the mainstream political vision.

Left in the background of historical and social analysis in the wake of the 1990s political and social insurgencies, the privatization of BiH industrial complexes was too often seen as a necessary, natural and neutral part of the historically inevitable transition to liberal democracy and free market, with workers having little or no say in the matter (Jansen, 2006: 186–190). Skilled and unskilled, former and current industrial workers were among the social groups most affected by the economic, social and cultural transformations of the last two and a half decades, and yet they were often seen as passive agents who did not understand their role within capitalism. It was often backgrounded to identity issues on research agendas[17] that deindustrialization, unemployment, pauperization, ethnic rivalry on the labor market and the persistence of structural disparities—all of which were particularly intensely felt by the working classes.

The unity of Yugoslav workers after the second world war until the 1990s wars was further damaged through a combination of the impact of, on the one hand, the dissolution of large enterprises during and after the war, and, on the other hand, what was—despite alleged media freedom—an acute lack of public space suitable for the articulation of workers' struggles (Dale & Hardy, 2011: 259–260; Musić, 2013: 10–11). In this period, public property was passed into the hands of private individuals or political parties, while the working class, its interests and its political subjectivity along with matters concerning social justice disappeared from public debate. The Yugoslav working class had been weakened by austerity measures introduced in Yugoslavia as early as the 1970s (Živković, 2014: 49) while the elites wanting to preserve their privileges in socialism and afterwards compromised much of the social equality discourse. By giving way to identity politics pushed by the elites after Tito's death in 1980 and later, the Yugoslav working class simply became "amputated from the social body it once served" (Lowinger, 2009: 78). Instead, the ethnic other had to be reimagined and even "phantasized as a fundamentalist" (Monument Group, 2011) that was constantly threatening "our" ethnical being, with the continuity of this threat explained by a variant of the "ancient ethnic hatreds" thesis (Kaplan, 2005).

The loss of social property and self-management —two imperfect but real artefacts of Yugoslav socialism, only furthered the peripheralization of the country. In this respect, it is also necessary to state that BiH has undergone three large waves of privatization. The first took place in 1989–1990, the so-called "Marković privatizations",[18] when it was still

[17] Sabrina Perić has highlighted this in an unpublished paper, claiming that "the Bosnian belongs to the world of 1992–1995: they can only be explained in terms of the paradigmatic war event. All sociality stems from the war and Bosnians of various affiliations are susceptible to nationalist ideologies, which were solidified in a terrifying moment of violence." Perić claims that war ushered what Gramsci calls "spontaneous consent" on ethnonationalist's operational logic both by those researchers who embrace it and those who barely acknowledge its existence.

[18] Named after the Prime Minister of SFRY, Ante Marković, whose government passed the Law on Social Capital in 1989–1990 and enabled privatization in SFRY.

part of Yugoslavia whereas the second, in 1997, was under the guidance of USAID. The third occurred between 2006 and 2008, during which time new laws regulating privatization processes in the two entities were introduced (Divjak & Martinović, 2009). The first wave of privatization had enabled workers of socially owned enterprises to buy shares at a discount relative to the enterprises' estimated values (based on the previous year's annual balance sheets), but these shares could not be traded on the stock market (Bayliss, 2005).[19]

Legal validation of the practice of denying formerly common ownership and self-management of Yugoslav workers by declaring socially owned property state-owned came through the USAID-guided privatization in 1997. State-owned enterprises were, in the postwar period, owned either by the BiH Federation or RS governments and the privatization continued through a voucher model. This policy enabled citizens to buy shares in the to-be-privatized state companies (Bayliss, 2005), consolidating "economic power in the hands of the few by enabling those with the means, connections and resources to engage in active secondary trading of vouchers" (Donais, 2002: 9).Voucher privatization failed to become an engine of economic growth (Bayliss, 2005; Donais, 2002)—a much wanted although contested desire of a worker in the periphery such as Bosnia.[20] Instead, ownership was "widely dispersed in the hands of unsophisticated and inexperienced shareholders" (Bayliss, 2005: 44–45), further entrenching the economic positions of BiH's nationalists and "reducing the prospects of ethnic reintegration" (Donais, 2002: 8). The third (and ongoing) wave of privatization further included the issuing of public tenders and bids, mainly intended for those enterprises deemed to be of strategic value (such as telecommunications, electrical companies and refineries). This last push was, moreover, meant to review

[19] A total of 585 (5.24%) socially owned companies carried out these privatizations, affecting organizations that employed 98,494 (12.87%) of BiH's workforce at the time.

[20] Even though capitalist growth cycles have been globally criticized, concepts like green growth or degrowth, as well as policy aiming at divestment of for example coal power plants or extractive industries have never taken off the ground in BiH. Also, most of the "successful" privatizations of socialist conglomerates were actually a part of the extractive economies of non-renewable resources that can only be partly processed in BiH and then exported. So we face a paradox whenever, for example, ArcelorMittal is criticized for not adhering to the bare minimum of ecological standards, and production grinds to a halt leaving thousands without work.

privatizations that had already concluded but were now deemed to have failed.[21]

Back to the Socialist Future?

What then would be alternative, possibly decolonial, conceptualizations and readings to the problems reflected in contemporary struggles on the ground? And how do we rethink (and reinsert) anew a socialist horizon that has been missing from a lot of the decolonial theory (especially from the decolonial work coming from former USSR, see for example Tlostanova, 2019)? Crucial here is that with the addressing of relevant theoretical grounds of peripherality and marginality, the vantage point of the decolonial perspective should not neglect the problems of the actually existing SFRY state socialism (Karkov & Valiavicharska, 2018), but instead "value its socialist emancipatory potential, especially in comparison to the post-1995 period marked by repatriarchalization and retraditionalization, international interventionism, and ethnonationalist capitalism" (Majstorović, 2019b: 133). One is invited here to ask are these struggles merely attempts at "becoming the center," do they call for a new socialism, and in what way do these struggles for survival open space(s) of resistance and alternatives to both capital and coloniality while striving to offer different, better lives for its people?

Working with activists and academics in Tuzla,[22] we found that workers have managed to voice their concerns and prevent the squandering of the factory by stopping its sale on three different occasions. With the little raw materials that they had, they managed to restart the production but

[21] For example, the Law on the Revision of Privatization of State Capital and Banks in FBiH was adopted in 2012, establishing an Agency for Revision of Privatization in FBiH that would review failed and suspicious privatizations. However, the Agency did not actually start work until the first quarter of 2015, and thus has so far been unable to provide any tangible results.

[22] We have been invited to provide linguistic analyses of twenty odd interviews with Dita workers by the Workers' University collective, comprised of researchers and activists who supported them throughout their "protest for production" occupation of the factory, and the restarting of production after they managed to expel the owner. The analysis was provided for the collective as a part of attempts to understand better the working class grievances and create potential bridges between activist, academic and workers, therefore it will not be published. For more information on the Tuzla Workers' University check their website at http://radnickiuniverzitet.org/. but also the work of DamirArsenijević, Jasmina Husanović, Larisa Kurtović, Andrew Gilbert, Boris Stapić and others.

eventually came to the realization that the factory needed to be privatized, the only thing left to insist on was a "responsible owner." Their goal was to continue working and producing, and they were well aware that reclaiming the factory as owners (for different examples see Kojanić, 2018) would be close to impossible. With the 2018 Justice for David movement in RS, issues such as police brutality, a weak legal system, public security and trust in the public institutions were voiced as additional elements of distrust, especially before and after the October 2018 state elections.

Another response to peripheralization that gained prominence since 2013 is migration—more and more BiH citizens are moving to the supposed "core," either through permanent or temporary arrangements, or through applying and reapplying for work visas in the EU. Since 2013, BiH citizens have been quietly taking either "grey economy" jobs or more permanent employment arrangements, mostly in Germany and Austria, but also in other EU countries. Germany is the target country, for which the Sarajevo Embassy approved 13,300 visa applications in only for the first nine months of 2017, and the number is estimated to have tripled since. Germany provides 24-h care for some 1.86 million elderly people, in which around 300,000 mostly female eastern Europeans already work (Lutz in Hanewinkel, 2015); young men get recruited too, as the need is growing. These new socio-economic migrants are mostly care workers, domestic and construction workers, as these are the most widely available entry-level jobs.

But parallel to people migrating, or rather fleeing much of the region,[23] BiH has become a transit country on the migrant route. Given that state capacities are rather meager, even with support from the EU and IOM it is questionable whether any humane treatment can come out of "managing" migrations. The scope of this management has been seen in the past two years: a migrant camp was set up on a former dumpsite in close proximity to a minefield, with no access to clean water; it has limited capacity in manpower and funds. The IOM—with direct oversight of parts

[23] The complexity of the latest migratory wave from the Balkan countries is hardly reducible to bad government or their accession to EU, with consequences still beyond comprehension or simple solutions. See: Judah, T. (2019, October 14). Bye-Bye Balkans: A Region in Critical Demographic Decline. *Balkan Insight*. Retrieved from: https://balkaninsight.com/2019/10/14/bye-bye-balkans-a-region-in-critical-demographic-decline/?fbclid=IwAR0Ef_OpCDxBU_7p_CryCxHzqXhkNayvKgn3fu5DAyBiRXbo6pb8_hIglk8.

of the country—has worked diligently to put civil society, like the many NGOs and the press, under more or less direct control, while investing in private security forces where the state has failed to provide the desired level of security. The looming humanitarian crisis and one of the "living dystopias in Europe" expose the conditions of coloniality of power, where the post-colonial migrant on their way from war and poverty gets stuck in the "desert of postsocialism" (Horvat & Štiks, 2012), on their route to the center. The entanglement between protests and migrations as well as relicts of socialist heritage offer a point of rupture and a place from where to rethink growth, ownership, production and a decolonial resistance that is simultaneously a socialist struggle—not for some restorable past but a future that is to come.

By Way of Conclusion

BiH powerfully shows that the "periphery" is not a homogenous container where everyone is marginalized—looking closer, we see a polarized society made up of "the people" and ethnonationalist elites (see Arrighi, 1985). While these elites promise nationalist fantasies bordering on neofascism, patriarchy and religious conservatism, after more than twenty years of largely incompetent and irresponsible rule, they have privatized, plundered and squandered the former social property leaving the country impoverished and indebted. Unlike the 1990s and early 2000s when international interventionism in BiH was at its peak (Majstorović, 2007), today neither the OHR nor the EU seem keen to intervene in BiH's internal affairs even though they are located in the constitutional framework of the country (OHR) and have legalized its protectorate in order to secure peace in BiH. Both local and international actors seem to have accepted the status quo.

We have also tried to show the constitutive elements of BiH peripherality, with a focus on the more than twenty years of experiments with new forms of sovereign rule, the active production of underdevelopment and a recruiting ground for both skilled and unskilled labor since the 1992–1995 war. Almost three decades after the fall of real socialism, BiH has dismantled most of its socialist heritage through war, deindustrialization, privatization, ethnic racism, historical revisionism etc. and shares with the other countries of the Balkans all of the conditions of neoliberal capitalism. Well after postsocialism in the former Yugoslavia, we have seen various resistance movements, public occupations of space for protest, a return to nationalism, as well as migration. Therefore, our text is an invitation to think with and about forms of resistance, situated geographically but also historically at the border of Europe. As we have tried to document here, Bosnia's peripheral position has shifted several times since the dismantling of socialist Yugoslavia—this has always had tangible consequences for bodies being violated, murdered or banished and property changing owners, being squandered, pillaged and stolen in its wake. Documenting the contemporary politico-economic contemporary history in a historical materialist kind of way should serve one goal other than the archiving "for the future"—the one of analysis. Only then can we start conceiving of new joint struggles and solidarities from where new socialities can emerge, doing away with peripherality altogether by delinking from global capitalist networks while striving for a more just and equal world.

References

Arrighi, G. (1985). *Semiperipheral development: The politics of Southern Europe in the twentieth century*. Sage.

Arsenijević, D. (2014). *Unbribable Bosnia and Herzegovina: The struggle for the commons*. Baden-Baden: Nomos.

Bartlett, W. (2009). Economic development in the European super-periphery: Evidence from the Western Balkans. *Economic Annals, 54*(181), 21–44.

Bayliss, K. (2005). *Post-conflict privatisation: A review of developments in Serbia and Bosnia Herzegovina*. London: Overseas Development Institute.

Bechev, D. (2012). *The Periphery of the periphery: The Western Balkans and the Euro Crisis*. European Council on Foreign Relations.

Blagojević, M. (2009). *Knowledge production at the semi-periphery: A gender perspective*. Institut za Kriminološka i Sociološka Istraživanja.

Bombelles, J. T. (1991). Federal aid to the less developed areas of Yugoslavia. *East European Politics and Societies, 5*(3), 439–465. https://doi.org/10.1177/0888325491005003003

Bonfiglioli, C. (2015). Gendered citizenship in the global European periphery: Textile workers in post-Yugoslav states. *Women's Studies International Forum (WSIF), 49*, 57–65. https://doi.org/10.1016/j.wsif.2014.07.004

Brubaker, R. (2002). Ethnicity without groups. *European Journal of Sociology, 43*(02), 163–189. https://doi.org/10.1017/S0003975602001066

Dale, G., & Hardy, J. (2011). Conclusion: The 'crash' in Central and Eastern Europe. In G. Dale (Ed.), *First the transition then the crash: Eastern Europe in the 2000* (pp. 251–265). Pluto Press.

Denzin, N. K., & Giardina, M. D. (2009). *Qualitative inquiry and social justice: Toward a politics of hope*. Left Coast Press.

Divjak, B. & Martinović, A. (Eds.). (2009). *Privatizacija državnog kapitala u Bosni i Hercegovini*. Transparency International BiH.

Donais, T. (2002). The politics of privatization in post-Dayton Bosnia. *Southeast European Politics, 3*(1), 3–19.

Dunaway, W., & Clelland, D. (2017). Moving toward theory for the 21st century: The centrality of Nonwestern Semiperipheries to world Ethnic/racial inequality. *Journal of World-Systems Research, 23*(2), 399–464. https://doi.org/10.5195/jwsr.2017.598

Hanewinkel, V. (2015). *Ausländische Pflegekräfte in Deutschen Privathaushalte—An Interview with Helma Lutz*. Bundeszentrale fur Politische Bildung. http://www.bpb.de/gesellschaft/migration/kurzdossiers/211011/interview-mit-helma-lutz?p=all. Accessed 11 February 2018.

Horvat, S., & Štiks, I. (Eds.). (2012). *Welcome to the desert of transition! radical politics after Yugoslavia*. Verso.

Jansen, S. (2006). The privatisation of home and hope: Return, reforms and the foreign intervention in Bosnia-Herzegovina. *Dialectical Anthropology, 30*, 3–4, 177–199. https://doi.org/10.1007/s10624-007-9005-x

Kaplan, R. D. (2005). *Balkan ghosts: A journey through history*. Macmillan.

Karkov, N., & Valiavicharska, Z. (2018). Rethinking East-European socialism: Notes toward an anti-capitalist decolonial methodology. *Interventions, 20*(6), 785–813. https://doi.org/10.1080/1369801X.2018.1515647

Kojanić, O. (2018). Flipping the transition script. *Anthropology News, 59*(2), e244–e248. https://doi.org/10.1111/AN.826

Lowinger, J. (2009). *Economic reform and the 'double movement' in Yugoslavia: An analysis of labor unrest and ethno-nationalism in 1980s*. The John Hopkins University.

Majstorović, D. (2007). Construction of Europeanization in the high representative's discourse in Bosnia and Herzegovina. *Discourse and Society, 18*(5), 627–651 (2007). https://doi.org/10.1177/0957926507079635

Majstorović, D. (2016a). (Un)Doing feminism in post-Yugoslav media spaces. *Feminist Media Studies, 16*(6), 1093–1108 (2016). https://doi.org/10.1080/14680777.2016.1150313

Majstorović, D. (2016b). Stvaranje "nove" jugoslovenskežene: Emancipatorski elementi medijskog diskursa s kraja 2. svjetskog rata. In T. Okić & A. Dugandžić (Eds.), *Izgubljena revolucija: AFŽ između mita i zaborava* (pp. 84–115). Crvena and Rosa Luxemburg Stiftung.

Majstorović, D. (2019a). Epistemes of contemporary nationhood. In M. Berocal & A. Salamurović (Eds.), *Political discourse in central, Eastern and Balkan Europe* (pp. 211–238). John Benjamins Publishing Company.

Majstorović, D. (2019b). Postcoloniality as peripherality in Bosnia and Herzegovina. In P. Manolova, K. Kušić & P. Lottholz (Eds.), *Decolonial theory and practice in Southeastern Europe* (pp. 131–148). Special issue of Diversia.

Majstorović, D. (2020). Labor and gender between "there" and "here": discourses of Bosnian-Herzegovinian third-wave migrant women in Germany after 2015. In R. Senković (Ed.), *Transformation of work: Practices, narratives, Regimes*. Institut za etnologiju i folkloristiku.

Majstorović, D., & Vučkovac, Z. (2016). Rethinking Bosnian postcoloniality: Challenges of the Europeanization discourse. *Journal of Language and Politics*, *15*(2), 147–172. https://doi.org/10.1075/jlp.15.2.02maj

Majstorović, D., Vučkovac, Z., & Pepić, A. (2015). From Dayton to Brussels via Tuzla: Post-2014 economic restructuring as Europeanization discourse/practice in Bosnia and Herzegovina. *Southeast European and Black Sea Studies, 15*(4), 661–682.

Monument Group. (2011). Artist's intervention: Matheme. *Future Anterior, 8*(2), 57–73. https://doi.org/10.5749/futuante.8.2.0057

Musić, G. (2013). *Radnička klasa Srbije u tranziciji 1988–2013*. Rosa Luxemburg Stiftung.

Mutua, K., & Swadener, B. (2004). *Decolonizing research in cross-cultural contexts: Critical personal narratives*. SUNY.

Standing, G. (2011). *The precariate: The new dangerous class*. Bloomsbury.

Tlostanova, M. (2019). The postcolonial condition, the decolonial option, and the post-socialist intervention. In M. Albrecht (Ed.), *Postcolonialism cross-examined: Multidirectional perspectives on imperial and colonial pasts and the neocolonial present* (pp. 165–178). Taylor & Francis.

Tokača, M. (2012). *Bosnian book of the dead*. Research and Documentation Centre.

Trouillot, M. R. (1995). *Silencing the past: Power and the production of history*. Beacon Press.

Vučkovac, Z. (2020). Against institutionalised forgetting: Memory politics from below in postwar Prijedor. In A. Milošević & T. Trošt (Eds.), *Europeanisation and memory politics in the Western Balkans* (pp. 231–262). Palgrave Macmillan.

Wallerstein, I. (1974). *The modern world system: Capitalist agriculture and the origins of the European world-economy in the sixteenth century*. Academic Press.

Živković, A. (2014). From the market... to the market: The debt economy after Yugoslavia. In S. Horvat, & I Štiks (Eds.), *Welcome to the desert of post-socialism: Radical politics after Yugoslavia* (pp. 27–38). Verso.

Ukraine and the (Dis)integrating "Empire of Capital"

Yuliya Yurchenko

The demise of the USSR marked the beginning of the biggest most recent expansion of the capitalist empire, as well as the sunset of the last significant counter-weight to the US-led capitalism-and-elections world order. The post-Soviet space—and Ukraine in particular—are positioned on the crossings of reinvigorated geopolitical rivalries, and conflicting agents of the "empire of capital" with its internal competitions and shifting spatial and social boundaries. It is torn by inequalities, economic crises, predatory capital (home-grown and from elsewhere), various forms of conflict, and a reinvigorated struggle for geopolitical presence between Russia and the new-old West (Yurchenko, 2018). The empire(s) and imperialisms cannot be reduced to states' boundaries and their assumed associated interests. They do have a geopolitical dimension, and it is in that sense that Ukraine fell victim to the relentless spread of the empire of capital, where Russian and Western capitalist geopolitical imperialisms collided (Ishchenko & Yurchenko, 2019).

Global and national economies alike are increasingly shaped by transnationalizing processes, societies and institutions, and so our analytical tools,

Y. Yurchenko (✉)
University of Greenwich, London, UK
e-mail: y.yurchenko@gre.ac.uk

A. Gagyi and O. Slačálek (eds.), *The Political Economy of Eastern Europe 30 years into the 'Transition'*, International Political Economy Series,
https://doi.org/10.1007/978-3-030-78915-2_6

terminologies and methodologies need to reflect and fit those ontological shifts. Transnational historical materialism i.e. "the application of the historical materialist method to the study of transnational social relations", as a method of inquiry makes that possible (Overbeek, 2002: 168).[1] It is a dialectical scientific method of the Italian communist Gramsci, further articulated by neo-Gramscian scholars (for example R. W. Cox, S. Gill et al., A. Bieler and A. Morton among others), that allows one to historicize the formation and role of social forces. In the study of Ukraine, such an approach is particularly useful in explaining how, through the process of privatization (that is, primitive accumulation of capital), oligarchic groups and financial industrial groups (FIGs) were formed (that is, concentration of capital); how from the body of employees of the same state-owned enterprises (SOEs), a few turned into oligarchs and the rest into workers/unemployed/dispossessed; how and why new political parties and movements emerged which were representative of—or in alliance with—concrete oligarchs, and in support of different directions of foreign policy, for example, the global West versus East. The method allows us analyze how public consciousness is transformed to consensually accept a concrete new regime, reforms and people in charge by bringing in the concept of passive revolution, that is, the gradual and consensual transformation of social order without the meaningful inclusion of the interests of the subject or affected social groups. This is achieved partly by the process of trasformismo, where political forces strategically align despite their differences until the differences are submerged in the initially dominant group's framework. Westernization in all its forms—marketization, cultural assimilation, and so forth—is precisely the process of passive revolution and trasformismo. In the process, the ruling bloc act as the often willing and responsible implementers and beneficiaries of marketization reforms; the masses too are being "transformed" on the level of consciousness to perceive those reforms as benefiting them, while in reality they are losing out and having social benefits taken away from them—and they know it too!

[1] A study which consists of:

(1) a materialist philosophy of history ... which leads to the ontological primacy of "social relations of production", (2) a rejection of separation between subject and object... and adoption of a dialectic understanding of reality as dynamic totality and as a unity of opposites [...], and (3) the method of abstraction as outlined by Marx in the Introduction to the *Grundrisse*.

Market fetishization, that is, treating marketization as the only viable reform option, is the myth on which the dominance of the neoliberal system of governance rests. International organizations, financial institutions, and lobby groups (associations) channel, further, and perform that governance. With the helping hand of those, both Russia and Ukraine underwent capitalist transformation, yet with their own idiosyncrasies; the first went through "shock therapy" to become a state-run paternalistic oligarchy, the second became a neoliberal kleptocracy. The crucial differences between the two unfolded in the remaking of the countries' institutional backbone, the state.

The institution of the state is pivotal for the empire of capital as state is the terrain where the interests of various social groups, parties, movements, and blocs are (re)negotiated, rules and boundaries of agency-space get redrafted, interests of some put over those of others, eighth to benefit the latter or to exploit. Various social groups and classes have different and often contradictory interests and as a result, the state embodies those contradictions. While advocates of the market liberalization doctrine argue for the state's withdrawal from the private economic sphere, the state is in fact a key institution without which capital and capitalism cannot function. In its neoliberal phase, however, the new transnational capitalist imperialism needs a specific type of state—one that accommodates the transforming mechanisms of accumulation and capitalist class structure globally, that there are classes and their fractions in each state that favor policies which effectively contradict the interest of the state's society as a whole and this is evidenced abundantly across the globe and historic eras. Elsewhere in my work I suggest to capture these contradictions embedded in the institution of the state by treating capital as a force that is shaped by and shapes the state and society alike, while is an autonomous force. Nation-states are then the categorical units of the past, the new unit is a state-society-capital complex (see Yurchenko, 2018; Powell & Yurchenko, 2020). On application of such an analytical lens, sovereign functioning of Ukraine's state, for example, is impossible in conditions where the interests of (transnational) capital take precedence, or when autonomy of state-level decision-making is compromised by complex economic dependencies (with geopolitical components) on the West or Russia, enshrined in law and at the expense of socially oriented reform and investment.

Ukraine's Capitalism With a Twist

Ukraine's entry into the global capitalist economy meant leaving in the past its planned economy and the welfare functions typical of a Soviet state, ironically trading state economic planning for planning markets instead. This trade was based on a mythological idea that the "transition to market"—designed in accordance with the International Monetary Fund (IMF), World Bank, and the European Bank for Reconstruction and Development (EBRD) modeling—had to occur in the ex-USSR republics. Economic models, however, cannot grasp the nuances of politico-economic complexity because apart from the (socio-)economic factors, there are also their political forms—institutional, ideological, cultural, etc.—and that means abundance of "unintended consequences", disruption on implementation. Secondly, the modeling presumes that there must be a transition to neoliberal market capitalism with no reasons given for that choice. Indeed, market (mis)planning and the weakening of the state were the main factors that have brought on the devastating socio-economic effects we are now seeing.

Since the 1990s, Ukraine's nascent ruling bloc has utilized the multiplicity of already available and constantly expanding mechanisms of accumulation in the global capitalist system. These mechanisms, both legal and extra-legal (for example, offshoring of revenue, capital recycling as FDI, tax avoidance and evasion, (in)direct subsidization of private enterprise/socialization of costs, etc.) were hastily adopted on the advice of the IMF and EBRD, and have produced a regime of neoliberal kleptocracy. Through domestic and foreign economic policies of selective liberalization and protectionism which favored oligarchic capital, and through the creation of virtual spaces of accumulation for offshoring profits and institutionalized expropriation, "black holes" were designed in the economy (Yurchenko, 2012). A regime of neoliberal kleptocracy evolved with its inevitable internal rivalry over access to power (social, economic and political). The inability to achieve a consolidated strategy between the dominant and contender blocs shaped Ukraine's post-Soviet history, escalating into an armed conflict with an element of foreign intervention, occupation and separatism that is still ongoing at the time of writing.

Survival Myths of Systemic Failure

Marketization and geopolitical games in the post-Soviet space were in contradiction with the potential construction of a cosmopolitan, egalitarian society and thus, different, divisive myths were used to shape the public imagination. As the empire of transnational capital was spreading with the EBRD, US Agency for International Development (USAID), IMF and World Bank, neoliberal reforms were planted into the transforming system (in Ukraine and Russia alike if with different consequences), undermining the best of intentions by their incompatibility with socio-economic development and exacerbated by the existing and, also, transforming system of economic activity, both legal and extra-legal. They needed a different backbone, one patch-worked from myths that would in effect compartmentalize the society: the myths of transition, democracy, "two Ukraines", and "the Other" (Yurchenko, 2018: 10–22 et passim).

The myth of (the necessity of) transition can be summarized in the idea that a "transition to the market" based on IMF, World Bank and EBRD modeling had to occur in the ex-USSR republics at all—no explanation was given as to why this was treated as an axiom, beyond Fukuyama's infamous "end of history" thesis which stipulated that capitalism won, communism failed and history thus has ended with the demise of the USSR.

The myth of democracy helps maintain the façade of "selection" of a market orientation, and of a functioning democratic system with representation politics. The feasibility of democratic rule, in a polity where private interests come before public, is one of the more insidious yet resilient myths that allows for the survival and spread of authoritarian neoliberalism in Ukraine and elsewhere. Instead of a functioning representative democracy—rather than a system of "transparent elections"—what can be witnessed in Ukraine is the further entrenchment of a regime of neoliberal kleptocracy, where political disempowerment of the voters was combined with their economic disempowerment, and the ideological hollowing out of political discourse; I shall return to this in more detail below.

The myth of "two Ukraines"—east and west, Russian- and Ukrainian-speaking—has been manufactured in what is a diverse and non-homogenous society just like any other country; its "heterogeneity is a historical norm, not the historical exception" (Menon & Rumer, 2015: 1 et passim). The Yanukovych vs Yushchenko presidential electoral campaign of 2004 became the defining moment where the boundary between the two—manufactured by political technologists—was demarcated in Ukraine's political discourse, making Riabchuk's 1992 declaration of there being two Ukraines (2001) a materialized prophecy.

The myth of "the Other" is the most recent and the most destabilizing, destructive for the country's social fabric and collective national consciousness. Ukraine is now locked into defining itself in opposition to the Russian "other" by the content of the infamous "de-communization laws". So, the "othering" occurs not only on the level of the separation of society into separatist/Russia sympathizers and "patriots", but also intrinsically, on an individual level through the rejection of a part of one's cultural, historical, linguistic, and religious identity.

Social Forces and the Making of Ukraine's Multilevel Crisis

The myth of democracy mentioned above was kept alive throughout Ukraine's "independent" years—with mixed success and necessary adaptations, by various combinations within the ruling bloc with its competing fractions, alternating cadre and their rivalries—while the core of the politics remind undoubtedly neoliberal and characteristically kleptocratic.

The myth of democracy goes complements the myth of transition by helping to discursively prop up the social consensus i.e. it helps "make" the passive revolution, that neoliberal capitalism is the path to be taken, wired in all policy as with markets supposedly comes democracy, comes freedom of enterprise and individual freedom too. How can a democratic rule be possible is in principle in a society that places private interests before the public—especially where social and institutional dialogue is corrupted, as it is in Ukraine—is unclear. Yet, pretence of democracy is both one of the more insidious and resilient myths that allows authoritarian neoliberalism to survive and spread. Instead, institutionalization of a regime of neoliberal kleptocracy, occurs where political and social disempowerment of the voters is aggravated by their economic disempowerment (as Kyiv Independent Institute of Statistics surveys confirm annually) and virtualization, ideological emptying of political discourse and party politics as an effect (Dyczok, 2005, 2006, 2009; Wilson, 2005, 2014).

After 1991 most of the old apparatchiks remained in power who, together with the criminals-turned-oligarchs, who will constitute the fractioned and rivaling ruling bloc and whose task it will be to maintain the façade of democracy and effectively destabilize the political order to the point of making an insurrection, and now armed conflict possible. Political disempowerment and the crisis of representation in Ukraine are amply evidenced by the declarative nature of Ukraine's party programs and politics and thus virtual rather than tangible performance which led to a general lack of trust in politicians and voter apathy (D'Anieri, 2007; Kuzio, 1999, 2005; Wilson, 2005). The latter is being "resolved" by "winning" voters for the oligarch-associated parties and politicians through bribes, which in conditions of economic deprivation is relatively cheap and is certainly cheaper than life quality improving reforms.

Capital accumulation ambitions of fractions of the competing, ruling—and eventually capitalist—class of the newly emerged kleptocratic regime were services by specially designed political shell parties (D'Anieri, 2007; Wilson, 2005). Survival of both depended on virtual politics and on materializing the next two myths—of the "two Ukraines" and of "the Other". Political differences between the parties associated with the fractions of the ruling and capitalist bloc are arbitrary which contributes to the myth of democracy and that means that no matter who you vote for you will get marketization and kleptocracy, with some rotation of faces albeit. Since the early 1990s a couple of rival fractions among many more dominated Ukraine's political scene who get conventionally referred to by the regional affiliation by origin and by location of most of their assets, Dnipropetrovsk and Donetsk. A more diversified ruling bloc replaced the latter in 2014 upon the ousting of Yanukovych. Power between the blocs shifted a number of times and can be summed up in a few periods.

The first period—1991–1998(9)—started immediately after Ukraine gained independence and was characterized by a clear dominance of the Dnipropetrovsk bloc, two presidents, Kravchuk (1991–1994) and Kuchma (since July 1994), and Prime Minister Lazarenko. The bloc comprised members of the neo-nomenklatura and the capitalists-in-the-making who came from the milieu of the criminal-political nexus and Komsomol (the all-USSR communist youth union). During the period, the first oligarchics emerged in trade of gas, oil, lubricants, and the fuel with Lazarenko, Tymoshenko, and Pinchuk in the lead (KUB and later YeESU companies). Simultaneously, a rival group was emerging in the Donetsk oblast and was characterized by its violent methods of accumulation and expropriation of resources and companies. Independent Ukraine's Constitution was finally adopted in 1996, making the country a Presidential-Parliamentary Republic thus helping to keep the centralized control in the hands of the presidential administration with Kuchma and his cronies from Dnipropetrovsk firm at the wheel.

In the second period of 1998(9)–2004 the growing leverage of the Donetsk bloc in both economic and political spheres of Ukraine became noticeable. It included a number of top state administration appointments, for example Prime Ministers Azarov and later Yanukovych. Capitalist class fractions formed through primitive accumulation of the SOEs and concentration of capital in the FIGs, with pronounced dominance of the Donetsk forces. By the late 1990s those forces emerged as class-fractions-for-themselves and formed the Party of Regions—and many other respectively—to pursue their interests through direct participation in the country's political decision-making. The gradual shift of power from the Dnipropetrovsk neo-nomenklatura to the Donetsk fraction commenced with Lazarenko's money laundering scandal, Tymoshenko's and YeESU's loss of control over the gas market, and the Kuchma and Pinchuk class fraction compromise with the Donetsk forces. In late 2004, prior to the re-run of the presidential election—that is, during the Orange Revolution—the Constitutional reform was adopted that shifted the power over to the Parliament, in order to guarantee the Party of Regions/Donetsk leverage on the decision-making process in case of Yanukovych's defeat in the election.

The third period was a short interregnum of 2004–2007. In late 2004, the power struggle of the rival capitalist fractions in the presidential election resulted in a two-month-long civil protest that became known as the Orange Revolution. It was led by the presidential candidate Yushchenko—and his backer Tymoshenko—who were supported by fractions of Donetsk (ISD of Taruta and Mkrtchan) and Dnipropetrovsk (Privat Group of Kolomoyskyi and Boholyubov) capital, and Ukraine's western partners, the USA and EU. The protest was a reaction to the electoral fraud by the Donetsk bloc's Yanukovych whose candidacy was supported by the outgoing president Kuchma, SCM/Akhmetov, Interpipe Group/Pinchuk, and Russia. Subsequently, the rival forces within the Orange bloc were unable to build a broad coalition across the branches of power and thus a political compromise was sought elsewhere, with elements of the Blue, Yanukovych bloc, the Party of Regions. Conflict between the parliament—dominated by the Party of Regions, opposition parties, and their associated rival capitalist class fractions—and the inability of president Yushchenko to maintain the allegiance of his previous backers, led to Tymoshenko's loss of office and the subsequent appointment of Yanukovych as the new prime minister. Parties associated with Yushchenko and Tymoshenko were rapidly losing support, and in the 2007 parliamentary election the Party of Regions won the majority of seats, thus marking the beginning of the formal centralization of power by the Donetsk bloc.

During the period between 2007 and 2013/4 the Donetsk bloc assumed power in the country. Following the 2007 parliamentary election and the formation of a coalition with Yushchenko's party Our Ukraine, Tymoshenko was once again appointed the prime minister. As the effects of the Great Recession hit Ukraine's economy, Tymoshenko's rivalry with Firtash over the gas markets turned into the so-called "gas wars" with Russia (that is, episodes when gas supply cutoffs and pricing were used for geopolitical blackmail by Russia in relations with Ukraine) which cost her popular support as the prime minister. This helped Yanukovych secure victory in the 2010 Presidential election, which in combination with the Party of Regions' parliamentary majority gave the Donetsk bloc control over both the executive and the legislative branches of power. Centralization of power now accelerated, and among other things, included the vertical concentration of power in the hands of the president through the reversal of the Constitutional reform of 2004. It also meant the extension of control to the judiciary by adoption of The law on the judiciary and the courts from July 2010, that "represented at one and the same time both an instrument for gaining and imposing power over the judiciary [by the president] and an attempt to improve the administration of justice" (Solomon, 2011).

The next period, which started in late 2013–early 2014, was marked by the insurrection, the annexation of Crimea, an intensification of civil strife and the outbreak of the armed conflict. The latter is the direct result of the "two Ukraines"—and more recently the manufacturing of "the Other"—without which Russia-supported separatism would not have been possible. The multi-vectoral foreign policy started by Kuchma was reaching its crescendo as the time to sign the trade agreement with the EU was approaching. Where lobbying efforts and IMF's SALs could not succeed, disciplining by debt and the extensive enforcement mechanisms of the Deep and Comprehensive Trade Area (DCFTA) Agreement with the EU would finish the job, and make the entry and functioning of transnational capital more comfortable. The Agreement was unprecedented in its scope and depth due to three particular features: "comprehensiveness, complexity, and conditionality" (Petrov et al., 2015: 2 et passim). The economy was weakened by the consequences of the armed conflict and the loss of industry in eastern Ukraine. By late 2014, this had already been estimated to cost $7–8 billion, or some six percent of GDP (Havlik, 2014). The combination of heavy foreign-debt dependency and a state budget on the permanent edge of default presented Yanukovych's administration with an impossible choice. Under pressure from the Donbas' industry-owning oligarchy, Yanukovych refused to sign the treaty at the Third EU Eastern Partnership Summit in Vilnius in November 2013. The long-term consequences of Ukraine's short-term approach to politics were about to spill into the deepest multi-level crisis the country has witnessed since the post-second world war famine.

The (often self-imposed) removal of the Donetsk bloc members and the effective dissolution of the Party of Regions in 2014 led to intensification of rivalry among the remaining capitalist fractions. In conditions of a lack of a democratic mandate, the precarious "new" ruling bloc relied increasingly on the compartmentalization of society, the myths of "two Ukraines" and each of them being the other's "Other". Such an intensely polarized society in a state of civil conflict could only be dominated by increased coercion which, paradoxically, is legitimized by the very conflict that needs resolving. However, underneath the polarizing rhetoric, everyday socio-economic struggle is what unifies the many Ukraines, and a conscious acknowledgement of that fact became the biggest fear of the precarious rulers, whose political longevity now directly depended on the longevity of the conflict that they allowed to unfold. Poroshenko's embrace of nationalist rhetoric, and his inopportune flirtations with neo-Nazis—alternating with a distancing from them in public discourse—were all telling signs of that dependency and the vulnerability of that kleptocratic regime, which paved the way for the most recent period of the ruling bloc transformation. With the 2019 presidential and parliamentary elections, the last period has commenced, as the country has rejected the nationalistic turn of Poroshenko with his "army, language, faith" slogan and instead opted for its first "collective president", to which I turn next in more detail.

Hope, Farce, and Paving the Way of the "Collective President"

The election of Zelensky would not have happened if not for the disruptive dialectic of instrumentalization, and the ill-prescribed reforms launched domestically and from abroad which—by early 2019—merged into a perfect storm. First, though, some context.

Since 1991 Ukrainian society has been divided in its opinion on multiple domestic and foreign policy issues: "electoral support for major presidential candidates and political parties, status of the Russian language, Ukraine's membership in the European Union and NATO, and its relations with Russia" (Katchnovski, 2014: 3). Such divergent views are common in any society, yet it is not everywhere that they lead to armed conflicts. The regional character of those divisions is important, and due to Ukraine's history of being under the rule of various empires simultaneously, they run particularly deep in pre-border areas of the country's east and west. That is not to say that concrete regions are homogeneous in their support of concrete political forces or foreign policy options, but to underline dominant political orientations.

Few expected that Ukraine would disintegrate, yet analyses warning of such a possibility did exist. Even once the rebellion had started the delusion carried on, and local support for separatism was downplayed by the West and the interim government in Kyiv. Instead, all responsibility for organizing and leading the breakaway was laid at the door of the Russian army and separatist brigades. In Russian media and political discourse, support was instead exaggerated, and portrayed as ubiquitous. Similar fictitious stories were manufactured and disseminated with a vengeance via Russian and separatist media about a "fascist junta" that allegedly took power in Kyiv by force. The "fascist coup d'état"—also known as Yanukovych's self-imposed exile—was then seen as a fascist threat and in that context "separatists, including Russian volunteers, defended people of Donbas from Ukrainian 'fascists'". The Novorossiya project (a reference to the Black Sea adjacent region of the Russian Empire—Ukrainian gubernias, that is imperial Russian territorial units—which since 1920s was part of Ukraine's territory) of confederating the ex-Russian Empire land of south–eastern Ukraine was fully launched and, according to Putin, included the territory of the Kharkov, Lugansk, Donetsk, Dnipropetrovsk, Kherson, Mykolayiv, Odesa, Zaporizhzhya oblasts.

It is hard to imagine, however, that the Novorossiya project could have taken off with little to no local support. Indeed, Serhiy Kudelia suggests that the Donbas insurrection was "primarily a homegrown phenomenon" where "political factors—state fragmentation, violent regime change, and the government's low coercive capacity—combined with popular emotions specific to the region—resentment and fear—played a crucial role in launching the armed secessionist movement there" (Kudelia, 2014). The seeds of separatism were indeed sown in the 1990s, took root in the Blue-Orange campaign, and sprung out of the Maidans and anti-Maidans in 2013. In the context of social divisions manufactured in accumulation rivalries over some two decades, Yanukovych and local Party of Regions leaders had paved the way for Girkin's army, the "polite people", and Russian "invisible" troops of the Novorossiya project. Emotions of resentment and fear towards the new rulers in Kyiv (Kudelia, 2014: 3–5; Petersen, 2002) resulted from the systematic portrayal of a regional identity separate from the rest of Ukraine. Negative emotions were fueled by a lack of trust that was made worse by the increasing dehumanization of eastern dwellers in the mainstream political and mass media discourse (Yurchenko, 2018).

The "Maidan and anti-Maidan movements were both highly complex phenomena where there was no clear political position", no identifiable ideological component (Ishchenko, 2016). There were elements that could be deemed progressive and/or reactionary in both to various extents (Ishchenko, 2016), yet neither managed to deliver on that "progressiveness" at the end. The Maidans were hijacked by the oligarchy, the anti-Maidans by Russian separatists and their self-proclaimed "republics" (Ishchenko, 2014; Yurchenko, 2018).

Instead of a systemic change in the country following the events of the Bloody winter, a civil armed conflict broke out while oligarchy was largely intact. Fearing prosecution and loss of assets and state control, the oligarchs utilized the country's urgent need for legitimate representatives in power to push for snap presidential, and then parliamentary, elections in the following months (Plokhy, 2015). The rule of oligarchy was once again restore Poroshenko become president and key state administration positions being given to the cadre aligned with oligarchy. The main change in the ruling bloc was not the displacement of the reign of capital as the Maidan protests demanded, but erosion of the centralized control and influence that the Donetsk bloc had enjoyed in the country since 2007–2010 (Goldstein, 2014; Yurchenko, 2012). The Party of Regions, the party of Donetsk oligarchy, "saw massive defections from its ranks and the pro-Yanukovych majority collapsed in the Rada" in the winter of 2014 (Shevel, 2015) and the party did not take part in the snap election that followed. While their MPs made it into the new parliament through constituency votes and the newly formed pro-Russian Opposition Bloc party, their leverage in the parliament was weakened (Shevel,

2015: 162). The regional composition of the state apparatus became more mixed (Goldstein, 2014; Shevel, 2015), marking the renewed intensification of rivalry among oligarchs, who were by then much more susceptible to foreign/IFIs' pressure, and had suffered financial losses (100 Richest, 2016). The country's labor, on the other hand, was impoverished and faced with IMF-enforced market-adjusted utility bills that exceeded average wages and pensions, with the civil armed conflict on both sides of the frontline, and with destitution and slave labor in the separatist republics in the east (Levy, 2016).

The oligarchy fully realized the extent of the crisis of representation in the country, and that they remained in power only due to the popular fears of a power vacuum in the midst of a military campaign. In an attempt to instill public trust in the newly elected parliament of predominantly corruption-stained representatives, three foreigners were appointed to ministerial positions in an unprecedented move—the US-born Natalie Jaresko as finance minister, Lithuania's Aivaras Abromavicius as Economy and Trade minister and Alexander Kvitashvili, from Georgia, as health minister ("Foreign Born Ministers", 2014). However, a schism between the government and the team of foreigners—hired to win, if temporarily, popular trust in the broken system they were asked to fix—was growing, as the change that oligarchs wanted was cosmetic. Instead of winning the trust of citizens, the kleptocrats would lose the last residue of it together with the tiny newly found trust of IFIs, monitoring institutions, and NGOs. The sacrificial and violence-hungry (ultra)nationalist brigades instrumentalized for the legitimation of the oligarchs' ongoing power grab have not gone down well with the voters tired of war, socio-economic destitution, and the empty rhetorical diversions of Poroshenko on questions of language, faith and, yes, the army. The ruling bloc heavily underestimated public frustration, their vision skewed by a shortness of memory of their rejection by protesters at Maidans in the winter of 2013–2014.

* * *

I concluded my book, Ukraine and the Empire of Capital in late 2017 with a foretelling that Ukraine is pregnant with the Third Maidan. One may consider that to have been a prophesy that was never to be. And yet it did happen via a protest in the voting booths.

Zelensky, "team Zelensky" or, as I call them, the "collective president" (referring to most presidential communications/decision-making being produced with "team Zelensky" as a signatory), came into power on the assumed promises to democratize the establishment, disempower the oligarchs, improve the standard of living, among other often ambiguous claims, and—most importantly—end the war. The positive slogans and the ambiguous, if any, implementation plan had little to do with the victory—the disenchantment of the demoralized masses with the establishment and moral bankruptcy of all but a few of the 39 presidential candidates, is what delivered it. Yet neither before nor after the election have Zelensky, or his party, the Servant of the People (named after a TV show where he played Ukraine's president…), managed to convincingly distance themselves from the oligarchy (Bond, 2019), or demonstrate politics and conduct significantly different (Clarke, 2019) from their predecessors.

The adoption of a set of laws in an extraordinary parliamentary session on 30 March 2019 necessitated by the IMF pressure in exchange for vital cash flows reaffirmed further neoliberal politics entrenchment. The laws, adopted in violation of the voting procedures, approved the sale of agricultural land, including to foreign parties; a previously imposed moratorium was lifted, although a referendum on foreign ownership had been promised. The last untouchable asset of the Ukrainian people guaranteed by the country's Constitution was being offered as a bargaining chip in dependency games with the IMF. Ukraine's remaining sovereignty is eroding. "Trumpgate"[2] was a striking illustration of the morbidity that permeates the (dis)integrating empire of capital. As legitimate consensualizing narratives fail, convincing by fraud and corruption become the instruments of persuasion, of manufacturing "consensus", and of dominance of one class and bloc over the other. While this morbidity corrodes the weaker and the dependent, it too offers an opportunity to expose the systemic rot and potentially build a progressive form of social organization. The political demand is for socialism that dare not speak its name in the "decommunizing" minds and institutions. Yet, under whatever name or banner it comes, the economic system that is in "demand" is the socialist.

[2] cf. "Trumpgate": the scandal involving records of phone conversations where political pressure was applied on Ukraine in exchange for military aid.

P.S. This chapter was completed with the world firmly in the grip of the COVID-19 pandemic, the future of the global and Ukrainian economies alike are uncertain. Many years of destabilizing "reforms" generated a "perfect storm", with the pandemic and debt dependency further exacerbating the state of ideological paralysis in the war-ridden country.

The (dis)integrating empire of capital does so faster in conjunctures of world (economy) vulnerabilities. As the death toll rises, national and global GDPs shrink, millions are made unemployed and/or furloughed (if lucky), and so on, the short term economic slowdown will have a lasting disruptive effect to add to those not quite metabolized since the Great Recession. It is difficult to ascertain what exactly this will mean for Ukraine with any accuracy. Its sovereignty increasingly compromised, the new wave of enclosures brought on by the land reforms around the corner as is the referendum on allowing foreigners become proprietors of that land. The vote will be telling of the pulse of the extorted people, as a sign of things to come. What comes after Maidans fail to deliver via voting booths we too are to find out in the near future as people are taking to the streets over unaffordable utility bills and selling off of the last remaining national assets. Not all Maidans are yet in the past.

References

самых богатых людей Украины: Полный список [100 Richest Ukrainians]. (2016). *Focus*. https://focus.ua/ratings/350253/. Accessed 20 February 2021.

Bond, I. (2019). *Will the "Servant of the People" be the Master of the People, Centre for European Reform*. https://www.cer.eu/insights/will-servant-people-be-master-ukraine. Accessed 20 February 2021.

Clarke, D. (2019, July 29). Ukraine's Volodymyr Zelensky cannot be a Servant of the People and of Oligarchy. *The New Statesman*. https://www.newstatesman.com/world/europe/2019/07/ukraine-s-volodymyr-zelensky-cannot-be-servant-people-and-oligarchy. Accessed 20 February 2021.

D'Anieri, P. J. (2007). *Understanding Ukrainian Politics: Power, Politics, and Institutional Design*. M.E. Sharpe.

Dyczok, M. (2005). Breaking through the information blockade: Elections and revolution in Ukraine 2004. *Canadian Slavonic Papers, 47*(3–4), 241–264.

Dyczok. (2006). Was Kuchma's censorship effective? Mass media in Ukraine before 2004. *Europe-Asia Studies, 58*(2), 215–238.

Dyczok. (2009). Do the media matter? focus on Ukraine. In Dyczok, M. & Gaman-Golutvina, O. (Eds.), *Media, democracy and freedom: The post-communist experience* (pp.17–42). Peter Lang.

Foreign-Born Ministers in Ukraine's New Cabinet. (2014). *BBC*. http://www.bbc.co.uk/news/world-europe-30348945. Accessed 20 February 2021.

Golstein, V. (2014, May 19). Why everything you've read about Ukraine is wrong. *Forbes*. https://www.forbes.com/sites/forbesleadershipforum/2014/05/19/why-everything-youve-read-about-ukraine-is-wrong/?sh=1483aa2b510e. Accessed 20 February 2021.

Havlik, P. (2014). Economic consequences of the Ukraine conflict. Wiener Institut für Internationale Wirtschaftsvergleiche, Policy Notes and Reports. https://wiiw.ac.at/economic-consequences-of-the-ukraine-conflict-dlp-3427.pdf. Accessed 20 February 2021.

Ishchenko, V. (2014, May–June). Ukraine's fractures. *New Left Review*, 87.

Ishchenko. (2016). The Ukrainian left during and after the Maidan protests, a report for the DIE LINKE delegation, GUE/NGL. http://cslr.org.ua/wp-content/uploads/2016/01/The_Ukrainian_Left_during_and_after_the.pdf. Accessed 20 February 2021.

Ishchenko, V., & Yurchenko, Y. (2019). Ukraine, US hegemony and inter-imperialist rivalry. In I. Ness & Z. Cope (Eds.),*The Palgrave encyclopedia of imperialism and anti-imperialism*. Palgrave Macmillan.

Katchanovski, I. (2014). The separatist conflict in donbas: A violent break-up of Ukraine? E*uropean Politics and Society, 17*(4), 473–489. https://doi.org/10.1080/23745118.2016.1154131. Accessed 20 February 2021.

Kudelia, S. (2014). Domestic sources of the donbas insurgency. *PONARS Eurasia Policy Memo*, 351. http://www.ponarseurasia.org/memo/domestic-sources-donbas-insurgency. Accessed 20 February 2021.

Kuzio, T. (1999). *State and institution building in Ukraine*. St. Martin's Press.

Kuzio, T. (2005). Regime Type and Politics in Ukraine under Kuchma. *Communist and Post-Communist Studies,* 38, 167–190

Levy, G. (2016, October 4). *Slave labour in Lugansk: What war in Ukraine has "Achieved"*. https://peopleandnature.wordpress.com/2016/10/04/slave-labour-in-lugansk-what-war-in-ukraine-has-achieved/. Accessed 20 February 2021.

Menon, R., & Rumer, E. B. (2015). *Conflict in Ukraine: The unwinding of the post-cold war order*. MIT Press.

Overbeek, H. (2002). Transnational historical materialism: Theories of transnational class formation and world order. In M. Rupert (Ed.), *Historical materialism and globalization*. Routledge.

Petersen, R. (2002). *Understanding ethnic violence: Fear, hatred, and resentment in twentieth-century Eastern Europe*. Cambridge University Press.

Petrov, R., van der Loo, G., & van Elsuwege, P. (2015). The EU–Ukraine association agreement: A new legal instrument of integration without membership?, *Kyiv-Mohyla Law and Politics Journal*, 1.

Plokhy, S. (2015). *The gates of Europe*. Penguin.

Powell, J., & Yurchenko, Y. (2020). The evolution of private provision in urban drinking water: New geographies, institutional ambiguity and the need for political economy. *New Political Economy, 25*(1), 91–106. https://doi.org/10.1080/13563467.2018.1562432

Riabchuk, M. (2001). Дві України [Two Ukraines], *Krytyka*, 4.

Shevel, O. (2015). The parliamentary elections in Ukraine, October 2014. *Electoral Studies, 39*, 159.

Solomon, P. (2011, March 2). Yanukovych's judicial reform: Power and justice. *Ukraine Watch*. https://ukrainewatch.wordpress.com/2011/03/02/yanukovychs-judicial-reform-power-policy/. Accessed 20 February 2021.

Wilson, A. (2005). *Virtual politics: Faking democracy in the post-soviet world* (1st ed.). Yale University Press.

Wilson. (2014). *Ukraine crisis: What the west needs to know*. Yale University Press.

Yurchenko, Y. (2012). "Black holes" in the political economy of Ukraine: The neoliberalization of europe's "wild east". *Debatte: Journal of Contemporary Central and Eastern Europe, 20*(2–3), 125–149.

Yurchenko, Y. (2018). *Ukraine and the empire of capital: From marketisation to armed conflict*. Pluto Press.

Reconfiguring Regimes of Capitalist Integration: Hungary Since the 1970s

Agnes Gagyi and Tamás Gerőcs

In the following chapter, we present an analysis of the new accumulation regime that emerged in Hungary after 2010 as part of the unfolding crisis of a global hegemonic cycle. Our study is based in the broader tradition of critical international political economy, inspired by world-systems analysis (for example, Becker, 2016; Gates, 2018; Szentes, 1988; Vliegenthart, 2010; Wallerstein, 1976; Weissenbacher, 2018). The methodological framework we apply in this paper is informed by dependency scholarship (Cardoso, 1972; Grosfoguel, 2000) and the French regulation school

This research was co-financed by the project "From developmental states to new protectionism: changing repertoire of state interventions to promote development in an unfolding new world order" (OTKA FK_124573), supported by the NRDIO (NKFIH) in Hungary.

A. Gagyi
University of Gothenburg, Gothenburg, Sweden
e-mail: agnes.gagyi@gu.se

T. Gerőcs (✉)
State University of New York, Binghamton, NY, USA
e-mail: tgerocs1@binghamton.edu

A. Gagyi and O. Slačálek (eds.), *The Political Economy of Eastern Europe 30 years into the 'Transition'*, International Political Economy Series,
https://doi.org/10.1007/978-3-030-78915-2_7

(Jessop, 1997; Lipietz, 1997). We look at the new Hungarian accumulation regime as a development in the history of Hungary's integration into capitalism's global cycles of hegemony (Frank, 1977; Wallerstein, 1976). We conceive of the global financial and economic crisis in 2008 as a moment in the longer downturn phase of the post-war hegemonic cycle (Arrighi & Silver, 1999; Brenner, 2006; Roberts, 2016; Van der Pijl, 2012). We use the concept of accumulation regime in a local context as a methodological focus to look at those geopolitical processes that link the formation of concrete local historic blocs to the global geopolitical environment.

Within this framework, we characterize Hungary's integration into the long crisis of the post-1945 global hegemonic cycle, beginning from the 1970's, by shifts between three accumulation regimes. The first regime, which crystallized by the 1960's, was characterized by a "bridge position" in international trade and the domestic political compromise it entailed. Throughout the crisis of the 1970s, this model was transformed into a neoliberal accumulation regime, which was dominant until the early 2000s. The third regime of accumulation was born out of the contradictions of the previous neoliberal regime, using the manoeuvre space provided by the financial crisis of 2008. We interpret transitions between these three regimes as the internalized development of global crisis, driven by reconfiguring internal–external geopolitical class alliances and mediated through state policies.

In the context of the global hegemonic crisis, and the concomitant emergence of new regional power-blocs, usually referred to as the multipolarization of the global power field, in the case of many East European countries, this process has resulted in growing Chinese and Russian interference with the regional formation of hegemonic blocs. In our analysis of the post-2010 regime, we show how Hungary has become exposed to multiple geopolitical forces that include the eastward expansion of German industrial capital, as well as expanding Russian and Chinese financial capital. We examine these geopolitical forces that shape the formation of the new historic bloc in Hungary, as part of the global hegemonic shift. We emphasize that the formation of the present historic bloc in Hungary is exposed to both external shocks as well as internal social contradictions. This analysis has been produced as part of a long-term collaboration within the Working Group for Public Sociology "Helyzet" in Budapest (Barna et al., 2019).

The Crisis of the Post-1956 "Bridge-Model"

Despite political conflicts, state socialist economies have always been embedded in relations of world economic trade and finance (Bettelheim & Dobb, 1965; Cliff, 1974; Chase-Dunn, 1980; Frank, 1977). In the decade preceding the 1970s crisis, Hungary's post-war state socialist regime of accumulation was based on a bridge-position that the country occupied in international trade. This model constituted a specific but vulnerable response to the fundamental contradiction of all import substitution industrialization efforts: the simultaneous pressure to import Western technology, and to pay for it by stepping up exports from traditional agricultural production (Gerőcs & Pinkasz, 2018b: 338; Hirschman, 1968; Tyson, 1986).

In terms of external integration, Hungary's bridge model answered this problem by a trade specialization within the international commerce between Western capitalist and Comecon economies (Lóránt, 1990; Gerőcs & Pinkasz, 2018a; Vigvári, 1990). It specialized in technology imports from the West, and in manufacturing exports to the Comecon market, based on those technologies. The incomes from Comecon exports did not produce enough convertible currency to cover Western trade. To compensate for this, the bridge model was based on the re-export of subsidized Soviet crude oil, together with more traditional agrarian exports to Western markets. The re-export of the Soviet crude oil, complemented with favorable terms of trade with newly independent southern countries, had to produce sufficient amounts of convertible currency to cover the costs of Western imports.[1] Otherwise, the country had to rely on international loans in order to cover the trade bills. This constituted a vulnerable exposure to international commerce in convertible currency, and to external funding, generally higher than in the case of fellow Comecon members which sustained either more autarchic economic models, such as the Soviet Union, or concentrated more on Comecon trade, like Czechoslovakia after 1968 (Ban, 2012; Gerőcs & Pinkasz, 2018a, 2018b).

In the internal dynamics, the bridge model rested upon a political compromise between three major economic lobby groups, the dominant

[1] Trade with the global South remained miniscule compared to Western trade and, because in some instances it did not deliver expected results, it had been deprioritized by the 1980s.

two of which were the so-called industrial and agrarian fractions (Berend, 1996),[2] and respective fractions of labor that this compromise aimed to reintegrate within the political system after the workers' revolution in 1956.

The structural division between industrial and agrarian fractions was the product of the contradictions of the import substitution industrialization effort, and was similar to the political conflict between industrial oligarchies favoring protectionism and agricultural and other extractive sectors promoting liberal trade policies in other global semi-peripheries (Cardoso, 1972; Gereffi & Evans, 1981; Grosfoguel, 2000). On the side of labor, this conflict was completed by tensions following from forced collectivization, which served surplus extraction from agricultural production, and the transformation of the peasant class into a proletarian and semi-proletarian labor force (Vigvári & Gerőcs, 2017). The political compromise after the 1956 Revolution was meant to meet the contradictory needs of agriculture and industry and recreate hegemony over labor, through an economic model that eased the pressure on agriculture by stronger reliance on external trade for industrialization, and allowed a limited growth of private consumption, with softened ideological repression. However, this political compromise was conditioned upon favorable trade relations both in the Comecon and in Western trade as well as cheap international funding.

After the oil crisis in 1973 and 1979, the terms of trade turned unfavorable for many semi-peripheral countries, including Hungary, creating a large gap in the country's balance of international payments (Gerőcs & Pinkasz, 2018b; Lóránt, 1990), which led to the acceleration of foreign debt accumulation.[3] In the internal balance of class forces, this situation opened space for a coalition between monetarist technocrats, corporate managers interested in privatization, a growing number of foreign investors, and international lenders promoting market liberalization (Bockman, 2000; Mong, 2012). While state investments into social reproductive functions were cut due to debt repayment, direct effects on popular life standards (and thereby on the political legitimation provided

[2] The third group, the energy lobby, played a more important role in the 1980s.

[3] On top of that between 1979 and 1981 US Federal Reserve raised the Fed-interest rate which caused turbulence in international money markets. The crisis culminated in a series of sovereign defaults all over the global semi-periphery from Latin America, Africa, Eeastern Europe, and southern Asia in the 1980s and early 1990s.

by growth of consumption) were muffled by legalizing popular second economy practices, where incomes from unpaid second shifts compensated for declining life standards. Supported by a newly forming neoliberal coalition within the politburo, and conditioned by unmanageable debt service, this shift constituted a turn towards export-oriented market liberalization, dependent on access to foreign capital, and ultimately the transition to post-socialist market economy.

Post-socialist Transition and the Neoliberal Accumulation Regime

In the context of mounting public debt, the collapse of the Comecon market and a dire need to import capital, Western capital's interests dominated the process of privatization and market liberalization during the post-socialist transition. Old industrial capacities nurtured during the time of ISI were sold at a suppressed price. The resulting deindustrialization opened space for foreign direct investment (FDI), created a market for imported goods, and depressed the wages of workers through mass unemployment. In the new FDI-based accumulation model, Hungary specialized in low value-added manufacturing dominated by foreign corporations in dedicated custom-free export-zones (Bohle & Greskovits, 2012).

While the dominance of foreign capital in the economy became inevitable, in this context a small group of national capital also emerged from the process of privatization[4] (Burawoy & Lukacs, 1994; Böröcz, 1999; Eyal et al., 1998; Laki & Szalai, 2004; Stark, 1996), comprised mostly of high-level technocrats with strong political affiliations. They often enjoyed the backing of old trade union members who were afraid of international investors. Still, domestic enterprises were largely devalued to the periphery of regionally expanding foreign production networks, or subordinated to the dominant fractions of international capital even in domestic services such as finance, media, and telecommunication. The majority of workers employed by former state enterprises lost their jobs during the transition period (Gerőcs & Pinkasz, 2018b).

[4] The background of these national capitalist classes traces back to state socialist reform-technocrats, corporate managers, and petit entrepreneurs who could partially turn privatization to their benefit thanks to political connections they had nurtured in the late socialist reform period.

Along hopes tied to the promises of Western-oriented democratic transformation, the social tensions resulting from the transformation crisis were tackled through a "divide and pacify" tactic of fragmented social policy schemes (Vanhuysse, 2006), a cross-party alliance in narrowing and fragmenting labor representation (Thoma, 1998), as well as by a boom of the informal economy (Stark, 1996), and urban–rural migration. Within politics, a coalition of Socialists and Liberals came to represent dominant interests tied to FDI-based development. The contending power bloc comprised conservative intellectual and political elites, a base of aspiring national capitalists and smaller entrepreneurs who lost out in the privatization process, and a larger base of voters targeted with discourses of pre-1945 nostalgia. Remaining in a subordinate position until the 2000s, this bloc developed a national-conservative critique of neoliberal integration which later became the dominant vocabulary of protests against the Socialist–Liberal coalitions' developmental paradigm, favoring the fast-track admission to the European Union.

In the early 2000s, the FDI-based model had temporarily been challenged by the exhaustion of privatization; Hungary's economy became more dependent on EU money transfers, and public and private debt accumulation accelerated again until German manufacturers –mostly in the automotive industry—resumed their investment activities (which happened only after the global financial crisis in 2008). Problems in the public budget attracted inspection by international lenders, while the cumulative effects of liberalization and austerity policies led to public discontent. Another source of delegitimation was that full dependence on European funds bound state practices to neoliberal EU policies. This happened to such an extent that not only traditional union allies, but also the remaining segments of the national capitalists were alienated from the Socialist–Liberal coalition—the latter regrouping around the contending nationalist politics of Fidesz. Fidesz's constitutional super-majority in 2010 was backed by the delegitimation of the symbolic "catching-up" message of late socialist and early post-transition period, and a reconfiguration of positions and alliances within the crisis of the neoliberal regime of accumulation (Böröcz, 2012; Wilkin, 2018).

State-Class Reconfiguration as Part of Dependent Development After 2010

The majority won in the 2010 elections empowered Fidesz to engage in reconfiguring internal–external capitalist alliances towards more benefits to the national capital (cf. Fábry, 2019; Gagyi, 2016; Gagyi & Gerőcs, 2019; Scheiring, 2020). This project was communicated politically as a fight against the domination by Western capital, and relied on the legitimating effect of popular discontent with decades of neoliberal austerity. This legitimating effect was complemented by introducing ideological and redistributive divisions according to status, invoking hierarchies of gender, ethnicity, and citizenship as necessary pillars of rebuilding national strength. Ideological campaigns against women's rights, Roma, migrants, and the homeless were paired with conciliatory messages praising honest work and promises of a new middle-class development. The development of a new layer of upper middle class capitalized through redistribution policies, with its savings and consumption channeled into protected circuits of domestic capital, also served as a tool of political stabilization, with polls showing higher support of the regime in these circles.[5] For the masses of unemployed who were largely the victim of post-socialist deindustrialization, an obligatory public workfare initiative was introduced to replace the former universal social transfer system that the rural poor were eligible for. This system became a major tool to discipline the reserve army of labor (Czirfusz et al., 2019), with regions with the highest unemployment providing the highest numbers of pro-government votes.

In order to carry out its project of increasing the space for maneuver of domestic capital the Fidesz government carried out a massive centralization of institutional power. This included media control, the centralization of local and regional government, and judicial reform. The government also launched a stock-repurchase program to increase the public share in private enterprises. In some instances, renationalization or hostile takeovers were also initiated. Increasing European transfers were used to subsidize domestic capital through state-supervised infrastructural investments and land lease programs.

Due to the heavy dependence on capital inflows, however, the government could not be entirely hostile either to multinationals or the EU.

[5] See the parallels on "neo-middle classes" with India and Turkey in Kumral and Karatasli (2020), and with the global South in Bello (2019).

Instead, it used the opportunity of the 2008 crisis to realign domestic classes with international capital. We distinguish three spheres of the economy according to three types of policies that were employed to reconfigure external–internal capital relations.

Dependent Neomercantilism in Export Manufacturing

First, the government needed trade surpluses in order to alleviate financial dependence and the concomitant influence of foreign lenders. For this purpose, economic policies encouraged large export manufacturers to increase their capacity and produce sufficient foreign currency for the reserves held at the central bank (Becker, 2016; Becker et al., 2015; Raviv, 2008). Due to the dominance of German automotive and electronic suppliers, industrial policy has largely been modeled as a peripheral version of Germany's neomercantilist regime, helping German export-manufacturers to relocate production outmoded because of the intense competition in the world market, such as combustion engines and other automotive parts (Bernaciak & Šćepanović, 2010; Gerőcs & Pinkasz, 2019; Pavlínek, 2015; Šćepanović, 2013).[6] This affected education, taxation, labor regulation, and social policies.

One telling example is the reforms of the labor code which reduced unions' maneuver space, and made it increasingly optional for companies to extend working time frames and force overtime work when demand is high, but put workers on under- or unpaid furlough when demand is low. As a consequence, working time frames pushed incomes down (Meszmann, 2016). Manufacturers double-benefited from the reform: they can use more flexible working conditions in their Hungarian factories, plus they also have a strong disciplining tool in discussions with stronger unions in Germany, where the effects of relocations have also been severe for the blue-collar workforce (Krzywdzinski, 2014). While the reforms reduced strike activity, new union capacities have also been built in parallel with reindustrialization, as shown, for instance, in 2018 protests against the "Slave Law" (Gagyi & Gerőcs, 2019). In education,

[6] Some of these industrial policies were co-drafted by Hungarian government officials from the Ministry of Innovation and Technology, and agents of German lobby organizations, for example the German-Hungarian Chamber of Industry and Commerce.

a vocational training system was designed by the German industrial lobby and their Hungarian counterparts, which provides companies with cheap and flexible labor, and with the same move, closes mobility channels, and solidifies low-skilled positions within the class system. (Gagyi & Gerőcs, 2019). Finally, the corporate tax level has since 2010 become the lowest in the European Union while the tax-burden on households (sales tax) is the highest.[7]

Building Domestic Capital in Domestic Services

The second type of policies targeted non-tradable production in domestic service industries, where the state has gained regulatory capacity to intervene and change market relations to the benefit of domestic capital. Here, international capital was targeted by discriminative and protectionist policies. Hostile takeovers and disputed renationalizations also took place, such as in the case of municipal utilities. Targeted areas were typically in retail, media, telecommunication, energy, and construction.[8] As a result of the influx of European funds, the state could also extend its redistribution capacity through infrastructural investments, which has become an effective means of subsidizing domestic capital.

Strengthening National Finance Capital and Reorganizing Financial Dependence

Banking and international finances have constituted a specific field in which sources of external funding intersect with the capitalization of domestic classes. In banking, conflicts among the national and international fractions of capital were relatively muted, due to a win–win situation

[7] The official corporate flat-tax rate is 9%, but the effective tax which companies paid in 2018 after specific allowances was only 7.2%, while the 30 largest multinationals—dominated by German manufacturers—were calculated to have paid an effective rate of 3.,6%. The Hungarian personal income tax system is similarly flat, with a universal rate of 15%. In contrast to the low corporate and income tax rates, Hungary introduced the highest value-added tax that was possible within the tax-harmonization framework of the EU, with a rate of 27%.

[8] The construction industry is probably one of the most traditional spheres where semi-peripheral states provide protected circuits for domestic capital, sometimes in collaboration with finance as well (cf. Arrighi, 1990; Gereffi & Evans, 1981; Radice, 2009; Wallerstein, 1976).

provided by generous bailouts provided to international capital in the management of the post-2008 debt crisis (Mihályi, 2015). Shifts in market relations helped government-associated financial institutions to overtake the private lending market which used to be under the control of foreign banks prior to the crisis. Since then, the private landing market experiences a massive concentration of capital; with the help of the government, newly acquired financial assets are integrated into a new giant bank that is hoped to dominate the oligopolistic market. Meanwhile, shifts in the balance of international forces helped Hungarian authorities to reorganize external funding (cf. Van Apeldoorn, 2009; van der Pijl, 2012). Russian and Chinese capital, in particular, has been favored by the Hungarian central bank in helping diversify away from the dependence on European funds.

In order to loosen its dependence on Western financial sources, the Fidesz government seeks alternative funding channels that it can use for its capital import needs. This need is met by China's and Russia's geopolitical endeavor of exporting their excess capital in the form of new infrastructural projects in countries that are in need of capital investment. In the case of Russia, important investment packages were agreed upon with the Fidesz government. This involved the extension of Hungary's nuclear power-block capacity by an international consortium led by Russia's Rosatom in the city of Paks which is already producing 40% of the country's energy supply. With the extension, the share of nuclear energy is planned to reach 80% of the supply; such a massive supply of cheap energy is hoped to serve both the needs of the eastwardly expanding German industrial complex, and Hungarian companies who cover up to 40% of the construction plan. 80% of the costs of this massive infrastructural project are covered by a $10 billion credit line agreement. According to the second agreement, the new headquarters of Russia's International Investment Bank (IIB)[9] was set up in Budapest in September 2019. As part of the agreement, the Hungarian state raised the joint stock of the bank's capital by 10 billion euros, making Hungary the second largest stakeholder in the IIB.

Unlike Russia's bilateral investment packages, China's Belt and Road Initiative (BRI) is a multilateral investment framework for China's capital

[9] The former Comecon Development Bank, established in 1970; members are Bulgaria, Cuba, Czechia, Hungary, Mongolia, Romania, Russia, Slovakia, and Vietnam.

exports. In the case of central, eastern, and south–eastern European countries, China has set up a special credit facility (CEEC-17), worth $10 billion to finance infrastructural projects in 17 countries. They are eligible to apply for preferential loans to be used for infrastructural projects, mostly in transportation and energy, if those are part of the broader BRI framework (Piroska & Gerőcs, 2018). This involves the building of a high-speed cargo rail line, part of which has been a Belgrade–Budapest line, to be built by a consortium led by China Communication Construction Company, with 85% of costs to be covered by China's Exim-bank (Rogers 2019). Hungarian state-backed construction companies are expected to participate in the construction too.

Another important initiative was launched by the People's Bank of China (PBC) in 2013 to promote the internationalization of its own currency, the renminbi (cf. Gao & Yu, 2011; Gerőcs, 2017; Van Noije & De Conti, 2017). The Hungarian central bank was among the first to sign a bilateral foreign exchange swap agreement with the PBC, which permitted the Hungarian central bank to use the currency as a reserve. In 2016 Hungary launched its own "Budapest RMB Initiative" which was aimed at attracting Chinese financial institutions to open regional branches in Budapest.[10] Hungary and Poland were also among the first countries in the EU to issue foreign sovereign bonds in RMB (Gerőcs, 2017: 180).

One of the most tangible effects of the multipolar geopolitical environment on the development of regional economies can be grasped by the structural breakdown of their external funding. Between 2013 and 2017 Hungary has eliminated European loans altogether, while the share of EU funds in the broader external funding structure became the smallest in comparison to other eastern European Union member states (however, measured as share of the GDP it is still among the highest), which is related to the fact that the Hungarian authorities seek alternative funding channels (Fig. 1).

[10] Since 2015, three out of the four largest Chinese banks by total assets, China Construction Bank, Bank of China, and Agricultural Bank of China, already use Budapest for regional offshore RMB transactions.

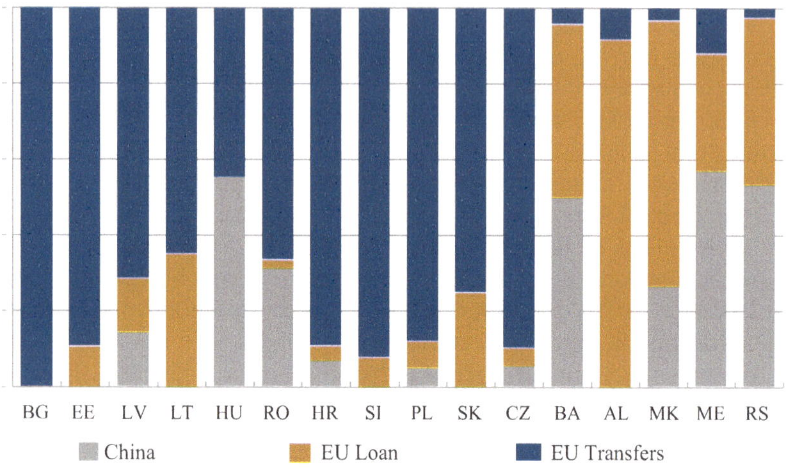

Fig. 1 Regional breakdown of external funding, 2013–2017 (Piroska & Gerőcs, 2018)

Conclusion

This chapter analyzed Hungary's current accumulation regime in the context of reconfigurations of global integration throughout the long crisis of the post-war global capitalist cycle. Since the 1970's, we differentiated three main regimes in Hungary's integration into the world economy. The first we described as a model of import substitution based on a bridge position between Western and Comecon markets in the 1960s and 1970s. The second was the neoliberal model of integration, which lasted from the dismantling of the import substitution model in the 1970s until the 2008 crisis. This model was characterized by increasing market liberalization and reliance on Western capital inflow—first by FDI through privatization, then through public and private debt accumulation. After the economic exhaustion and political delegitimation of this model, the conservative Fidesz government used the opportunity of the 2008 crisis to reorganize the country's position in global accumulation chains after 2010.

We conceive of the present regime as a new constellation of dependent development, which combines three main aspects of world-economic integration. The first entails making space for the development of national capital as a junior partner of external capitalist coalitions. The second aspect, which we called dependent neomercantilism, integrates the local economy in a subservient position with crisis management measures of regionally dominant industrial capital. The third aspect is a reorientation towards alternative sources of external funding. As domestic capitals' accumulation largely depends on EU transfers and their favorable redistribution controlled by the state, efforts to diversify financial dependence from the EU drive the regime towards new deals with Chinese and Russian capital, internalizing the effects of global multipolarization into Hungary's dependent development.

The external and internal accumulation enabled by the regime puts a double burden on local labor's reproduction, the effects of which become visible as imminent signs of a social-reproductive crisis. Despite the increasingly authoritarian measures used by the regime to stabilize its accumulation model, these tensions, together with the instability of the global automotive industry and fragile financial markets on which the regime depends, point towards new sources of vulnerability that follow from its own contradictions.

References

Arrighi, G. (1990). The developmentalist illusion: A reconceptualization of the semiperiphery. In G. W. Martin (Ed.), *Semiperipheral states in the world-economy* (pp. 11–42). Greenwood Press.

Arrighi, G., & Silver, B. (1999). *Chaos and governance in the modern world system*. University of Minnesota Press.

Ban, C. (2012). Sovereign debt, austerity, and regime change: The case of Nicolae Ceausescu's Romania. *East European Politics and Societies, 26*(4), 743–776.

Barna, E., Csányi, G., & Éber M. Á. (Eds.). (2019). 2008–2018: Válság és hegemónia Magyarországon (2008–2018: Crisis and hegemony in Hungary). *Fordulat* 2019/2, special issue.

Becker, J. (2016). Europe's other periphery. *New Left Review, 57*(99), 39–64.

Becker, J., Jäger, J., & Weissenbacher, R. (2015). Uneven and dependent development in Europe: The crisis and its implications. In J. Jäger & E. Springler (Eds.), *Asymmetric crisis in Europe and possible futures: Critical political economy and post-Keynesian perspectives* (pp. 81–93). Routledge.

Bello, W. F. (2019). *Counterrevolution: The global rise of the far right*. Fernwood Publishing.

Berend, T. I. (1996). *Central and Eastern Europe, 1944–1993: Detour from the periphery to the periphery*. Cambridge University Press.

Bernaciak, M., & Šćepanović, V. (2010). Challenges of upgrading: The dynamics of East Central Europe's integration into the European automotive production networks. *Industrielle Beziehungen, 17*(2), 123–146.

Bettelheim, Ch., & Dobb, M. (1965). Socialism and the market. *Monthly Review, 17*(4), 30–39.

Bockman, J. K. (2000). *Economists and social change: Science, professional power, and politics in Hungary, 1945–1995*. San Diego: University of California.

Bohle, D., & Greskovits, B. (2012). *Capitalist diversity on Europe's periphery*. Cornell University Press.

Böröcz, J. (1999). From comprador state to auctioneer state: Property change, realignment and peripheralization in post-state-socialist Central and Eastern Europe. In A. D. Smith, J. D. Solinger, & C. S. Topik (Eds.), *States and Sovereignty in the Global Economy* (pp. 193–209). Routledge.

Böröcz, J. (2012). Hungary in the European union: "Catching up." *Forever. Economic & Political Weekly, 47*(23), 22–25.

Burawoy, M., & Lukács, J. (1994). *The radiant past. Ideology and reality in hungary's road to capitalism*. University of Chicago Press.

Brenner, R. (2006). *The economics of global turbulence: The advanced capitalist economies from long boom to long downturn, 1945–2005*. Verso.

Cardoso, F. H. (1972). Dependency and development in Latin America. *New Left Review, 1*(74), 83–95.

Chase-Dunn, C. (1980). Socialist state in the capitalist world economy. *Social Problems, 27*(5), 505–525.

Cliff, T. (1974). *State capitalism in Russia*. London: Pluto.

Czirfusz, M., Meszmann, T. T., Kovai, C., Ivanics, Z. S. (2019). A magyarországi munkásság a hosszú lejtmenetben. *Fordulat, 26*, 142–172.

Eyal, G., Szelényi, I., & Townsley, E. (1998). *Making capitalism without capitalists: Class formations and elite struggles in post-communist central Europe*. Verso.

Fabry, A. (2019). *The political economy of hungary: From state capitalism to authoritarian neoliberalism*. Palgrave MacMillan.

Frank, A. G. (1977). Long live transideological enterprise! socialist economies in the capitalist international division of labor. *Review, 1*(1), 91–140.

Gagyi, Á. (2016). "Coloniality of power" in East Central Europe: External penetration as internal force in post-socialist hungarian politics. *Journal of World-Systems Research, 22*(2), 349–372.

Gagyi, Á., & Gerőcs, T. (2019, January 1). The political economy of Hungary's new 'slave law'. *LeftEast*. http://www.criticatac.ro/lefteast/the-political-economy-of-hungarys-new-slave-law/. Accessed 02 November 2020.

Gao, H., & Yu, Y. (2011). The internalisation of the renminbi. *BIS Working Papers 61.*

Gates, L. (2018). Populism: A puzzle without (and for) world-systems analysis. *Journal of World-Systems Research, 24*(2), 325–336.

Gereffi, G., & Evans, P. (1981). Transnational corporations, dependent development, and state policy in the semiperiphery: A comparison of Brazil and Mexico. *Latin American Research Review, 16*, 31–64.

Gerőcs, T. (2017). Challenges of internationalisation from the perspective of the Chinese currency. *Financial and Economic Review, 16*(1), 170–185.

Gerőcs, T., & Pinkasz, A. (2018a). Debt-ridden development on Europe's Eastern periphery. In M. Boatcă, A. Komlosy H. & Nolte (Eds.), *Global inequalities in world-systems perspective: Theoretical debates and methodological innovations* (pp. 131–153). Routledge.

Gerőcs, T., & Pinkasz, A. (2018b). Conflicting interests in the comecon Integration: State socialist debates on East-West-South relations. *East Central Europe, 45*(2–3), 336–365.

Gerőcs, T. (2019a). The formation of a New Patrie in the multipolar world-system. In T. Gerőcs & M. Szanyi (Eds.), *Market liberalism and economic patriotism in the capitalist world-systems.* Palgrave, 213-226.

Gerőcs, T. (2019b). The transformation of African–Russian economic relations in the multipolar world-system. *Review of African Political Economy, 46*(160), 317–335.

Gerőcs, T., & Pinkasz, A. (2019). Relocation, standardization and vertical specialization: Core-periphery relations in the European automotive value chain. *Society and Economy, 41*(2), 1–22.

Gerőcs, T., Meszmann, T. T., & Pinkasz, A. (2020). Uneven development in the European automotive industry: Labour fragmentation and value added production in the Hungarian semi-periphery. In A. Komlosy, & G. Musić (Eds.), *ITH global commodity chains and labour relations.* Brill.

Grosfoguel, R. (2000). Developmentalism, modernity, and dependency theory in Latin America. *Nepantla: Views from South, 1*(2), 347–372.

Hirschman, O. A. (1968). The political economy of import-substituting industrialization in Latin America. *The Quarterly Journal of Economics, 82*(1), 1–32.

Jessop, B. (1997). Twenty years of the regulation approach: Has it been worth it? *New Political Economy, 2*(3), 503–526.

Krzywdzinski, M. (2014). How the EU's Eastern enlargement changed the German productive model: The case of the automotive industry. *Revue De La Regulation, 15*(1), 1–61.

Kumral, S., & Karatasli, S. S. (2020). Capitalism, labour and the global populist radical right. *Global Labour Journal, 11*(2), 152–155.

Laki, M., & Szalai, J. (2004). *Vállalkozók vagy polgárok?* Osiris.

Lipietz, A. (1997). The post-fordist world: Labour relations, international hierarchy and global ecology. *Review of International Political Economy, 4*(1), 1–41.

Lóránt, K. (1990). Adósságcsapda. In A. Vigvári (Ed.), *Adósság: Tanulmányok adósságunk múltjáról, jelenéről és jövőjéről* (pp. 53–84). Szakszervezetek Gazdaság- és Társadalomkutató Intézete.

Meszmann, T. T. (2016). The rise of the dual labour market: Fighting precarious employment in the new member states through industrial relations (Precarir) country Report: Hungary. CELSI Research Report 12. https://celsi.sk/media/research_reports/12_CELSI_RR_1.pdf. Accessed 01 February 2021.

Mihályi, P. (2015). A privatizált vagyon visszaállamosítása Magyarországon 2010–2014. *Műhelytanulmányok 7.* Budapest: MTA Közgazdaság- és Regionális Tudományi Kutatóközpont Közgazdaságtudományi Intézet.

Mong, A. (2012). *Kádár hitele: A magyar államadósság története 1956–1990.* Libri.

Pavlínek, P. (2015). Foreign direct investment and the development of the automotive industry in Central and Eastern Europe. In B. Galgóczi, J. Drahokoupil, & M. Bernaciak (Eds.), *Foreign investment in Eastern and Southern Europe after 2008: Still a lever of growth?* (pp. 209–255). European Trade Union Institute.

Piroska, D., & Gerőcs, T. (2018). International organization of credit in the liberal leviathan post crisis: The case of China CEEC nexus. Presentation in the Workshop on International Political Economy of Finance and Financialization in BRICs. The M.S Merien International Centre of Advanced Studies 'Methamorphoses of the Political', Erfurt 2018.06.01.

Radice, H. (2009). Halfway to paradise? Making sense of semi-periphery. In O. Worth & Ph. Moore (Eds.), *Globalization and the new semi-peripheries* (pp. 25–40). Palgrave Macmillan.

Raviv, O. (2008). Central Europe: Predatory finance and the financialization of the new European periphery. In J. Robertson (Ed.), *Power and politics after financial crisis: Rethinking foreign opportunism in emerging markets* (pp. 168–186). Palgrave Macmillan.

Roberts, M. (2016). *The long depression: Marxism and the global crisis of capitalism.* Haymarket Books.

Šćepanović, V. (2013). *FDI as a solution to the challenges of late development: Catch-up without convergence?* Doctoral dissertation, Central European University.

Scheiring, G. (2020). *The retreat of liberal democracy. Authoritarian capitalism and the accumulative state in Hungary.* Palgrave.

Stark, D. (1996). Recombinant property in East European Capitalism. *American Journal of Sociology, 101*(4), 993–1027.

Szentes, T. (1988). *The political economy of underdevelopment*. Akadémiai.

Thoma, L. (1998). Védtelen társadalom. A rendszerváltás és a szakszervezetek (1988–1992). In T. Krausz (Ed.), *Rendszerváltás és társadalomkritika. Tanulmányok a kelet-európai átalakulás történetéből* (pp. 245–269). Napvilág.

Tyson, L. (1986). The debt crisis and adjustment responses in Eastern Europe: A comparative perspective. In E. Comisso & L. Tyson (Eds.), *Power, purpose, and collective choice: Economic strategy in socialist states* (pp. 63–110). Cornell University Press.

Van Apeldoorn, B. (2009). The contradictions of 'embedded neoliberalism' and Europe's multi-level legitimacy crisis: The European project and its limits. In J. Drahokoupil & L. Horn (Eds.), *Contradictions and limits of neoliberal European governance* (pp. 21–43). Palgrave Macmillan.

Van der Pijl, K. (2012). *The making of an Atlantic ruling class*. Verso.

Vanhuysse, P. (2006). *Divide and pacify: Strategic social policies and political protests in post-communist democracies*. Central European University Press.

Van Noije, P., & De Conti, B. (2017, November 9–11). China: Capital flight or renminbi internationalization? Presentation at the 21st FMM Conference: The crisis of globalization. Berlin, Germany.

Vigvári, A. (1990). *Visszapillantás a magyar eladósodás történetére* (pp. 54–65). Aula.

Vigvári, A., & Gerőcs, T. (2017). The concept of 'peasant embourgeoisement' in the perspective of different historical conjunctures. *Studia UBB Sociologia, 62*(1), 65–84.

Vliegenthart, A. (2010). Bringing dependency back in: The economic crisis in post-socialist Europe and the continued relevance of dependent development. *Historical Social Research/Historische Sozialforschung, 35*(2132), 242–265.

Wallerstein, I. (1976). Semi-peripheral countries and the contemporary world crisis. *Theory and Society, 3*(4), 461–483.

Weissenbacher, R. (2018). Peripheral integration and disintegration in Europe: The 'European dependency school' revisited. *Journal of Contemporary European Studies, 26*(1), 81–98.

Wilkin, P. (2018). The rise of 'illiberal' democracy: The orbánization of Hungarian political culture. *Journal of World-Systems Research, 24*(1), 5–42.

Czechia 30 years On: An Imperfect Oligarchy Without Emancipatory Alternative

Ondřej Slačálek and Daniel Šitera

Why is there so much popular discontent in Czechia thirty years after the regime change? Indeed, the capitalist Czechia does not look bad on paper. Surpassing the 90 percent of the European Union GDP average per capita, it outstrips now the formerly richer southern European periphery in terms of economic output. The unemployment rate is the lowest on the continent. The Gini index ranks it among the most equal societies in the world. The global indices of liberal democracy are also less alarming than the rest of the region.

On the ground, the real picture does not look as good. Czechia has a dependent economy with the highest rates of foreign ownership in the region (Chmelař et al., 2016). Its export-oriented manufacturing industries are moreover reminiscent of a European quasi-colonial maquiladora (Švihlíková, 2015). Wages and working conditions thus remain among the

O. Slačálek (✉)
Department of Political Science, Faculty of Arts, Charles University, Prague, Czechia
e-mail: Ondrej.Slacalek@ff.cuni.cz

D. Šitera
The Institute of International Relations, Prague, Czechia
e-mail: sitera@iir.cz

A. Gagyi and O. Slačálek (eds.), *The Political Economy of Eastern Europe 30 years into the 'Transition'*, International Political Economy Series,
https://doi.org/10.1007/978-3-030-78915-2_8

lowest in the EU. Around 10 percent of the whole population, mostly the working poor (Uhlová, 2018), are subject to the debt collection schemes, due to their inability to pay back private debts (Rychlíková et al., 2018). These segments of society are ever more concentrated in excluded peripheral regions (Prokop, 2019). Given such growing socioeconomic contrasts, the absence of a credible emancipatory or left-wing force to provide an alternative asks for reexamination.

In this chapter, we try to explain this absence through a historical comparison. Czechia is generally compared with Hungary, Poland, and Slovakia due to their shared political and economic history (Drahokoupil & Myant, 2015; Nölke & Vliegenthart, 2009). While accepting these similarities, we look for the specificities of the Czech case. Czechia has not experienced any explicit national conservative challenge against neoliberalism in the economy and liberalism in politics as Hungary and Poland. The Czech difference consists in the so-called technocratic populism (Císař, 2017; Šitera, 2020) which is manifested in the state capture by the Czech oligarchs as an open political force.

This crisis of democratic capitalism in Czechia and the wider central and eastern Europe is often understood as a backlash against the post-socialist transition to liberal democracy, a market economy, and the return to the West (Buštíková & Guasti, 2019; Hanley & Vachudová, 2018; Pehe, 2018). We counter this liberal narrative by historicizing the oligarchic turn as a fairly logical (while not necessary) result of the three post-socialist decades. These three decades, as we show in our analysis, gave rise to two blocs of pro-capitalist social forces which provided fertile soil for the oligarchic turn. Meanwhile, the third possible force, the left-wing alternative, failed to become both an intellectual and political force, although this might change in the future.

This chapter, first, periodizes Czech capitalism to historicize its development. Second, we identify the key hegemonic discourses which shaped this development. Third, we conclude by briefly setting out why this model helps in exploring the failure of a left-wing alternative.

Periodizing Czech Capitalism

There are various approaches conceptualizing the historical development of Czech capitalism (Drahokoupil & Myant, 2015; Nölke & Vliegenthart, 2009; Offe, 1991). We go beyond the tendency to compare central and eastern Europe as a less successful derivation of the Western-type institutions of democratic capitalism because it does not properly address the asymmetric political relations of central and eastern Europe capitalist integration. Our periodization complements then the existing historicizing studies of Czech capitalism (Císař & Navrátil, 2017; Drahokoupil, 2009; Šitera, 2020), by extending them with a refined interpretation of turning points in its historical development. This involves identifying the dominant elite forces in the Czech state (Šitera, 2021), and key discursive struggles which shaped these turning points.

Therefore, we identify a competition between two leading forces in Czech state-society relations: the *neoliberal nationalist* and the *liberal globalist*. Both succeeded in developing their own hegemonic discourse, representing either nationalist or foreign capital. We focus on longer periods of rule, but especially the pivotal moments of conflict and change. These moments we denote as interregna.

The standard periodization (Císař & Navrátil, 2017; Drahokoupil, 2009) recognizes two to three phases of state projects and social movement protests: *nationalist* in the 1990s; *globalist* in the 2000s; and *austerity* between the late 2000s and mid-2010s. We extend these to identify an *oligarchic* period since the mid-2010s (Šitera, 2020). At the same time, we do not evaluate the austerity period as a successful state project comparable with previous hegemonies. We consider austerity to be part of a conflict which marked the last interregnum, and which ended up not with the victory of austerity neoliberals (a mixture of some globalists and some neoliberal nationalists), but with the ascendancy of oligarchical populism.

Our periodization is proposed in Table 1. The first period is characterized by the leadership of nationalist neoliberal forces, which strived to establish a Czech national capitalist class. This period was one of nationalist neoliberal rule (1992–1997), under the coalition governments led by the Civic Democratic Party (ODS). After the economic and political crisis of this rule, liberal globalist rule followed (2002–2010), characterized by active international competition over foreign direct investment (FDI). The liberal globalists consisted of a heterogeneous coalition which included the Czech Social Democratic Party (ČSSD) as well as comprador managers aligned with the interests of foreign capital. Following the fall of the ČSSD-led governments by the mid-2000s, it was replaced by a coalition promoting austerity measures after the onset of the global economic

Table 1 Periodization of Czech post-socialist capitalism

Period	*Era*	*Leading forces*	*Main conflicts and issues*	*Key discourses (present in the whole era, but playing decisive role in the interregnum)*
1990–1992	First interregnum	Neoliberal nationalists vs. dissident gradualists/globalists	National question and the Czecho-Slovak break-up, gradualist vs. shock-therapy reforms	Market justice/anti-Communism
1992–1997	Nationalist rule	Neoliberal nationalists	Privatization, democracy in the new Czech nation state	
1997–2002	Second interregnum	Neoliberal nationalists vs. heterogeneous forces (Social Democracts; comprador managers, liberal globalists)	Defense of public media and division of power vs. majoritarianism, NATO accession and EU accession talks, FDI inflows (incl. bank privatization)	Party-based majoritarianism vs. elitist civil society
2002–2010	Globalist rule	Globalists (including both comprador managers and Social Democrats)	EU accession, US radar base, corruption, FDI	
2008–2013	Third interregnum	Austerity coalition (including the liberal globalists and neoliberal nationalists)	Global economic and Eurozone crisis, Austerity reforms, anti-austerity protests	Discourse of corruption vs. discourse of colony

(continued)

Table 1 (continued)

Period	*Era*	*Leading forces*	*Main conflicts and issues*	*Key discourses (present in the whole era, but playing decisive role in the interregnum)*
2013–	Oligarchic rule	Oligarchs	Corruption, refugee crisis, position in the EU	

crisis in 2008 which, among other factors such as corruption scandals, deprived it of legitimacy. After 2013, we can identify the oligarchic rise, whereby its key figures such as Andrej Babiš and other prominent oligarchs skillfully harvested the discursive products of previous eras to assert their autocratic rule.

As Table 1 shows, we consider as decisive the turning points (interregna) which were characterized by both economic and political crises. Only some of these contestations are becoming key to the next period of capitalist development, but even those others are important for connecting multiple crises and defining the atmosphere over time. Hegemonic discourses become more visible in the interregna as they become contested. We identify three interregna: the first (1990–1992) was marked by the conflict between gradualists/globalists and neoliberals, with the nationalist neoliberals ascendant; the second (1997–2002) was marked by the failure of the nationalist neoliberal project which led to the globalist victory; and the third (2008–2013), marked by conflict over austerity governance and the shift to an oligarchic turn. The rest of this section presents the most important aspects of these three longer-term ruling periods and three interregna.

First Interregnum (1990–1992) and Neoliberal Nationalist Rule (1992–1997)

After the Velvet Revolution of 1989, an uneasy pro-democratic and pro-capitalist coalition of humanist dissidents, reform communists, and neoliberal technocrats faced important dilemmas. This coalition was built around Václav Havel´s dissident opposition, Václav Klaus´ neoliberal technocrats and the broad managerial movement of middle-ranking

Communist cadres (Eyal, 2003; Kopeček, 2019; Sommer, 2019). Their demands for pro-Western democratic and economic reform turned out to be divisive very early on (Krapfl, 2013; Pullmann, 2011). During the first interregnum, these forces had to resolve following issues: What did democracy mean in practical terms? How to restore market society and the capitalist class after decades of state socialism?

Their answers differed (Myant, 2003). Ex-reform communist economists around the centrist post-dissident Czech Prime Minister Petr Pithart promoted a gradualist privatization with the strategic partnership of foreign capital. The federal minister of finance, Klaus, opposed this solution, winning popular support with the Czech Way reform program of a "market without adjectives" oriented at generating a Czech capitalist class. The program centered on the voucher privatization, where everybody could participate by buying vouchers to become a shareholder in the newly established privatization funds. Klaus exploited anti-Communism, a new enthusiasm for entrepreneurship, voucher privatization, and the partition of Czechoslovakia, to establish nationalist neoliberal leadership in the Czech state. In 1991, he left the common platform of the Civic Forum and established the ODS, going on to win the 1992 parliamentary elections. In these pivotal years, the neoliberal nationalists prevailed and established their rule.

The nationalism of neoliberal forces was limited in this period: "Return to Europe" became the ethos of the decade, aimed at making Czechia a normal Western country. Klaus worked hard on integrating Czechia into NATO and the EU. Thus his nationalism at that time was more economic than political.

Before collapsing in the national currency crisis of 1997, the Czech Way succeeded in forming a nascent national capitalist class. However, despite the shock-therapy rhetoric, Klaus accepted many gradualist concessions to avoid strong social turbulence (for example, rent regulation, and an emphasis on high employment). In addition, Klaus resisted privatizing the banks through which he could exert influence on granting credits, and thus the whole economic transition. As the amount of bad credit to the newly privatized national enterprises accumulated, international trust in the state-owned banking sector was undermined, and consequently led to the monetary crisis. Domestically, the regime lost popular legitimacy due to the growing scale of economic crime, including the asset stripping colloquially known as *tunelování* (tunneling).

Second Interregnum (1997–2002) and Globalist Rule (2002–2010)

The economic recession in 1997 and the ongoing corruption scandals—which Havel labeled "mafia capitalism"—led to the second interregnum between 1997 and 2002. A new caretaker government of globalist technocrats set the future program of the subsequent minority government of social democrats. Led by pragmatic leader Miloš Zeman, the ČSSD dropped its humanist socialist election demagoguery in favor of the co-option by liberal globalists, and cooperation with foreign capital. At the same time, it was harshly criticized by the globalists for brokering a novel political deal—the Opposition Agreement with the ODS—where power positions in the state apparatus were shared in return for the ODS' promise not to initiate a no-confidence vote. This arrangement (1998–2002) was viewed as the culmination of the rise of corruption and crony capitalism. The Left was thus caught between both the neoliberal nationalists and liberal globalists.

This interregnum was marked by the mobilization of huge middle class protests, the most significant of which were connected with efforts to revive the ideals of the Velvet Revolution, and use them against the Opposition Agreement. These protests twice gathered over 100,000 people in the streets, but without a viable electoral alternative. Instead of economic critique of the transition, they proposed a moralistic political critique. One of their most important slogans—"Thank you, now go"—was aimed at the leaders of the transition period. It showed that this movement accepted and appreciated the transition consensus, only adding disgust of "corrupt" representatives (Dvořáková, 2003; Slačálek & Svobodová, 2017).

The new government coalition was based on the ČSSD, liberal globalists in smaller center-right parties, Václav Havel's presidential office, and the comprador networks (Drahokoupil, 2009). It came to power through a twofold legitimization: the crony years of the nationalist project would be redeemed by the EU accession and the arrival of foreign capital. The EU accession returned Czechia to the democratic path and opened it to the foreign investment with the new productive spillovers. This involved privatization of the banks, and competition over the FDI in the manufacturing industries. If the nationalist project was *internally* corrupt according to the globalists, the globalist project was *externally* colonial according to the nationalists. Indeed, the accession conditions of

EU membership restructured the Czech state according to the neoliberal design and supervision of the European Commission (Vliegenthart & Horn, 2007). Later simply labeled as "Brussels", mainly—but not exclusively—by the (neoliberal) nationalists (Drulák & Beneš, 2015), EU membership was interpreted as a kind of political colonization by the Western bureaucrats. For the liberal globalists, this however promised a trade-off: the FDI-led neoliberal integration into the EU internal market harnessed developmental assistance through the EU structural funds, and promised a convergence with the European economic core. This proved to be only an illusion which rather trapped the economy into an integrated semi-periphery (Pavlínek, 2016) which remains a cheap but skilled assembly line for western European and east Asian corporations in the EU internal market.

The ODS returned to power in 2006; moreover, Klaus replaced Havel as president in 2003. By this time, the ČSSD was compromised as both internally corrupt, and representing an external colonizing power. The compromised political Left gave way to the ODS-led coalition with center-right globalist parties. Paradoxically, the ODS-led governments retained the anti-colonial discourse against the EU and FDI, but hardly challenged it in practice.

Third Interregnum (2008–2013) and Open Oligarchic Rule (2013–)

Already before the 2008 crisis, the new coalition government between the neoliberal nationalist and liberal globalists started self-imposed austerity reforms. The crisis became a prime opportunity for it to deepen its austerity bias (Šitera, 2021). This expected the private financial capital to enter areas ranging from the educational and social to healthcare sectors (Saxonberg & Sirovátka, 2014). The combination of the ongoing corruption scandals and the unpopular austerity measures undermined and delegitimized both leading forces in government.

Despite proving itself as a powerful protest force, the Left failed once again to become a leading force. The oligarchic force took the center stage as a result. Since 2010, new austerity measures faced constant opposition from the newly formed anti-austerity movements ProAlt and Alternativa zdola, as well much stronger trade unions (Císař & Navrátil, 2017). Despite this left-wing renovation, the Left remained rather a co-opted or protest force. While in the 2013 parliamentary elections the ČSSD won (with 20.5 percent), the new (centrist) anti-corruption populist party ANO of Andrej Babiš won almost the same share of the vote (18.7 percent). They became coalition partners in the new, post-austerity government. In the 2017 election, ANO gained the most votes (29.6 percent), with both the ČSSD (7.3 percent) and the Communists (7.8 percent) as its junior coalition partners.

Unlike Poland and Hungary, the Czech state capture is primarily economic, rather than political. Oligarchs Babiš, Zdeněk Bakala, and Petr Kellner symbolize this turn, albeit with differing strategies of state capture. Recently deceased Kellner was the main beneficiary of the 1990s voucher privatization through his investment fund PPF acquiring shares in over 200 companies, and sponsored the neoliberal nationalists (Biler, 2019). Ranking at number 68 in the *Forbes* list of billionaires (in July 2020) with a net worth of $14.9 billion, he is by far the richest oligarch in the whole of post-socialist Europe with the exception of Russia. Babiš used to be the second richest Czech and at number 616 on the *Forbes* list, with a net worth of $3.2 billion. Bakala became billionaire only in the mid-2000s while being formerly associated with the ČSSD and liberal globalists, including Havel.

Babiš chose the direct strategy of political state capture after establishing his ANO movement in 2011 (Císař, 2017). Kellner's group around PPF controls a large part of the political field from afar. Bakala openly promotes liberal globalist parties and organizations. All of them, however, share the same features. They all own domestic media empires, which they bought from the foreign publishing houses during the crisis. Babiš as oligarch-prime minister has gone the furthest. In an ironic twist, he was initially helped to power by the anti-corruption liberal globalist NGOs (Hanley & Vachudova, 2018). Having declared his intention to govern the state-as-firm, Babiš uses this economic power to directly finance and enhance his political career, and the political arena for his financial benefit in return (Patočka & Vlasatá, 2017).

However, rather than producing or relying on any civil society organizations like the liberal globalists and neoliberal nationalists along with their oligarchs, the ANO political strategy is just a hybridized product of past discourses which is skillfully wrapped in the flexible PR package. ANO could thus pride itself as being led by a domestic capitalist, without practically solving the rising problems with the FDI dependency. This happens at a time when the question becomes more acute, due to the outflow of profits (Chmelař et al., 2016; Švihlíková, 2015). While only around two billion Czech Crowns of foreign-owned profits left Czechia in the mid-1990s, 81 billion were withdrawn from the national economy—mostly by the Western owners—by the time of EU accession in 2004. With the 2008 global crisis, this number skyrocketed to 200 billion and reached almost 300 billion Czech Crowns in 2019. While other Czech oligarchs are headquartered abroad—Kellner's PPF Group based in the Netherlands, and Bakala permanently living in Switzerland—Babiš resides in Czechia, as does Agrofert.

Babiš skillfully profited from the discourse of Czechia as a political colony of the EU during the 2015 refugee crisis (Heřmanová, 2018). Moreover, this brought him into an ever-tighter alliance with president Zeman, who replaced Klaus by becoming the first directly elected president in 2013. Zeman turned from an early pragmatic Social Democrat in the late 1990s, to an anti-refugee nationalist in the mid-2010s, who willingly collaborated with Kellner´s financial interests. Therefore, the alliance between Zeman and Babiš could underpin the third leading oligarchic force to fill the power vacuum which the Left failed to take as an opportunity for the transformation from the protest to the leading force.

Hegemonic Discourses

Some key topics were constitutively present in the hegemonic discourses of the last three decades: markets, democracy, and Western integration. The intensity, context, emphases—and to some extent even content—of such discourses changed. Albeit schematically (see Table 1), we note that the pivotal moment for the market justice discourse coincided with the first interregnum; democracy, and civil society became the primary topic of key debates in the second interregnum; and the dependent and unequal position of Czechia in the EU has emerged since the third interregnum.

Market as Normalcy, Reparation, Efficiency and Justice: Neoliberalism and Anti-Communism

After the Velvet Revolution, the market economy was promoted by the leading post-socialist forces, with a mixture of both practical and moral arguments. The practical argument was based on the supposed efficiency and superior performance of markets, which was demonstrated by contrasting Western market economies and the Czech experience with ineffective management of state planning, parallel economy, corruption, and socially tolerated thefts of "socialist property". The moral complement was based on anti-Communism. The alleged criminal nature of communism was underlined, to discredit not only the past regime but a much broader group of actors—often the whole Left, or even centrist liberals. The reintroduction of the market could in this context not only repair defects of the Communist past, but could also work as moral rehabilitation, re-educating a spoiled society, and introducing sound and normal relations and values (Eyal, 2000; Kolářová, 2014; Roubal, 2015; Šitera, 2021).

Both arguments led to a perception of the moral and practical inferiority of state ownership and the public commons. The private sector, working effectively because of direct control by private interests, was also considered as morally superior, being the product of free entrepreneurial energy and invention, not that of state machinery. This discourse also distracted criticism from some areas in society and directed it disproportionately to others. Thus, the newly reborn public sphere and political arena were invested with hopes. They inverted into bitter disillusionment with politics. On the other hand, the private sphere was much more shielded from criticism. Criticism of social inequalities was excluded politically—as a manifestation of the Communist past—as well as morally—connected with negative human characteristics like envy. An emphasis on the supposed trickle-down effect was another component in this discourse: the wealth of some would bring prosperity to the whole society, which should thus tolerate inequalities, and even support and encourage its most skillful members in their pursuit of wealth and happiness. Critiques of class division were excluded and stigmatized by the anti-Communist rhetoric.

"Civil Society" Elitism vs. Aggressive Majoritarianism: Discourses of Democracy

The 1990s were marked by the conflict of the two interpretations of the meaning of democracy, personified by Havel and Klaus. The second interregnum became the moment of their open conflict which made visible many of the limits of the post-socialist democratic imagination.

Havel's idea of civil society rested on an elitist democracy of "values" and "personalities". Havel was the leader and icon of the Velvet Revolution and the subsequent democratic transition, but his thinking was also heavily informed by the experience of the crisis of democracy. His thinking can be considered to some extent as paralleling that of the western New Left (Barša, 2015), but he was at the same time heavily influenced by anti-democratic thinkers like Heidegger.

The Civic Forum was originally built as a movement without formal membership, and with the leadership only having informal power. As soon as Havel became president, he became distant to the movement, and even more so to political parties. As a self-proclaimed corrective of democracy, he promoted the heavy moralization of politics by "values" (which included humanism and a kind approach to minorities, as well as unclear rhetoric about an "order of being", with conservative undertones), and strong "personalities" with the trust of their fellow citizens. Against the reduction of "politics" to political parties, Havel underlined the role of "civil society" as the corrective to political parties and agenda-setters. He thus mixed some radical democratic impulses with a strong elitism. Havel and his followers sometimes articulated a moral and aesthetic disillusionment with politics and with the results of the Velvet Revolution. His position can be characterized as "moral populism" (Znoj, 2015), with Havel in the unique position of "moral authority" and pastoral power.

In contrast, Klaus' "standard political parties" rested on majoritarianism. Beyond a primacy in economic knowledge, Klaus triumphed over Havel and his followers because he had a strong sense for political organization (Hadjisky, 2001). According to him, politics was a sphere only for political parties, and their electoral struggle. Anything beyond this sphere—such as NGOs and social movements, the judiciary, or international organizations— suffered from a deficit of legitimacy, and posited a danger to democracy. In Klaus' mind, the competition of "standard political parties" looked similar to market competition. Most important was the act of election, not the quality of public debate or the division of power. Those who gained the majority of votes should rule. If Havel´s elitism meant the moralization of politics, Klaus' majoritarianism meant the marketization of it (cf. Bělohradský, 2010).

What resonated on both sides was the conservative lesson from the twentieth century: that democracy can be dangerous. With references to the electoral successes of the Nazis in Germany (1933), and the Communists in Czechoslovakia (1946), the danger of democratic voting for anti-democratic forces was emphasized. To prevent this, the division of power and some "safety valves" (Senate, constitutional court) were included into the political system to "defend democracy" against the *demos*. "Dangers to democracy" could come from the masses, which could be influenced by "extremists" or "populists" and attack the basic parameters of the system—be it democracy, human rights, or private property.

The rights of minorities became part of this discourse. Havel´s camp underlined the defense of minorities such as the Roma as one distinctive aspect of its moralism. The majority was viewed with a moralistic distance and distaste, as inclining to racism and xenophobia (often quite legitimately), which had to be put under the tutelage of a humanist elite. The radical left was another strong anti-racist force, which sometimes led to strange cooperation. The "defense of minorities" by elites sometimes led to the connection of the unpopular minorities with unpopular elites, and exposed both groups to a broader backlash.

Market, Corruption, Colony: Explaining Inferiority in the European Context

There was a strong feeling of catching up with the West during transformation. As Czechia became a formally equal member of the EU, the equality was complemented by the semi-peripheral position, for a long time considered as temporary, and not problematized. The unfulfilled promise of full Westernization had been historically nothing new, but later fueled resentment against the West (Eberle, 2018; Slačálek, 2016).

Czechia soon became a strongly Eurosceptic country, both in opinion polls and in the positions of president Klaus, but the declared motives were more political than economic. During the third interregnum and later, the economic position of Czechia in the EU also became a hotly debated topic (Chmelař et al., 2016; Myant & Drahokoupil, 2017; Švihlíková, 2015). In the mid-2010s, the trade unions started a campaign against cheap labor comparing Czech and German wages. The topic of profits leaving the country started to be highlighted at roughly the same time. We can schematically identify three discourses which provide an explanation of the dependent and inferior Czech position.

The first discourse can be termed as *transition and market justice*. This cast the subordinate position as a deserved punishment for anti-market sins, be they the Communist past or lower labor productivity. This discourse also proposed a cure: the comparative advantage of post-Communist countries could be a higher level of market orthodoxy, and lesser scope of regulations than in the EU. Of course, this is analogous to the discourse in neoliberal rhetoric about poor individuals, peripheral regions, and excluded minorities such as Roma or the "underclass".

The second one was a ***discourse of corruption***. It located the main problems not in relations with external forces, or the internal division of wealth, but to the cronyism and corruption of domestic politicians. This criticism includes two elements. First, it made possible an uncritical interpretation of external penetration, with Western standards seen to be bringing a higher civilizational level against the backdrop of corrupt domestic politics. Second, it delegitimizes the political class much more than the domestic capitalist class. Corruption is often connected with the fraud in the EU structural funds. This discourse implies that Czechia could have reached Western living standards but it didn't due to the non-transparent state.

Third is the ***discourse of colony***, which emphasizes the unequal relations between the EU core and Czechia. In this view, the inferior position is the responsibility of western Europe and its approach to Czechia based on a power imbalance and unequal integration into the EU. It had both neoliberal nationalist and left wing varieties. The neoliberal version was already articulated by Klaus and ODS during the late 1990s in the context of accession negotiations. This form of Euroscepticism underlined the political dimension of the EU, its "socialism", "regulations", as well as criticism of structural funds as deforming the market. Brussels became the new Hapsburg Vienna or the new Moscow in this discourse, the capital of "imperial rule". The leftist version of this critique was formulated later. Švihlíková (2015) articulates an economic criticism of the outflow of profits, the FDI model, and the internal inequalities of the EU. She concludes by proposing a nationalist industrial policy, and a return to the nation as central to development. Therefore, this discourse has both—leftist and rightist—which meet in the economic nationalism.

In Place of Conclusion: Is There a Space for Any Left-Wing Alternative?

We opened this chapter with the basic left analysis of the socioeconomic polarization. In this conclusion, we discuss why the Czech Left—trade unions, social democrats, and civil society—failed to develop as an autonomous force able to represent Czech labor in a hegemonic struggle with the two dominant—neoliberal nationalist and liberal globalist—forces. During the 2010s, oligarchs have become the third leading force instead. What is more, while the Left was a leading anti-austerity protest force in the early 2010s, it is no longer a leading one in the case of anti-oligarchical protests.

To summarize briefly: trade unions have a mass constituency, but with few exceptions they do not have the capacity for militant (or almost any) activity and industrial action. Social democrats are contaminated by the legacy of participating in the liberal globalist project, as well as by being Babiš's junior partners. The Communists remained a strange residuum of Brezhnevism, blocking the space for an authentic radical left. The only promise can be given to the rejuvenation of the leftist civil society. The establishment of online dailies *Deník Referendum* and *Alarm* in the 2010s are evidence of this development.

As we conclude this chapter on the brink of a COVID-19 crisis, the vitality of the Left is ever more crucial because it only "accelerates the departure of the past epoch" of neoliberal capitalism in Czechia and globally (Barša, 2020). This puts us all—and the Left in particular—at the crossroads. Either the Czech Left fails again in giving way to a more entrenched technocratic-oligarchic rule, or it is able to articulate its own hegemonic discourse of emancipation within or beyond capitalism. Having a strong party representation, the Czech Left has always been weak in terms of active civil society which would intellectually embed this political representation. No wonder the ČSSD was either co-opted by—or torn between—other dominant forces, and unable to articulate a hegemonic discourse of a positive future. We see the nascent potential for this articulation thanks to emergent groups like Alarm or Deník Referendum, among others. Further, the trade unions are finally able to actively participate in defense of Czech "cheap labor" (Myant & Drahokoupil, 2017). There is thus a nascent social basis for a future leading force, but hardly any hegemonic discourse. Although we provide only a selective overview, our chapter still shows that the Czech left-wing analysis has become more diverse and articulate. First, it autonomously identifies important topics such as excluded regions or the working poor and makes them a mainstream topic in public discussions when attacking the discursive trap of "market justice" (Uhlová, 2018, Rychlíková et al., 2018; Prokop 2019). Second, it is critical to the Czech semi-peripheral position in the global division of labor, but looks for internationalist solutions without falling into the trap of economic and cultural nationalism (Chmelař et al., 2016; Heřmanová, 2018). Third, it convincingly identifies the ills of oligarchy, without being consumed by the old anticorruption discourse which would blame it all on the whole population as a failed case of Westernization (Biler, 2019). The problem is that this analysis has not come up with its own positive visions. But this is, anyway, a challenge for the Global Left generally.

References

Barša, P. (2020, April 7). Něco jako třetí světová válka? Pandemie koronaviru urychluje odchod minulé epochy, *Právo Salon*.

Barša, P. (2015). *Cesty k emancipaci*. Academia.

Bělohradský, V. et al. (2010). *Kritika depolitizovaného rozumu*. Grimmus.

Biler, S. (2019, July 30): Noblesa Petra Kellnera. *Alarm*. https://a2larm.cz/2019/07/noblesa-petra-kellnera/. Accessed 1 February 2021.

Buštíková, L., & Guasti, P. (2019). The state as a firm: Understanding the autocratic roots of technocratic populism. *East European Politics and Societies and Cultures, 33*(2), 302–330.

Chmelař, A., Pícl, M., Bittner, J., Volčík, S., & Nechuta, A. (2016). *Analýza odlivu zisků: Důsledky pro českou ekonomiku a návrhy opatření*. Úřad vlády ČR.

Císař, O. (2017). *Czech Republic: From post-communist Idealism to economic populism*. Friedrich Ebert-Stiftung.

Císař, O., & Navrátil, J. (2017). Polanyi, political-economic opportunity structure and protest: Capitalism and contention in the Post-communist Czech Republic. *Social Movement Studies, 16*(1), 82–100.

Drahokoupil, J. (2009). *Globalization and the state in central and Eastern Europe: Politics of foreign direct investment*. Routledge.

Drulák, P., & Beneš, V. (2015). Czech metaphors about Europe: Havel vs Klaus. *Journal of International Relations and Development, 18*(4), 532–555.

Drahokoupil, J., & Myant, M. (2015). Putting comparative capitalisms research in its place: Varieties of capitalism in transition economies. In E. Matthias, I. Bruff, & Ch. May, (Eds.), *New directions in critical comparative capitalisms research* (pp. 155–171). Palgrave.

Dvořáková, V. (2003). Civil society in the Czech Republic: 'Impulse 99' and 'thank you, time to go'. In C. Mudde & P. Kopecky (Eds.), *Uncivil societies in Eastern Europe* (pp. 134–156). Routledge.

Eyal, G. (2000). Anti-politics and the spirit of capitalism: Dissidents, monetarists, and the Czech transition to capitalism. *Theory and Society, 29*(1), 49–92.

Eyal, G. (2003). *The origins of postcommunist Elites: From Prague spring to the breakup of Czechoslovakia*. University of Minnesota Press.

Eberle, J. (2018). Desire as geopolitics: Reading the glass room as Central European fantasy. *International Political Sociology, 12*(2), 172–189.

Hadjisky, M. (2001). The failure of the participatory democracy in the Czech Republic. *West European Politics, 24*(3), 43–64.

Hanley, S., & Vachudova, M. A. (2018). Understanding the illiberal turn: Democratic backsliding in the Czech Republic. *East European Politics, 34*(3), 276–296.

Heřmanová, M. (2018, September 21). Babiš ve své nejpopulističtější formě. *Alarm*. https://a2larm.cz/2018/09/babis-ve-sve-nejpopulistictejsi-forme. Accessed 1 February 2021.

Kolářová, K. (2014). The inarticulate post-socialist crip. *Journal of Literary & Cultural Disability Studies, 8*(3), 257–274.

Krapfl, J. (2013). *Revolution with a human face. Politics, culture and community in Czechoslovakia 1989–1992*. Cornell University Press.

Kopeček, M. (Ed.). (2019). *Architekti dlouhé změny: Expertní kořeny postsocialismu v Československu*. Argo.

Myant, M. (2003). *The rise and fall of czech capitalism*. Edward Elgar.

Myant, M., & Drahokoupil, J. (2017). *'An end to cheap labour'—How a public campaign may become a turning point for Czech unions' strength*. Friedrich Ebert Stiftung.

Nölke, A., & Vliegenthart, A. (2009). Enlarging the varieties of capitalism: The emergence of dependent market economies in East Central Europe. *World Politics, 61*(4), 670–702.

Offe, C. (1991). Capitalism by democratic design? Democratic theory facing the triple transition in Eastern Central Europe. *Social Research, 58*(4), 866–892.

Pavlínek, P. (2016). *Dependent growth: Foreign investment and the development of the automotive industry in East-Central Europe*. Springer.

Patočka, J., & Vlasatá, Z. (2017). *Žlutý baron*. Referendum.

Pehe, J. (2018). Czech democracy under pressure. *Journal of Democracy, 29*(3), 65–77.

Prokop, D. (2019). *Slepé skvrny*. Host.

Pullmann, M. (2011). *Konec experiment*. Scriptorium.

Roubal, P. (2015). Anti-communism of the future. In M. Kopeček & P. Wciślik (Eds.), *Thinking through transition* (pp. 171–200). CEU Press.

Rychlíková, A., Uhlová S. & Mahdalová, K. (2018, December 3). Exekuce: černé svědomí Česka. *Alarm*. https://a2larm.cz/2018/12/exekuce-cerne-svedomi-ceska/. Accessed 1 February 2021.

Saxonberg, S., & Sirovátka, T. (2014). From a garbage can to a compost model of decision-making? Social policy reform and the Czech government's reaction to the international financial crisis. *Social Policy & Administration, 48*(4), 450–467.

Slačálek, O. (2016). The postcolonial hypothesis. Notes on the Czech "Central European" Identity. *Annual of Language & Politics and Politics of Identity, 10*(1), 27–44.

Slačálek, O. & Svobodová, E. (2017). Professionalised "civil society" vs. grassroots "uncivil society"? *Socio.hu, 7*(5), 23–52.

Sommer, V. (2019). *Řídit socialismus jako firmu*. Nakladatelství Lidové noviny.

Šitera, D. (2020). Trilema demokratického kapitalismu na východní semiperiferii Evropy. In P. Barša, & M. D. Škabraha (Eds.), *Za hranice kapitalismu* (pp. 69–92). Rybka.

Šitera, D. (2021). Exploring neoliberal resilience: The Transnational politics of austerity in Czechia. *Journal of International Relations and Development*, online first (to be published).

Švihlíková, I. (2015). *Jak jsme se stali kolonií*. Rybka.

Uhlová, S. (2018). *Hrdinové kapitalistické práce*. Cosmopolis.

Vliegenthart, A., & Horn, L. (2007). The role of the EU in the (trans)formation of corporate governance regulation in Central Eastern Europe—The case of the Czech Republic. *Competition & Change, 11*(2), 137–154.

Znoj, M. (2015). Václav Havel, his idea of civil society, and the Czech liberal tradition. In M. Kopeček & P. Wciślik (Eds.), *Thinking through transition* (pp. 109–137). CEU Press.

Post-dissent and the New Right: Problems and Potential of post-Communist Dissent in Slovakia and Beyond

Joseph Grim Feinberg

The Phenomenon of Post-Dissent: Still Fighting the Last War

When the results of Slovakia's last parliamentary elections came in on 29 February 2020, pundits were shocked, not least in Slovakia itself. A party known as "Ordinary People and Independent Personalities" (OĽANO in its Slovak acronym), which until the previous month had been polling at under 10 percent, placed first with 25 percent. Throughout most of the campaign, political discussion had paid little attention to OĽANO, framing the election as a duel between the ruling left-nationalist party Smer ("Direction") led by Robert Fico and the liberal anti-corruption platform Progressive Slovakia. Smer had been losing support since 2018,

This paper was written under the auspices of the project Media of the Cultural Opposition in Czechoslovakia, LTC18040, supported by the INTER-EXCELLENCE program of the Ministry of Education, Youth, and Sports of the Czech Republic.

J. G. Feinberg (✉)
Czech Academy of Sciences, Institute of Philosophy, Prague, Czech Republic
e-mail: feinberg@flu.cas.cz

A. Gagyi and O. Slačálek (eds.), *The Political Economy of Eastern Europe 30 years into the 'Transition'*, International Political Economy Series,
https://doi.org/10.1007/978-3-030-78915-2_9

when figures close to leading party officials were implicated in the murder of a journalist named Ján Kuciak, who had been investigating the government's ties to organized crime. Progressive Slovakia initially appeared poised to gain from popular demands for good government, but soon its appeal waned and an array of other parties rose under the banner of anti-corruption. Only in the final two weeks of the campaign, during a moratorium on opinion polling, did OĽANO rise to the top, while Progressive Slovakia's support fell beneath the threshold needed to enter parliament.

But what was it that voters had elected? OĽANO was known for the sensationalist accusations of criminality made by its leader Igor Matovič, and otherwise for its ostentatious refusal to espouse any consistent worldview. Although it eventually posted a program on its website, what it publicly presented as programmatic priorities were a series of unconnected proposals on a loose variety of topics, while its electoral campaign was comprised primarily of publicity stunts, such as traveling to a posh neighborhood in Cannes to denounce the corruption of a former minister alleged to own a villa there. OĽANO, in fact, hardly presents itself as a party at all. It is supposed to be a loose collection of "independent personalities" unbound by ideology or strict party discipline. It went largely unremarked that many of these personalities, including Matovič himself, happen to oppose abortion access, LGBTQ and women's rights, and immigration (Kobová, 2020), and that a new government led by OĽANO would likely be Slovakia's most culturally conservative since the second world war.

This lack of attention to political programs is nothing new. Since the regime change of 1989 it has been an integral part of the phenomenon I call "post-dissent." Under the very different conditions that prevailed until 1989, the dissidents of Central and Eastern Europe had developed an approach best known today by the terms "antipolitics," theorized by Hungarian dissident György Konrád (Konrád, 1984), and "apolitical politics" (or "antipolitical politics"), popularized by Czech dissident Václav Havel (Havel, 1988). Until 1989, "apolitical politics" meant refusing to participate in corrupt and ossified political institutions and, from a position outside power, demanding basic civil rights and the just application of the law. After 1989, leading former dissidents, along with others who invoked their legacy, maintained this focus on rights and law, but they shifted the standpoint from which they spoke of politics, re-positioning themselves as defenders of political institutions. Their attitude, wrought in the repressive conditions of dissent, presented politics as something to be done well or badly, something that protected rights or infringed on them, rather than a contest from which multiple legitimate outcomes might result.[1]

The "post-dissidents," as I call them, established a system of discourse that would set the terms of public discourse for decades to come, even while post-dissidents themselves typically enjoyed only brief periods of political power. In fact, the success of OĽANO can be seen as in the context of a long development in which the discursive dominance of post-dissent sets the stage for post-dissidents' repeated political failure. Post-dissidents have successfully framed politics as a struggle between decent people and immoral threats to political institutions; but their focus on individual morality and institutional integrity draws attention away from social and economic problems, ensuring that the public will be continually frustrated by institutions that fail to address their problems. "Social" problems appear as questions of morality and corruption, to be addressed by finding uncorrupted administrators and politicians with "social feeling," willing to make concrete, and often isolated, gestures that help the poor. And so post-dissident discourse encourages precisely the kind of unsystematic response to social problems that post-dissidents denounce as "populism": while post-dissidents continue to insist that social problems will be resolved when good governance is established, figures like Matovič—and like Robert Fico, whom Matovič replaced—gain popular support by mobilizing popular frustration and showing off their concern for "ordinary people" (as OĽANO calls them). Instead of systemic change, they offer public declarations of indignation and highly visible but usually superficial or short-term programs of aid.

The post-dissident attitude was central to the protest movement that erupted in Slovakia after the murder of Ján Kuciak. Its central slogan, "For a decent [*slušné*] Slovakia," reasserted the basic post-dissident dividing line of politics: between "decent" people who defend democratic institutions and other people whose actions are beyond the pale of decency. It was a minimal demand that journalists not be murdered and that those responsible for maintaining the murderous system be held accountable. When this demand—easy to support in itself—was made into the movement's central idea, masses of angry protesters came to appear as "decent"

[1] For more on the intellectual shifts that took place in the transition from dissident to post-dissident thought, see Feinberg (2008, 2020).

people who played by established rules and upheld established institutions, while the protesters' opponents in government appeared not as representatives of established institutions, but as threats to the institutions. Once the situation was framed in this way, the goal was not to change the system but to remove the threats that had attached themselves to it. It was unsurprising, then, that liberal and moderate conservative media would frame the 2020 parliamentary election in similar terms, as a struggle between corrupt rulers and proper, decent citizens.

Roughly these same terms have framed liberal and conservative political narratives in Slovakia—and, with some local variation, in much of Central and Eastern Europe—for over thirty years: On one side of the arena stand the anti-Communist dissidents and those who claim their legacy by fighting for democratic principles, good government, common-sense reform, and the rule of law. On the other side stand the Communists before 1989 and those who have allegedly stepped into their shoes since then: anti-democratic, populist, nationalist, and corrupt. On the first side fall political forces that identify as centrist, liberal, moderate-conservative, and sometimes center-left. On the other side stand forces that, from a variety of ideological positions, rail against the centrist establishment. This basic discursive structure is not significantly altered by the fact that the direct institutional successors of the historic Communist Parties have, in different contexts, fallen on opposite sides of this divide. In the Czech lands the Communist Party of Bohemia and Moravia remains to this day a principle target of post-dissident hatred and fear, while in Poland and Hungary Communist successor parties became proponents of political liberalism and economic neoliberalism, and post-dissidents have generally focused their criticism on the national-conservative right. In Slovakia, where the Communist Party's direct descendants fairly quickly lost political relevance, their place in post-dissident discourse has been occupied by left-nationalist figures like Robert Fico or, before him, the centrist-nationalist Vladimír Mečiar.

But the anti-liberal forces that have been rising in opposition to post-dissident discursive hegemony are also in important ways products of the rhetoric of post-dissent. In Hungary and Poland, the authoritarian right capitalized on and radicalized the anti-Communism that liberals, moderate conservatives, former-Communists-turned-neoliberals had already established and legitimized. Liberal and post-dissident formations spent the first decades of post-Communist rule unmaking the economic and social system that was associated with the already-defunct political system. Taking responsibility for mass privatization and the dwindling of the welfare state, they were eventually outflanked by a more radical right that was less orthodox in its economic anti-Communism but more insistent in its symbolic anti-Communism. The new right was able to redefine the terms of political engagement, channeling anti-Communist resentment into a culture war against liberals and the left, whose efforts in introducing market capitalism could be framed as a continuation of anti-traditional "leftist" modernization. The countries' centrists had been so focused on the old authoritarians, enacting policies that would distinguish them from the old regime, that they were slow in developing a program that might secure popular support against a new authoritarianism.

In Slovakia and the Czech Republic, no such authoritarianism has yet risen to dominance. But the discursive structure there is similar to the structure that helped clear the stage for the radical right across their borders. Czech protest leaders condemn Prime Minister Andrej Babiš for having been a "Communist" decades ago, rather than for being a capitalist today, while radical right-wing forces strengthen within established opposition parties, facing little public scrutiny. In much the same way, Slovak protest leaders' post-dissident narrative lent legitimacy to the simplistic anti-corruption declarations of figures like Igor Matovič, whose general conservatism appeared beside the point.

Post-dissent is a variation on the more general theme of anti-Communism, but it involves a narrative with its own, a specific configuration of protagonists and plot. In 2018, when the Hungarian government cleared the area by its parliament of a statue of the Communist Imre Nagy, who led the country's 1956 democratic socialist revolution against Soviet domination, this was clearly an attempt to retell history in the interest of today's rulers. In 2015, when the newly elected Polish government launched a campaign to remove memorials to Communists from public spaces and remove Communists' names from streets and squares, this was an unabashed attempt to mark territory for the current regime. But when Czech protesters speak of their corrupt rulers as "Communists," or when Slovak protesters depict themselves as if their fight against contemporary rulers were the same as the dissidents' light against Communists thirty years ago, something else is going on.

Classic anti-Communism, as it developed in places like the United States and Latin America and has been taken up with renewed vigor by post-Communist autocrats, is a tool used by those in power who justify their rule in the name of fending off subversive threats. Post-dissent, by contrast, ever since 1989 has ascribed to itself the role of a democratic opposition while ascribing Communist attributes to those in power—and in doing so it has concealed the non-Communist aspects of actually existing power. Classic anti-Communism has claimed to be struggling against the past, while in fact it functions as an effective technology of repressive contemporary rule. Post-dissidents, by contrast, claim to be struggling against the present, but they do so in terms borrowed from the past. At the same time, by linking dissent rhetorically to Communism, post-dissent stands in the way of developing effective contemporary dissent—that is, radical disagreement from currently hegemonic discourse and radical opposition to actually existing, non-Communist regimes. The post-dissident narrative stands in the way of other stories being told.

Slovakia's Left and Right in Transition: Crony Capitalism vs. The Race to the Bottom

The phenomenon of post-dissent tends to be strongest in places where former dissidents and their allies were least successful after 1989. In Hungary and Poland, significant numbers of former dissidents held prominent positions in years of liberal and moderate governments, and to a lesser extent even in governments of the liberals' national-conservative opponents. In the Czech lands (already before the 1993 breakup of Czechoslovakia), the political scene was dominated by Václav Klaus, a radical market reformer who was as disdainful of the allegedly ineffectual and moralistic former dissidents as he was of the defeated Communists. Quickly crushing the post-dissident political formations in the electoral arena, Klaus's free-market radicalism won considerable support among urban liberals and liberal-conservatives, and the post-dissent attitude suffered in the Czech lands from the lack of a clear target for its moral outrage. Klaus was an imperfect understudy for the role bequeathed to him by the Communists—a role today played more convincingly by the slightly more corrupt and less ideologically neoliberal prime minister Andrej Babiš. But in few places has the tradition of post-dissent been stronger than in Slovakia, where former dissidents and their liberal-conservative allies were kept out of power for most of the 1990s by the moderate authoritarian Vladimír Mečiar, who formed a national-populist alliance with former-Communists-turned-businessmen. When Mečiar's popularity declined, he was overtaken by a similar alliance that formed around Robert Fico and his party Smer.

Mečiar and Fico have contributed to Slovakia's reputation as a conservative, nationalist country—an image further bolstered by the rise of fascist Marian Kotleba and xenophobic populist Boris Kollár (who has joined the current government). But opposition to illiberal nationalist leaders has also consolidated post-dissident liberalism, which remains relatively strong at a time when it has lost much of its erstwhile public appeal in Slovakia's neighbors. In recent years Slovakia has even become a minor exporter of intellectual liberalism, as the liberal daily Denník N founded a Czech subsidiary in 2018. When Zuzana Čaputová won Slovakia's 2019 presidential elections, the country became a beacon of hope for those otherwise horrified by the rise of illiberal authoritarianism all around. But genuine public enthusiasm for liberal freedoms continually fails to translate into progressive policy, thanks to the way the battle lines of Slovak politics are drawn, which leads political liberals to ally with economic neoliberals and cultural conservatives while shunning association with the left.

When Vladimír Mečiar's Movement for a Democratic Slovakia (HZDS) emerged as the most powerful political force in the 1990s, it rejected labels of left and right and explicitly invoked the legacy of the struggle to overthrow Communist Party rule. But Mečiar was often identified as leftist by his opponents, partly because he adopted a policy of slower privatization and more moderate austerity than that favored by his leading opponents (including many with more convincing dissident credentials than his), partly because he offered positions of power to former Communist Party functionaries and managers, and partly because he showed only moderate enthusiasm for the projects of NATO expansion and European integration. In 1998 Mečiar lost power to the liberal-conservative right, who pursued unpopular austerity policies that eventually led to the 2006 electoral victory of the explicitly leftist—but on many issues national-conservative—Smer party, which subsequently dominated Slovak politics up until its recent defeat.

In effect, the post-1989 division between "left" and "right" in Slovakia was largely a reflection of competing strategies of capitalist investment. While the left generally favored local capital—and has sometimes justified this explicitly as a struggle against "globalization" (see, for example, Blaha, 2018)—the right favored foreign investment through enthusiastic participation in the neoliberal race to the bottom, offering direct tax breaks to potential investors and pushing deregulation and reductions in social spending designed to make the country attractive to international businesses (Becker & Lesay, 2019:141–143; Polák, 2004). In the long run, however, the left quietly accepted much of the development strategy introduced by the right. The country's low wages and low taxes, coupled with a strong industrial base inherited from before 1989, helped it become a center for manufacturing, earning it the label of "the Detroit of the East." The label is, for now, a misnomer, if one considers that Detroit boasted high union density and high wages, while Slovakia's development strategy has depended on keeping workers docile and wages low. But if neoliberalism runs its usual course and investment moves elsewhere as soon as workers organize and wages rise, then the "Detroit" label may turn out to be rather apt, and Slovakia's now-bustling industrial hubs may turn into Michigan-type ghost towns.

While the rule of a populist left might have dampened some social tension, it has not satisfied those parts of society that hope, in the post-dissident spirit, for cultural tolerance and clean government. And even in the economic sphere the governmental left's results have been mixed. Slovakia was spared some of the worst shock therapy suffered elsewhere, but austerity, mass unemployment, and the loss of public property came all the same. Although the bases of the welfare state were still partially intact when Smer took power in 2006—during a time of significant economic growth that continues up to the time of writing—over a decade of leftist rule has managed only marginally to improve on the social system that it inherited. Economic development has been regionally uneven, with wealth heavily concentrated in the capital Bratislava and poverty still rampant elsewhere. Healthcare, the school system, and public transportation have hardly improved, and housing prices in Bratislava—where new wealth has also meant high levels of stratification—have gone through the roof.

What's more, the governmental left's moderate defense of welfare and regulation has been coupled with ethno-nationalist and conservative rhetoric that justifies social welfare for the national majority and the culturally normative, while blaming the system's inadequacies on those who draw on resources they supposedly don't deserve: immigrants (or hypothetical future immigrants) who might take advantage of supposedly generous welfare policies, Roma who are accused of not wanting to work, intellectuals whose work is unproductive and a waste of state funds. In the early 1990s, the self-described right positioned itself as the defender of minorities, intellectual elites, and moral statesmanship against national-populism. When the self-described left emerged as a formidable electoral force, it hardly made an effort to change the terms of political discourse, seeming content to play the part assigned to it by the right. When it has failed to relieve economic discontent, it has channeled this discontent into personalized hatred and fear.

In the midst of all this, Slovakia's liberals have spoken about the country's economic problems in largely technical terms, as problems to be solved by bringing more effective managers into government. It is telling that Progressive Slovakia, which emerged in late 2017 as the leading claimant to the liberal mantle, declared the left–right spectrum to be obsolete seemed determined to hide the fact that its founders were former leftists (see Slovak Spectator staff, 2018). Progressive Slovakia's public statement of "What We Believe" makes no mention of economic equality, defining equality purely in terms of "dignity" and "rights." (Progresívne Slovensko n.d.-b) Its statement on the economy expresses support for the free market and "balanced growth," without mention of poverty (Progresívne Slovensko n.d.-b). Only buried more deeply among the party's online statements does one find a promise of "a just redistribution of (...) produced value between (...) wages and (...) capital" (Progresívne Slovensko n.d.-c), although, to be fair, this does mark a change from the attitude of earlier post-dissident formations that actively promoted economic inequality. Another of Progressive Slovakia's programmatic statements explains with typical passion that "We cannot solve our problems simply by pouring more money into things. And we do not even have resources that would allow us to do so. The European agreement about a strict budget policy set (...) boundaries that we cannot (and do not want to) ignore. Hence, what is left is the unpopular way of trying to achieve 'more for less,' and the faith in economic growth that would be faster than that of our neighbors." (Progresívne Slovensko n.d.-a). It is hardly surprising that voters showed more enthusiasm for conservative populists like Matovič and Boris Kollár, and even fascists like Marian Kotleba, who add flamboyant promises of social welfare to their condemnations of immorality and corruption.

Dissent in Defense of Consensus

On the level of superficial rhetoric, this is what post-dissent has become: an appeal to decency and competence rather than daring vision, a push to improve political and administrative culture rather than economic structure, a call to change personnel rather than society. The great irony is that dissident thought, now so moderate and narrowly focused, gained prominence in 1989 as the leading idiom of a revolution. And before that revolution the dissidents' visions were remarkably far-reaching (Bolton, 2012; Feinberg, 2008). What is crucial to post-dissent is precisely that it is no longer dissent, but underwent significant change when it became post.

The dissidents' critique of power was shaped by the regime under which they lived. They rebelled against demoralizing and amoral mechanisms of political and bureaucratic domination. Insofar as they criticized not only communism but also capitalism—which they frequently did—they tended to view capitalism as a system of bureaucratic manipulation analogous to the system they experienced in Central and Eastern Europe. While they tended to take for granted basic socialist values like economic equality and the dignity of the poor, they also paid them relatively little attention. Problems of labor exploitation and economic inequality became secondary to problems of political representation and civic freedom. This shift in emphasis, though problematic already before 1989, in some respects fit well within a system that did in fact make the political sphere into the dominant factor of social organization, and in which the limitations of the political sphere were widely and rather justifiably perceived as the most serious limitations on freedom and happiness in everyday life.

What is remarkable is how this exclusive emphasis on political morality remained in place even after the changes of 1989 radically transformed the society that dissent had confronted. Economic reforms affected nearly every aspect of life, but critical thought continued to act as if the economy were hardly worthy of attention. Reforms were typically characterized as "necessary" and, therefore, beyond the scope of critique. Debate focused on a narrow range of possibilities, such as the speed and ideal beneficiaries of privatization. In Czechoslovakia this culminated in a highly publicized conflict between Václav Klaus, who proposed "coupon" or "voucher" privatization (allowing citizens to select shares in newly privatized property), and the many former dissidents who favored privatization to individual owners. The possibility of not privatizing at all, and instituting worker self-management—an idea that had been popular up until the end of 1989—was hardly considered in post-dissident debate at all. Although those who invoked the dissident legacy after 1989 were wary of the new class of people enriched by privatization, post-dissidents did not criticize their role in the economy—that fact that they enriched themselves—but their role in politics—the fact that they enriched themselves through their connections to political power and then used their wealth to influence politics. Insofar as the newly rich acted like "Communists" (that is, like managers and bureaucrats who venally and cynically mixed economics and politics), they would be opposed. But insofar as they acted like capitalists (exploiting workers and accumulating capital), there was nothing to criticize.

Post-dissent is thus "post" in two different ways. Post-dissent is, of course, the leading discursive tradition that claims the legacy of dissent from before 1989. Post-dissent "came after" dissent and has tried to preserve the dissident principle of criticizing illegitimate power. But post-dissent also comes after dissent in a second sense: it places dissent in the past. Post-dissent presents radical dissent as a phenomenon of a time that is already gone. It justifies the end of dissent and its replacement by a defense of what the dissident tradition allegedly achieved, which now needs to be protected and cultivated: "democracy," "freedom," and "civil society." The attitude of post-dissent presents its critique of power not as dissent from social consensus, but as a defense of social consensus against its enemies. Even when these enemies are so internal to the system as to be its presidents and prime ministers, they appear as if they were external threats, explicable not by the functioning of the system itself, but as irrational dangers that should be quashed. Because potential struggles against conditions of capitalism are framed as if they were struggles against Communism, post-dissident subjects fight as if against a specter that is no longer there. All the significant Communist successor parties are capitalist parties, fully integrated into and committed to the market economy. All the former Communist Party members who remain powerful have done so by mastering the rules of the capitalist political game. All the major problems that provoke popular discontent are typical problems of capitalism. But problems of capitalism are defined in terms derived from Communism, and capitalism goes unseen. Post-dissent has played the illusionist to post-Communist capitalism. The capitalist rabbit disappears in the magician's black top hat.

The disappearance of capitalism helps make possible a separation between the high ideals of post-dissent and the low obsessions of post-Communist economic actors, which post-dissidents abhor. Post-dissent makes it possible to see the post-Communist oligarch and the post-dissident intellectual as opposites, locked in a battle that has been going on for thirty years. The social relation of waged labor and commodity production, which connects the fields, and which is upheld by both the oligarch and his critic, goes virtually unseen. By keeping criticism out of economic relations and within the bounds of the political sphere, post-dissent criticizes corruption while simultaneously justifying and concealing the conditions of private economic interest and inequality that produce corruption. Meanwhile, a stranger observing liberal and conservative political discussion for the first twenty years of post-Communist Slovakia could easily come away believing that no labor was taking place in the country at all. But in the third decade after the change in regimes, this consensus gradually began to unravel, its elements developing in new directions.

From Engaged Citizens against the State to "Ordinary People" against Difference

For years, illiberal nationalists had generally joined liberals in speaking of economics without class. Rather, they nationalized economic discourse, which in Slovakia meant presenting rapid market reforms as Czech and presenting their own crony privatization as an attempt to keep the economy in Slovak hands (Gould, 2013: 106). When Robert Fico's explicitly leftist Smer party gained prominence, workers began slowly to make their appearance as well. But now workers, like the economy as a whole, would be symbolically nationalized. Smer's most influential ideologue on this point has been Ľuboš Blaha, an MP and self-styled Marxist philosopher whose vociferous denunciations of liberals as people who "hate Slovakia" and "support immigration, gays, big finance, and the liberal media mafia" (Parlamentní listy staff, 2019) have earned him, as of this writing, 128,216 followers on Facebook. Blaha calls instead for a "left" that rejects the claims of ethnic and sexual minorities in favor of "workers," who supposedly have "more conservative and authoritarian views" (Blaha, 2016). In Blaha's hands, the old national-conservative opposition to liberalism has donned work clothes. The liberal image of the worker as a danger to pluralist democracy remains unchanged, but it is now elevated as the basis of a political project to defend conservative sexual values and ethnic homogeneity—alongside social welfare for those who conform to norms and protect their borders from foreign dangers.

Yet even while anti-liberalism has attacked post-dissident discourse for its Western orientation and its tolerance for minorities, in other respects anti-liberalism has developed in conformity with central post-dissident values. Already in 2012, the liberal-conservative Slovak Democratic and Christian Union (SDKÚ) would employ the same rhetorical call to "decency" (*slušnosť*) later invoked by the protest movement against the murder of Ján Kuciak, in order to justify cracking down on Romani squatters as a defense of "proper citizens" (*slušní občania*) (Webnoviny staff, 2012). The fascist People's Party–Our Slovakia would employ the same rhetoric when it began to organize marches against Roma and, later, when it organized armed militias to defend against Muslim immigrants (RTPS staff, 2017). Proper citizens would be mobilized against the imagined threat of improper citizens—or, we might say, of non-citizens and second-class citizens characterized as uncivil (*neslušní*) and accused of not working hard enough or not sharing the majority's cultural practices and norms. Anti-liberal discourse has brought the category of work back into the ideal of citizenship as a marker of the citizen's exclusive value, and it has maintained the denigration of laziness that was an aspect of pro-market liberalism since the beginning. Now the image of the lazy worker corrupted by the weak Communist work ethic has been melded with an image of the improper citizen or immigrant non-citizen who threatens the polity of hard-working Slovaks.

Meanwhile, the mainstream liberal and conservative parties have shown increasing willingness to work with radical national populists. Nationalist xenophobia has also made a strong showing within the liberal camp, as Richard Sulík, the leader of the (ironically named) Freedom and Solidarity (SaS) party, has tried to position himself as one of the country's foremost critics of the EU's supposedly welcoming immigration policies.

In the midst of this, Igor Matovič has risen to the top of the political pack by taking up the post-dissident opposition to corrupt politics and forming a party of "ordinary people" that rejects even the most basic parliamentary conventions. As of this writing it remains rather unclear how his rejection of programs, plans, polite debate, and party discipline, an approach honed in opposition benches, will function in government, but what is clear is that Matovič has taken certain post-dissident principles to more radical conclusions than post-dissident discourse itself allowed. Unlike traditional post-dissident commentators who decry bad politicians but support established procedures and structures, Matovič seems to offer structural changes that would bring the democratic process in line with post-dissidents' anti-state rhetoric, mediating political expression without the need for politicians. And more effectively than post-dissident activists and politicians, he has developed a tactic that removes large areas of political discourse from view. While invoking the referendum as an expression of popular will, he has deflected attention away from the specific policies that might be enacted through referenda, even while he advocates lowering to 25 percent the turnout threshold needed for a referendum to be binding. Although Matovič claims that his party list is open to people of a wide range of views, liberal centrists are a small minority among party MPs, strongly outnumbered by ultra-conservatives who only now, once elected, have begun to suggest they will pursue a concerted conservative shift in policy. Voters were told to vote against corruption; they received a radical political vision that had barely been debated during the campaign. The post-dissident celebration of undefined citizens against the state has turned into a celebration of particular law-makers, elected without clear mandate, hailed as if they were an immediate expression of the general will and direct democracy.

Towards a New Dissent?

After a kind of proto-liberalism symbolically established itself as the leading dissident tendency in the late 1980s, liberal-conservative post-dissent became established as the leading critical voice of post-Communism. But the symmetry between dissent versus Communism on the one hand, and post-dissent versus post-Communism on the other hand, is imprecise. Dissent developed into a radical and external opponent to Communist Party rule. Post-dissent became post-Communism's loyal and internal opposition. And while dissidents did not consistently oppose communist ideals, they opposed the system that had made a mockery of those ideals. Post-dissent, by contrast, not only criticizes Communist practice, but has altogether rejected communist values, while it supports the fundamental pillars of the post-Communist system that it criticizes. Post-dissent is, structurally speaking, more analogous to the so-called revisionism or reform Communism of the 1950s and 1960s than to dissent itself. Its fundamental outlook is still grounded in the struggle against a previous system; its primary mode of critique is to call the current system to task when it fails to make good on its own promises. As anti-Stalinist revisionism became the conscience of the Communist movement, anti-oligarchic post-dissent has become the conscience of post-Communism.

But there came a moment when the revisionist Communist denunciation of its system's failures took a radical turn and began to point beyond the system as it was then configured. By contrast, the critical reach of post-dissent remains limited by the political consensus of post-Communism. As a tendency that upholds consensus, post-dissent celebrates the legacy of past dissent by limiting possibilities for dissent in the present. Is it possible to dissent from the contemporary consensus without threatening the emancipatory legacy that was at least one part of the contradictory revolutions of 1989? Is it possible to revive the emancipatory visions that many still held in 1989, before the course of revolution and the intervention of elites foreclosed the possibility of democratic socialism and made neoliberal capitalism the only permissible outcome of "democracy"? Is it possible, in other words, to make the principle of dissent present again?

Dissent in Central and Eastern Europe crystallized into an intellectual tendency by drawing attention to and organizing around what the regime of the day left out. Dissent gathered together disaffected youth, avant-garde artists, nonconformist hikers, intellectuals with publication bans, expelled Communist Party members, manual laborers who preferred free time over work. Out of the fragments of experience and ideas that were excluded from official discourse, they began to form a vision of an alternative society. What is excluded today from the post-Communist consensus codified in the morality of post-dissent? The single most significant omission from the post-dissident vision is the experience of labor exploitation. This is what the post-dissident critique of post-Communism is unable to see. It could offer the basis for formulating a new dissent that confronts this experience, re-draws the dividing lines of politics, and points forward. The new conservatism and the extreme right accept the post-dissident framework that substitutes political morality for class, while they reject post-dissident ideals of inclusion and outward-looking emancipation. A new dissent—a dissent true to the radical meaning of disagreement that was once contained in the word—a dissent based in the excluded position of labor, might finally bring life to the critical capacity that has been worn thin by long cohabitation with power.

References

Becker, J., & Lesay, I. (2019). Slovakia's development model: Contours, vulnerabilities and strategic alternatives. *Journal of Contemporary Central and Eastern*

Europe, 27(2–3), 139–154. https://doi.org/10.1080/25739638.2019.1692521
Blaha, Ľ. (2016, July 6). Ľavica sa musí vrátiť späť k pracujúcim ľuďom! *Vaše Věc*. http://vasevec.parlamentnilisty.cz/vip-blogy/lubos-blaha-postmaterialisticka-priepast-lavica-sa-musi-vratit-spat-k-pracujucimludom. Accessed 15 February 2021.
Blaha, Ľ. (2018). *Antiglobalista*. Veda.
Bolton, J. (2012). *Worlds of dissent: Charter 77, the plastic people of the universe, and Czech culture under communism*. Harvard University Press.
Feinberg, J. G. (2008). The unfinished story of Central European dissidence. *Telos, 145*, 47–66.
Feinberg, J. G. (2020). 1989: The triumph of truth and the burial of philosophy. In J. N. Beránková, M. Hauser, & N. Nesbitt (Eds.), *Revolutions for the future: May '68 and the Prague spring* (pp. 300–317). Suture.
Gould, J. A. (2013). Vladimír Mečiar and the politics of privatization in Slovakia, 1992–1998. *Slovakia, 61*(76–77), 102–144.
Havel, V. (1988). Anti-political politics, Trans. E. Kohák, & R. Scruton. In J. Keane (Ed.), *Civil society and the state* (pp. 381–398). Verso.
Kobová, Ľ. (2020, March 2). Neobyčejní reakcionáři v novém slovenském parlamentu. *A2larm*. https://a2larm.cz/2020/03/neobycejni-reakcionari-v-novem-slovenskem-parlamentu/. Accessed 15 February 2021.
Konrád, G. (1984). *Antipolitics: An* essay, Trans. R. E. Allen. Harcourt, Brace, Jovanovich.
Parlamentní listy staff. (2019, March 17). Ľuboš Blaha, největší čert fanoušků Čaputové: Bojíte se pravdy o vaší favoritce, ale ona stejně vypluje na povrch. A bude velmi bolavá. *Parlamentní Listy*. https://www.parlamentnilisty.cz/arena/monitor/Lubos-Blaha-nejvetsi-cert-fanousku-Caputove-Bojite-se-pravdy-o-vasi-favoritce-ale-ona-stejne-vypluje-na-povrch-A-bude-velmi-bolava-574300. Accessed 15 February 2021.
Polák, M. (2004). Slovakia: From "national capitalism" to EU liberalism (and beyond?). *Kurswechsel, 1*, 70–78.
Progresívne Slovensko. (n.d.-a). *Move on*. https://www.progresivne.sk/en/move-on/. Accessed 13 March 2020.
Progresívne Slovensko. (n.d.-b). *Our values*. https://www.progresivne.sk/en/our-values/. Accessed 13 March 2020.
Progresívne Slovensko. (n.d.-c). *The vision for the country*. https://www.progresivne.sk/en/the-vision-for-the-country/. Accessed 13 March 2020.
RTPS staff. (2017, September 14). Prečo chce EÚ odzbrojiť slušných občanov v čase, keď sa zvyšuje hrozba terorizmu? Aby sa pred teroristami nemali čím brániť? *RTPS.Sk—Robíme to Pre Slovensko*. http://www.rtps.sk/preco-chce-eu-odzbrojit-slusnych-obcanov-v-case-ked-sa-zvysuje-hrozba-terorizmu-aby-sa-pred-teroristami-nemali-cim-branit/. Accessed 15 February 2021.

Slovak Spectator staff. (2018, January 22). Newly launched Progressive Slovakia aims for 20 percent of the vote in the next election. *Slovak Spectator*. https://spectator.sme.sk/c/20743889/newly-launchedprogressive-slovakia-aims-for-20-percent-of-the-vote-in-the-next-election.html. Accessed 15 February 2021.

Webnoviny staff. (2012, September 11). SDKÚ chce chrániť slušných občanov v spravodlivom štáte. *Webnoviny*. https://www.webnoviny.sk/sdku-chce-chranit-slusnych-obcanov-v-spravodlivom-state/. Accessed 15 February 2021.

The Shame Movement in the Context of Georgia's 30 years of Transformation: A Gramscian Analysis of Civil Society

Nino Khelaia and Tornike Chivadze

In this paper, we analyze one of the most recent civil society movements in Georgia, the Shame Movement. We choose this movement as it enables us to discuss some of the aspects of Georgia's 30 years of post-socialist transformation from today's perspective. Our key thesis is that the movement has been reinforcing the hegemonic neoliberal order in Georgia. To develop this argument, we apply the political economy perspective of Gramscian analyses of the state and civil society and speak from the position of Georgia's newly emerging left-wing academic criticism. From that standpoint, this is one of the very first attempts to evaluate Georgia's post-socialist state-society-economy relations. We hope that this attempt will be followed by further explorations of the emancipatory potential of civil society in Georgia.

N. Khelaia (✉)
Humboldt-Universität zu Berlin, Berlin, Germany
e-mail: khelaian@hu-berlin.de

T. Chivadze
Corvinus University, Budapest, Hungary
e-mail: tornike.chivadze@stud.uni-corvinus.hu

A. Gagyi and O. Slačálek (eds.), *The Political Economy of Eastern Europe 30 years into the 'Transition'*, International Political Economy Series,
https://doi.org/10.1007/978-3-030-78915-2_10

On June 20, 2019, the Parliament of Georgia hosted an Inter-Parliamentary Assembly on Orthodoxy that was attended by the delegations from 25 countries. The Assembly was chaired by the Communist Party deputy of the Russian State Duma, Sergei Gavrilov. During his opening address, Gavrilov took the seat of the chairman of the Parliament of Georgia. Due to the high sensitivity of Georgian-Russian relations in Georgian politics and the experience of Russian territorial occupation, the opposition parties[1] found a good moment for protesting and exposing to the wider population the "pro-Russian" and "traitorous" nature of the ruling "Georgian Dream" party. The opposition party leaders presented the event as a "doomsday" for Georgian sovereignty, and as an insurmountable insult to national pride. The ruling party on the other hand, also condemned the situation, apologized for under-planning the event, and reaffirmed that under the conditions of Russian occupation they also did not see the place of a Russian Duma member in the Georgian parliament. The event was canceled, and on the same evening, thousands of people—in an anti-occupation spirit—gathered in front of the the legislative body and demanded the resignation of the chair of the Parliament. The opposition parties took advantage of the general protest spirit, and later that night, appealed for people to occupy the Parliament. This was seen as a coup attempt and was followed by violent clashes between the police and demonstrators with almost 300 injured as a result. On the following day, the Chair of the Parliament resigned, but the protest continued. This time, however, not only with an anti-occupation spirit, but also demanding the resignation of officials responsible for the previous night's violent clashes, and rather surprisingly, a shift from a mixed to a fully proportional electoral system for the 2020 elections.

These events gave birth to the anti-occupation movement, which named itself "Sirtskhvilia" (that is, "The Shame Movement"). The movement's first wave of organized street protests lasted for about 100 days and took center stage in the political and media agenda. Over the course of time, it was transformed from an anti-occupation to an anti-government movement. However, unlike previous anti-government protests in 2003 or 2012, this time, protest organizers assertively framed themselves as "civil society" representatives and claimed to be completely

[1] Former ruling party during the years of 2003–2012, the "United National Movement" (UNM) and their proxy "European Georgia (EG)".

distanced from political parties. "Civil society" thus became one of the most repeated terms in the movement's discourse.

In this chapter, we contextualize the movement's proclaimed civil society discourse in the light of Georgia's post-socialist transformation. Out of such contextualization, several features become evident: even if the Sirtshkhvilia movement—proclaiming itself as a part of civil society—was a relatively novel tactic, due to its general politics and ideological choices (such as a proximity to right-wing neoliberal parties), the movement echoed the dominant discourse created by post-socialist economic elites and its servant civil society, and formed itself as a conjunctural movement that subordinated its logic to the existing political and economic regime of neoliberal hegemony.

In our analysis, we consider The Shame Movement as a party movement in order to better illustrate the purposefully concealed presence of the link between the movement and the political parties under the "civil society" label. On the other hand, we see the party movement itself as part of civil society. However, our interpretation is informed by the Gramscian analytical framework of civil society, and fundamentally differs from how the movement depicts itself. If the movement frames itself using the popular understanding of civil society—in strong opposition with state and political society—we argue that 30 years after the end of state socialism, civil society activism in Georgia—as demonstrated by the movement Sirtskhvilia—renewed its existence as part of an extended state.

The concept of an "extended state"[2] (discussed in more detail below) finds its roots in the Gramscian critical perspective, uniting political society and civil society, as demonstrated in the famous equation "civil society + political society = state" (Cox, 1999). This theoretical tradition allows us to challenge established meanings of civil society and think about alternative conceptions that better reflect existing power struggles. In the case of the Sirtskhvilia movement, it helps us understand that despite the movement's strong inscription within the frame of popular meaning of civil society, in reality it embodies a type of civil society that has close links with the political society (especially political parties), and ultimately strives to seize state power through these political actors. Hence, the movement is not contesting, or confronting the neoliberal state and its power in general, but rather, just the current government.

[2] In "Prison Notebooks" the concept appears as "integral state" (Gramsci 1999: 210, 540).

For that reason, we refer to the movement also as an anti-government movement that strengthens and reinforces the current neoliberal order.

To illustrate our claims, in the following sections we first review some key features of the discourse on civil society in post-socialist settings and discuss the theoretical foundations of the civil society concept as part of an extended state. To elucidate our second argument about the anti-occupation movement as an actor reinforcing Georgia's neoliberal hegemony, we then analyze some of the key aspects of Georgia's post-socialist civil society in the context of state-society-economy relations. In the final part, we discuss the "anti-occupation" movement's discourse in light of the theory and put forward our claims.

Civil Society in Post-Socialist Settings: How to Understand Civil Society as Part of a Gramscian Extended State?

The concept of civil society in the post-socialist context is one of the most widely addressed phenomena in scholarly writings as well as in the political realm. There is already a significant body of scholarship that depicts rather negative development of civil society organizations and activism in these societies. In post-socialist states, this concept has been central for referring to a social change from below, but its practice was extensively professionalized and, due to its focus on policy issues and proximity with state power, has restricted the development of stronger movements and wider mobilizations (Ivancheva, 2015). In line with the assumptions of foreign assistance programs, civil society was primarily embodied through formalized NGOs that were understood as essential prerequisites of democracy and democratization (Aksartova, 2005); types of community activism that did not fit to this criterion of democratic action (e.g. right-wing extremist organizations) have lost the right to be included in "civil" and fallen under the category of "uncivil" societies (Kopecký & Mudde, 2003); being a novel type of externally sponsored action, the concept also gave birth to the debates with regards to the diverse political consequences—opportunities or constraints—foreign funding dependence created for local actors (Císař, 2010). Civil society was also subjected to multiple interpretations, but essentially it came as an ideologically loaded idea produced in the very specific historical period of post-socialist democratic transition, incorporating the hierarchical markers of social progress between "backward" East and "developed" West and acquiring a neoliberal character by presenting state as an "evil" and free market as a virtuous idea (Gagyi & Ivancheva, 2017). Overall, the idea of civil society in the historical context of post-socialist transformation has operated as an essential prerequisite for democratic transformation and servant of the capitalist integration. As a discourse of political and economic elites, civil society was supposed to exert continuous pressure on state power and contest communist and totalitarian vicious legacies "left alive" from the previous era.

Post-socialist Georgia's civil society has essentially shared most of these features of being foreign-funding dependent, professionalized, embodied mainly in the form of NGOs, and being ideologically driven idea for serving the free-market ideology by permanent neglect of social and economic aspects of rights. Most importantly, such conception saw its central purpose in challenging the state and its functions and shared more resemblance with American conception that began to dominate the nineteenth-century interpretation of the concept. Such interpretation in accordance with the American political context of that time, has put much faith in associational culture, autonomous mobilization, and citizen participation.

Beyond the American interpretation, the concept of civil society—as a realm of action distinct from the state—takes its roots in the eighteenth-century European Enlightenment, and since then has acquired various meanings. One of the central aspects guiding the change of discourse around the concept has been its relationship with state and capital. In European tradition, civil society was mainly equated with bourgeoisie, as it was mainly a private interest sphere distinct from a state that sought to advance its influence broadly (Cox, 1999). Since the nineteenth century, civil society has no longer been linked with capitalism and the bourgeoisie, but with voluntary citizen participation vis-à-vis state and economic powers (Cox, 1999). The American way of voluntary associationism profoundly differed from nineteenth-century European class and status-inherited societies, where state leaders in industrialized societies have brought "organized workers into a consensual relationship with the state for management of the economy" (Cox, 1999: 7).

Unlike the bottom-up initiatives conceived by American interpretation, post-socialist Georgian civil society landscape could only afford to pursue a foreign donor-driven agenda. In such a setting, instead of identifying genuine societal grievances and strengthening and building on already existed associational practices, the civil society organizations rejected all possible realms of civil society activities that existed in the past (including trade unionist realm) and created completely new professional structures of policy research and advocacy of their own. In this process, issues of economic power, inequality of wealth, and subsequent distribution of political power, have been excluded from the public sphere dominated by neoliberal discourse. When these issues accidentally reached the political agenda, influential NGOs have transformed from civil watchdogs to defenders of capital interests by launching an organized struggle against socially-oriented reforms.[3] It is through this process that they became ideological agents of economic liberalization and marketization and deflated the civil society concept from any emancipatory potential.

Gramsci's formulation of civil society, that can be seen as part of his theory of state and concept of hegemony (Gramsci, 1999), appeared in this context in the early twentieth century and presented a rather different field of power relationships among state, civil society, and economy. This view rejected economic reductionist understandings of civil society (economism) that reduced it to capitalist economic action and methodologically served the argument that the state must not intervene and regulate the economic sphere (Gramsci, 1999: 371). While Gramsci's definition of civil society looks rather ambivalent in different places of his writings, in its central characterization this conception considers it a theoretical error to fully distinguish political society from civil society, and includes all institutions—such as family, churches, cultural institutions, schools and political parties—in the civil society sphere. In this line of thought, civil society is a larger field of power relations, and it relates to existing powers of state and market by either supporting or opposing them (Cox, 1999).

Normative assumptions behind such a view of civil society are one of the central features of Gramscian definition, and rests on "a normative desirability of a future (socialist) civil society", whereas he treats actually existing civil society as a "function for a system of domination" that

[3] The clear example of this in Georgian case is that in 2017, the largest non-governmental organizations that declare themselves ideologically neutral (i.e. Transparency International Georgia, or International Society for Fair Elections and Democracy), have united against the removal of the "Economic Liberty Act" from the constitution. The Act constitutionally defined that Parliament had no right to increase taxes. Any tax increase would require a referendum. However, progressive taxation could not become the subject of a referendum.

should be rejected (Cohen & Arato, 1994: 118). This tradition thus puts to the fore two meanings of civil society: one, that it potentially reinforces the status quo of existing hegemony; and second, that it potentially disrupts it. While the former acts as a hegemonic actor, the latter is able to have emancipatory potential. If Gramsci's political aim in theorizing about civil society was to think of the emancipatory or counter-hegemonic potential of civil society, in our analysis the Shame Movement movement emerges as a supporter of existing neoliberal order and its dominant structures.

Unlike the established conception spread in post-socialist societies, civil society in this tradition is not an entirely autonomous realm existing by itself, but represents an instrument that participates in shaping the foundations of the state and new social order in the dialectical process of struggle for domination. As this is a realm that enables participation in political processes, civil society is presented as a political and ideological realm and is connected with political society. In that way, civil society is placed outside the state, but as it aspires to the creation of a particular type of state, it is seen as part of the extended state. A politically desired type of state in this tradition would be one that eradicates alienation between state and people.

Civil Society in the Context of Georgia's 30 years of Post-Socialist Transformation

Georgia's last 30 years of post-socialist transformation can be divided into two distinct periods. The first period lasted from 1990 to 2003, and can be seen as the initial transition to a market economy. The post-Soviet primary accumulation and distribution of formerly state assets went hand-in-hand with Shock Therapy—a doctrine promoting the fast transition to a market economy. This meant the creation of fundamental institutions for a market economy that generated conditions for new, capitalist types of inequalities. With the merging of political and economic elites, there was a competitive battle for resource distribution among former state nomenklatura representatives, political elites, and criminal coalitions. Also, formal democratization and liberalization processes represented an announcement of the country's pro-Western course.

The second period began with the so-called "Rose Revolution"—that marked the 2003 change in government, bringing to power the right-wing United National Movement (UNM) party—and continues up until the present. This period was characterized by the consolidation of market institutions and their implementation in practice. The second period in itself can be divided into two different sub-phases. The first was the phase of the UNM party governance under the leadership of President Mikheil Saakashvili, when the neoliberal order was aggressively established through extensive economic and political reforms. The second phase began in 2012, with the removal of the UNM and the election of the coalition "Georgian Dream – Democratic Georgia" under the leadership of Bidzina Ivanishvili. During this phase the neoliberal order was essentially maintained, however, the ruling party set businesses and private property owners free by removing previously existing informal state pressures.

The Gramscian type of political and civil society nexus, was empirically evidenced in Georgia already in the period preceding the 2003 Rose Revolution. At that time, foreign-funded non-governmental organizations—known as civil society organizations—played a significant role in political change and were openly allied with political actors. In 2001, under the influence of the Serbian "Otpor" movement, a new anti-corruption student movement "Kmara" ("It's Enough") emerged. The movement was supported by the Open Society Foundation—an international funding organization founded by the business magnate George Soros—and the aggressively liberal local advocacy organization "Liberty Institute." On April 1, 2003, the movement organized a mass protest, during which activists condemned Shevardnadze's government for being a remnant of the Soviet Union, and burnt the Soviet flag as a symbolic manifestation of their anti-communist attitudes (an act that was repeated 16 years later by the anti-occupation movement Sirtskhvilia). Anti-Communist rhetoric also occupied a central role in Saakashvili's entire pre-election campaign, in which Kmara played one of the central roles. The movement actively cooperated with the UNM party and openly positioned as the party supporter. Finally, it joined the anti-government protests of the Rose Revolution. At that time, three organized actors of civil society can be distinguished in the anti-Shevardnadze-government movement that prepared the ground for the change of power by 2003: the student anti-corruption movement Kmara, NGOs, and the private television station Rustavi2. Anti-corruption, anti-Communist and anti-government rhetoric was the key feature that united these three actors. At that time, the mobilization managed to acquire wider legitimacy through the discursive line of anti-corruption.

Pre-2003 civil society elites largely relied on the idea that future development rested on liberation from the Soviet past and its "vicious" imaginaries of statehood as well as state control. This idea in itself not only meant getting rid of corruption, but also limiting the state's possible realm of activities in economic relations. This discourse successfully managed to substitute the antagonism between labor and capital with the opposition between citizens and a state bureaucracy. This not only rejected the idea of class struggle, but also excluded from the debate the potential conflict between private and public realms.

After the popular National Liberation Movement of the 1990s, the new vanguard role of civil society in Georgia was played by the Western-funded non-governmental sector. Actors in this sector saw themselves as leaders of society with special knowledge and skills for democratization (Muskhelishvili & Jorjoliani, 2009), and through this solely avant-gardist spirit never managed to attract trust and legitimacy in the wider population. Pre-revolutionary civil society of the 2000s—which largely consisted of Western-educated young leaders fundamentally strengthened the ideas of the free market as an absolute good, and the state as an obstacle to progress. It was under such ideological conditions that the new, Rose Revolution government took power and began to engage in what was later to become a "neoliberal experiment".

"Post-Revolutionary" Civil Society—Civil Society in Government

Following the change of the government after the Rose Revolution in 2003, the level of overflow of civil society representatives into government positions and state structures proved so high that some researchers have used this fact as an argument to explain the insufficiency of civil society control, and the subsequent authoritarian concentration of power in the UNM (Cheterian, 2008).

According to the liberal distinction between civil and political society, traditionally, economic activities were seen as part of the civil realm: this very assumption defined the central interest of civil society to avoid state interference in the economy and provided justification for free trade politics (Gramsci, 1999). Such liberal understanding of civil society in "post-revolutionary" Georgia is transformed into a civil society which no longer represents an actor directly engaged in economic activities but embodies an actor that ideologically pursues the interests of economic elites. For this kind of civil society, the only "real" realm of rights is negative rights with the centrality of the right on private property.

As the UNM assumed power in 2003, the narrative which previously existed in anti-government movements shifted to the state policy level. The government persistently tried to form a new universal ideology by an active cultural policy and civil mobilization. With that motivation, the government initiated a relentless battle against the Soviet heritage, including its cultural and architectural aspects, and celebrated the launch of the "Museum of Soviet Occupation". As a symbolic gesture to highlight Georgia's rupture with the Soviet Union and affinity to Europe, the time zone was also changed (Isaacs et al., 2016).

The ruling UNM party ideology also shaped its conception of statehood as a reaction to the Soviet Union and Russia. In this narrative, the Soviet Union is equated with contemporary Russia, and a new patriotic narrative is being created by merging anti-Soviet and new neoliberal narratives. In this discourse, Georgia is depicted as an organic part of Europe, and the Soviet intervention as an interruption of this natural development path. Returning to that European road is seen as a historic mission, initiated and led by the Rose Revolution elites. Primacy of individual and economic freedoms are depicted as a natural characteristic to the Georgian nation: As President Saakashvili declared in his parliamentary speech in 2006: "our natural state is liberalism and this distinguishes us from Russia; the central difference between us and Russia is our human and entrepreneurial aspiration towards freedom" (president.gov.ge., 2006).

Such a mix of anti-Communist, anti-Russian and economic freedom-based narratives created a fundament for the formation of a new type of neoliberal nationalism. Finally, this discourse was instrumentalized as a means of discrediting political opposition and critiques of the government. The new hysterical invocation of anti-Russian slogans became introduced in the public sphere as the new normal way of political debates, and these debates were run by marking off the friend and enemy through such distinctions. At the same time, the rare attempts of university students to demand inclusive social policy were interpreted as Soviet-protagonist claims, and were marginalized from the public sphere.

As social and economic policies failed and repression increased, massive dissatisfaction grew in the country, finding its outlet in anti-authoritarian (and not anti-neoliberal) resistance. This created the conditions for politically marginalized representatives of big capital to appear on the political scene as more "humanistic" and non-authoritarian actors, and gain momentum for attracting people's support. In winning the 2012 elections, the "Georgian Dream—Democratic Georgia" coalition—which united liberal and conservative parties under the leadership of the billionaire Bidzina Ivanishvili—used this anti-authoritarian movement spirit to generate support. This made the UNM the main opposition force and since then, has shaped Georgia's political agenda by the false dichotomy dictated by these two parties. The anti-occupation movement Sirtskhvilia emerged in such a political and ideological setting.

Sirtskhvilia as a Party-Movement and a Part of an "Extended State"

Following the events of June 20, 2019, the spirit of protest was shared among the wider groups of the youth, non-governmental organizations, and urban and creative classes. Based on the widespread belief that these segments of society regarded party politics as a discredited and undesirable idea, the protest organizers from the very beginning distanced themselves from the opposition parties. However, such distancing lost its credibility already by the second day, when the activists began to demand proportional elections instead of the existing mixed electoral system. The focus on proportional voting, for long a part of the opposition party agenda, was in the interests of the UNM party. The united opposition, led by the UNM, was in 2018 already demanding early parliamentary elections with proportional voting (Civil.ge., 2018). Proportional elections were seen as a mechanism that could help the UNM get more electoral votes and change the power configuration in its own interests. At that time, however, the opposition parties failed to mobilize popular support and the proportional system was not achieved. Interestingly, the procedural debate about elections has its own history in Georgia: as a rule, it was a debate inside political elites and was oriented not on the real increase of representation and popular participation, but on finding better and more favorable ways for political groups to get closer to power. A clear illustration of this is the fact that in 2008, as well as in 2011, the then-ruling UNM party rejected the abolition of a majoritarian system and the introduction of proportional representation, with the same arguments as were later applied by its successor, the GD party (ISFED, 2015).

As political parties had failed to agree on this procedural issue during years of political negotiations, an actor with a "civil society" image was supposed to achieve it through street protests. Moreover, the tactics of organizing around civil society activism ensured more supporters than organizing in the youth party branch would: in Georgia's party politics, as there is no tradition of mass-based party organizations, youth participation is associated more with careerists rather than ideological and value-based aspirations. With this motive, Sirtskhvilia persistently sought to present its central demand about electoral change as a claim organically produced from within society, and effectively described it as a central societal grievance around which universal consensus existed.

Yet, it appeared rather non-organic from the young activists, who repeatedly distanced themselves from the political sphere, only to put up demands of political elites about such procedural issues of formal democracy without any serious argument. The activists equated the existing mixed (majoritarian and proportional) electoral system with some form of authoritarianism, and never profoundly elaborated on this inconsistency of reasoning. In fact, the political demand raised by the movement was not a debate between democracy and non-democracy, but was a conjunctural discussion within democratic projects in search of better procedures and methods. The entire debate not only belonged to the political elites (parties), but due to its highly technical details about the number of seats and representatives to be changed, its features were never comprehended by the wider public. Thus, the movement's central claim did not represent a value-driven issue which suggested a new and different imaginary about social and political change, but it was an instrument for preparing favorable conditions for the homogenous right-wing opposition parties.

All this situation conferred on the movement was the image of an actor manipulated by a political party and did not present it as an autonomous, organically emerged social movement with an authentic voice on genuine societal concerns. The Shame Movement did not establish itself as a creator of its own alternative political agenda. For that reason, it cannot be seen as a movement carrying a progressive value-based politics. In the same way, it cannot be considered as a representative of a civil society carrying an emancipatory potential. During the movement's almost 100 days of street protests, it established itself as a subordinate actor to the UNM and its satellite parties and took the form of a party-movement—a movement carrying the interests of a party. During the protests, a large share of the movement activists was directly linked with the UNM and its cultural and intellectual elites and their families: many of the activists were simply the new generation—sons and daughters—of the UNM associated figures; the UNM opposition party members and their supporters had no barriers to come onstage and speak to the audience.

However, this is not decisive in assessing the protest movement as actors appropriated by the opposition parties; what was decisive was that the movement followed the identical ideological and discursive agenda as the UNM and its cultural, economic and intellectual elites had been pursuing in recent decades. This could be illustrated in three main pillars of the discursive agenda: anti-government; anti-occupation (anti-Russian and anti-communist); and anti-corruption (anti-bureaucratic).

i. Anti-government discourse

On the level of claims, anti-government attitudes during the protests were articulated in demands for a change of electoral system, and contesting the one-party rule. The anti-government spirit radicalized as the GD leader Ivanishvili first announced that the country would shift to proportional elections with zero barriers, only to have his party reject the proposal. However, such criticism questioned the power concentration within the ruling party but never criticized the neoliberal character of it. This was identical to the criticism emanating from the UNM, and also resonated with the vision of democracy which had been established in Georgia over the last 30 years. According to this view, the key challenge of a state's political system is a nature of electoral system (majoritarian or proportional) and a pluralist party system. Such a conception of democracy mechanically reiterates that proportional electoral and pluralist party systems automatically create foundations for democratic order and entirely excludes questions of economic democracy from democratization debates. Notwithstanding its strong focus on the idea of pluralism, it does not problematize the absence of genuinely pluralist social groups in the political field, and the domination of the economic elite interest. Further, such a view does not regard it necessary to find answers to the key questions regarding what socially good democracy should bring.

The anti-government spirit was also demonstrated by the tactics applied by the movement to attract supporters. In the process of defining political allies or adversaries, the movement politics did not rely on any fundamental ideological differences and similarities (that is, about views on social, economic or foreign policies), but on the attitude toward the ruling party: those critical of the ruling GD party were considered as tactical allies and like-minds. Such a policy of mobilizing supporters was identical to the political technologies characteristic to the UNM and its affiliate TV channel Mtavari Arkhi.

ii Anti-occupation discourse

The anti-occupation discourse is characterized by aggressive manipulation of the issue of Russia's occupation and the existing pro-Western consensus in the country. Such a narrative, as promoted by the UNM, sees as pro-Russian and anti-Western any force hampering their aspiration toward power. In the Georgian context, the anti-occupation discourse was established by the UNM party in the post-2008 war period and presents an amalgam of anti-Russian and anti-communist ideas.

In the case of the Sirtskhvilia movement, the anti-occupation discourse did not entail any real interest in changing foreign policy and hence, the movement activists did not demand the implementation of such change from the government. Instead, it suggested that the ruling party was itself the central problem and its removal was therefore seen as necessary. The government was simply considered as "pro-Russian" notwithstanding the fact that the ruling party actively continued European integration policies. In this discourse, the existing government did not sufficiently oppose Russia's occupation of Georgia, and activists believed that this was symbolized by allowing Russia's Duma deputy in the Parliament of Georgia, and later, "punishing the people for protesting occupation". Finally, all this was considered as a threat to the idea of Georgia's independence and freedom.

Instead of offering an alternative project for resolving conflicts with Russia, the protesters expressed their positions with hysterical, provocative and quasi-heroic performances, such as singing non-normative language (swear words) containing songs to Russia's president Vladimir Putin; or burning a flag of the Soviet Union. Similar "heroic" acts were conducted by the UNM oppositional channel, whose speaker gave an abusive live address to Putin. As in the case of the post-revolutionary government of the UNM, Sirtskhvilia's anti-occupation discourse was part of the general post-Soviet anticommunism that divided society into progressive and competitive liberal subjects on one side, and the "backward Soviet remnants" on the other.

Overall, such a chain of logical argumentation of anti-occupation sought to create a legitimation framework for the idea that the UNM should again be in government due to its "exclusive rights" to pro-Western and anti-Russian narratives because of the 2008 Russian-Georgian war. The fact that the anti-occupation movement set proportional elections as its central claim, can be seen as a good illustration of this.

iii. Anti-corruption discourse

Even if the anti-corruption discourse was not central to Sirtskhvilia's claims, its leader Shota Dighmelashvili, along with other key activists, were associated with anti-corruption activism, and have been actively deploying liberal anti-corruption language in their speeches. The liberal framework of anti-corruption relies on the antagonism between the state bureaucracy and the people; it aims to pressure the state on all levels in order to reveal its "natural" inclinations to corruption and reduce it to a "small state". In this battle against state institutions, civil society is seen as a morally superior actor that is best positioned to implement such pressures.

The anti-corruption framework has been actively applied for more than two decades by the Rose Revolution elites, but as they were the ones who defeated lower-level corruption, by the time, this discourse became an anti-bureaucratic one, criticizing state spending on administration (such as on salaries), and the existence of certain state institutions–such as the Georgian Public Broadcasting–seen as unnecessary for whatever reason. This discourse saw such spending as a key source of poverty and suggested its own version of wealth distribution—not by taxation or other systemic economic and social policies—but by cutting state expenditure they famously call "waste". By putting the emphasis on cutting "unnecessary state spending", the anti-corruption discourse deliberately obscured the problematization of any systemic issues of economic power and redistribution.

Conclusion

During Georgia's 30 years of post-socialist transformation neoliberal hegemony emerges as a form of depoliticization that has narrowed the political debate, excluding aspects of social and economic equality and alternative economic policies from the agenda. That these issues are not debated anymore, only reaffirms the success of this historical structure. The very idea of controlling economic processes in one way or another, involves a strong state and its distributive mechanisms, whereas Georgia's post-socialist politics and civil society has mostly been structured "against the state" and been stuck in the reactionary (anti-corruption, anti-occupation and anti-government) discourses. In this situation, it is no surprise not to observe the movement openly willing or able to reinforce the role of state and claim control over the economy: neoliberal hegemony did not accommodate such claims. In this context, the movement Sirtskhvilia can only be seen as a civil society extension of established order. The idea of civil society has been foremost a space to stabilize and reinforce the current neoliberal hegemony, blocking attempts to think about emancipatory politics.

The Gramscian perspective allowed us to examine The Shame Movement as an actor of civil society which is not separate from state and political actors. By mobilizing this perspective, our aim was not only to critically evaluate movement's politics and ideology, but also to bring to the fore a rather different idea of civil society and raise questions regarding the worth of reclaiming back the civil society idea in the process of striving for more just societies. Following the Gramscian tradition, "first, to understand the strength of the status quo, and then to devise a strategy for its transformation" (Cox, 1999: 4), we have tried to provide the first steps toward this enterprise.

References

Aksartova, S. (2005). Why NGOs: How American donors embraces civil society after the Cold War. *International Journal of Not-for-Profit Law, 8*(3), 16–21.

Cheterian, V. (2008). Georgia's Rose revolution: Change or repetition? Tension between state-building and modernization projects. *Nationalities Papers, 36*(4), 689–712. https://doi.org/10.1080/00905990802230530

Císař, O. (2010). Externally sponsored contention: The channelling of environmental movement organisations in the Czech Republic after the fall of communism. *Environmental Politics, 19*(5), 736–755. https://doi.org/10.1080/09644016.2010.508305

Civil.ge. (2018). *United opposition announces 'Non-stop' protest rallies.* https://civil.ge/archives/271352

Cohen, J. L., & Arato, A. (1994). *Civil society and political theory.* MIT Press.

Cox, R. W. (1999). Civil society at the turn of the Millenium: Prospects for an alternative world order. *Review of International Studies, 25*(1), 3–28.

Gagyi, A., & Ivancheva, M. (2017). The rise and fall of civil society in East-Central Europe: Transnational discursive and funding hierarchies. In N. McCrea & F. Finnegan (Eds.), *Funding, power and community development* (pp. 55–69). Policy Press.

Gramsci, A. (1999). *Selections from the Prison notebooks*. ElecBook.

Isaacs, R., Polese, A., & Polese, A. (2016). *Nation-building and identity in the post-Soviet space: New tools and approaches*. Routledge.

ISFED. (2015). Position of ruling parties on electoral system—Before and after the elections. *ISFED*. http://old.isfed.ge/main/915/eng/

Ivancheva, M. (2015). "The spirit of the law": Mobilizing and/or professionalizing the women's movement in post-socialist Bulgaria. In A. Krizsan (Ed.), *Mobilizing for policy change: Women's movements in Central and Eastern European domestic violence policy struggles*. CPS Books. Central European University Press.

Kopecký, P., & Mudde, C. ([2003] 2012). *Uncivil society? Contentious politics in post-communist Europe*. Routledge.

Muskhelishvili, M., & Jorjoliani, G. (2009). Georgia's ongoing struggle for a better future continued: Democracy promotion through civil society development. *Democratization, 16*(4), 682–708. https://doi.org/10.1080/13510340903083000

president.gov.ge. (2006). Annual parliamentary report of the President Mikheil Saakashvili. President.Gov.Ge. https://www.president.gov.ge/eng/Mikheil-Saakashvili-en.aspx

The Roots of the Moralization of Politics in Post-1989 Bulgaria and What It Means for the Left

Georgi Medarov

Bulgaria has one of the highest rates of social inequality in the EU, along with rising poverty levels. Nevertheless, the country seems to have produced no strong progressive left alternative. This chapter discusses the broader process of depoliticization of political discourses as one–albeit not the only–factor impeding the formation of such an alternative.

Dominant anti-corruption rhetorics, together with the moralization of politics, impede the articulation of viable left progressive alternatives. Post-political discourses deny the existence of antagonistic interests and advocate universally beneficial "best practices". The post-1989 changes were presented in very broad terms ("Europeanization", "catching up with the West"), leaving debates over economic policies outside of public scrutiny. This framing, however, naturalized and dehistoricized class antagonisms, and produced the illusion that the policies simply needed to be implemented by honest technocrats. Thus, discontent with rising inequalities appears not as a critique of pro-business policies, but only of its political representatives—dishonest and corrupt politicians.

G. Medarov (✉)
Institute of Philosophy and Sociology, Bulgarian Academy of Sciences, Sofia, Bulgaria

A. Gagyi and O. Slačálek (eds.), *The Political Economy of Eastern Europe 30 years into the 'Transition'*, International Political Economy Series,
https://doi.org/10.1007/978-3-030-78915-2_11

Vicious Circle of Austerity and Poverty in Post-1989 Bulgaria

Bulgaria is frequently referred to as the poorest EU member state. Together with Lithuania, it is the fastest shrinking country in the world (Hruby, 2019). Since 1989, Bulgaria has lost 20% of its population, and according to United Nations, Department of Economic and Social Affairs (2019) estimates it will lose another 25% by 2050.

This deep demographic crisis is not surprising given the dire social context (Vassilev, 2005). Social inequalities have increased since Bulgaria joined the EU in 2007. Even the European Commission (2019) claims that Bulgaria's "growth-friendly" flat taxation "has little power [to] reduce poverty, which is the highest in the EU". According to Bulgarian unions, in February 2020 the living wage for four-member households amounted to the equivalent of €1300 (Draganov, 2020). Yet close to 80% of wages are less than €450 (Draganov, 2019). Furthermore, 20% of wage earners earn the minimum wage, which in 2020 amounts to €240 net.

Regardless of this dire social situation, proposals for progressive reforms are marginalized. The ruling and opposition parties stand united against progressive welfare and taxation. The dominant political discourse is anti-corruption, with each party accusing the others of being corrupt. Corruption seems to be a catch-all ideology, capable of explaining practically all social ills. Anti-corruption, however, puts an overemphasis on visible political actors, and conceals where true power lies–in powerful economic elites.

Despite looming social inequalities and practically non-existing welfare, Bulgaria's economic policies are still being subjected to wild neoliberal experiments. Since the 1990s, the imperatives of "balanced budgets" and austerity, along with privatization of public assets, have dominated the policy-making universe. Three decades later, policies have only furthered austerity and economic liberalization. Even with this social crisis in plain view, economic liberalization remains largely unquestioned. The most politically visible condemnation of neoliberalism came from the far-right. Nevertheless, their "anti-neoliberalism" amounts to criticizing the political aspects of liberalism (for example, gender equality, minority rights, etc.), while supporting economic liberalism (see Marinos, 2015).

The Bulgarian Socialist Party (former communists), the major center-left party in the country, did not capitalize on the criticism of rising social inequalities. Instead of shifting to the left, the BSP has been moving to the right for twenty years now. While in government from 2005 to 2009, the BSP was mostly concerned with market efficiency, entrepreneurialism, and competition. The post-2016 BSP leadership moved further to the right (from liberalism to conservatism), and solidified its nationalist and conservative agenda. The BSP's leader, Kornelia Ninova, openly identified as part of "the conservative left"—in opposition to gender equality, refugees, and to the progressive, but marginalized democratic-socialist fraction of the BSP. What remains of the left in this new conservative BSP is unclear, as the party failed to shed its economic liberalism. The new leadership has even praised Hungary's Viktor Orbán, and Kornelia Ninova made it known that her political role models are the British conservatives Margaret Thatcher and Theresa May.

In the last decade, and partly due to BSP's rightward turn, a number of new left organizations managed to establish themselves. They have not achieved any electoral successes and rarely unite around a wider platform, apart from attacks on the far-right and the BSP's conservative turn. Some of the new left groups are composed of students in the humanities without links outside of Sofia or workers' organizations. Their intellectual bias and lack of wider social base make it hard for them to appeal to the wider public. However, there are a growing number of positive examples, where new leftist groups managed to organize around wider social campaigns and cooperate with unions.

The reasons for the relative weakness of the left in Bulgaria are multifaceted. This chapter focuses on the processes of depoliticization and moralization of politics. Popular anti-corruption discourses exclusively address the moral integrity of politicians rather than the political integrity of policies. The preoccupation with politicians' morals makes anti-corruption ideologies ubiquitous, as both left-wing (over lack of welfare) and right-wing (over a lack of competition) political actors argue that all evil stems from politicians' insincerity and corruption.

The Ideology of Anti-corruption and the Post-political Condition

The focus on anti-corruption discourses and ideologies requires justification. The notions of ideology and/or discourse here are not reduced to orthodox Marxist assumptions about "base and superstructure". The latter often imagine politics and ideas as functions of the economy, masking class interests, and understand the economy only through a simplistic class analysis. This chapter does not attempt to invert this scheme by arguing that ideas are situated beyond material reality and practice, overdetermining society from outside. Traditional Marxist and idealist schemes share a common fallacy—they assume that ideas are immaterial and disembedded from practices and institutions. Discourses and ideologies have material conditions, for example, institutions which produce and disseminate them. They can also be used for purposes not intended by their initial producers.

For instance, neoliberal think-tanks produce expertise on corruption, the media transmit those ideas, and political actors use them for their own aims. Nevertheless, anti-corruption discourses do not simply conceal class interests. Anti-corruption may be mobilized by popular movements against neoliberal elites. Dominant anti-corruption discourses were designed to repack Washington consensus policies when they started to be delegitimized (Krastev, 2004: 1–41). Anti-corruption campaigns after the Cold War, such as those of the World Bank, transformed an earlier understanding of corruption as the effect of poverty and social inequalities into a conviction that it was their cause. As Krastev (2004: 37) frames it, "It was commonplace in the 1960s that poorer countries tend to be more corrupted. In the 1990s the commonsense opinion was that it is not that poor countries are more corrupted, but that corrupted countries are poor". This reconceptualization of corruption meant that the former critique of the effects of neoliberal policies is now an opposition to corrupt political elites. Relying on the language of anti-corruption, the left can legitimately question the economy's influence over the political sphere, while the liberal right can put the blame on politics' influence over the market. This interpretive scheme is limited as it does not allow movements to oppose the economic elites who corrupt politicians. Another underlying assumption in anti-corruption discourses is that policies could be universally beneficial, which obscures the fact that some groups benefit and others suffer from the same policies.

In that sense, both nationalism and liberalism remain blind to class conflicts—they presume that universally beneficial technical policies are possible. If they do not benefit everyone in practice, this is due to their incorrect implementation by morally corrupt politicians. It is no coincidence that all mass social protests in Bulgaria in the last decade have combined their social justice demands with anger at political parties and political representation in general. One can often hear proposals to reduce the number of members of parliament. Most large protests are staged in front of Parliament, rarely in front of governmental buildings, and never in front of corporate or business associations' headquarters. Other representative institutions such as trade unions suffer from the same suspicion (Tsoneva, 2017: 121). Reflecting these popular attitudes, political parties started presenting themselves as catch-all "movements", beyond left and right, rather than as parties, which sow division. The name GERB, the center-right party that has governed Bulgaria, with short breaks since 2009, stands for "Citizens for European Development of Bulgaria". This process is paralleled in the rest of central and Eastern Europe, with a plethora of parties trying to erase all traces of politics from their titles. Demonstrative examples are the party "Ordinary People and Independent Personalities" in Slovakia, or Andrej Babiš's ANO 2011 in Czechia.

The anti-corruption consensus and the widespread calls for more transparency are linked to the post-political condition (see Mouffe, 2005) and the rising distrust of representative institutions. According to Mouffe, the post-political attempts, witnessed in the rise of the neoliberal Washington consensus after the end of the Cold War, do not erase confrontation, but only amplify it. Repressed antagonisms and social contradictions return, but in non-political and ahistorical forms. They take naturalistic and cultural forms, as when social contradictions appear as ethnic. This facilitates the technocratization of governance, as it is no longer a question of right or left, but of good and bad policies. Technocrats tend to reimpose neoliberal policies, reinforcing popular discontent, distrust in "corrupt politicians"'. The vicious circle of technocratic neoliberalization, discontent with "corruption", and more technocratic neoliberalization is thus reproduced.

The post-political condition and its negative effects have been analyzed by a number of critical authors. For the peculiar post-socialist situation, I find insightful Boris Buden's (2016) analysis, which shows how depoliticization relates to the erasure of social contradictions' historical background. The subsequent naturalization of conflict intensifies it. More importantly, political confrontation is seen not as a clash between different parts of society or a zero-sum game, without universally beneficial policies. Instead it is understood as a conflict between the totality of the nation and the corrupt elites, usually imagined as serving foreign interests. This applies to both nationalist and liberal framings: liberals have painted all their adversaries as Putin's pawns, especially since the 2014 annexation of Crimea.

From Economic Liberalization to the Moralization of Politics

Reducing politics to technocratic administration and imagining a society in post-class terms is not reserved to post-socialist neoliberalization. By the late 1960s, the Bulgarian Communist Party (BCP) elites had pushed for limited economic liberalization and even attempted to couple wages to productivity levels (see Baeva & Kalinova, 2006: 152–153). The introduction of market mechanisms within central planning increased productivity, but following the collapse of Bretton Woods and the 1970s crises, Bulgaria started to experience public debt problems (see Vatchkov & Ivanov, 2012: 157–165). The BCP resorted to austerity measures, and further liberalization. The push towards efficiency, and the late socialist investments in the IT industry (see Petrov, 2018), coincided with a technocratic and corporatist turn evidenced by elites' fascination with Japan's technological advancements, supposedly overcoming class (and political) antagonisms.

Economic reforms coincided with a cultural shift towards nationalism, in sharp contrast to the politics of minority recognition of the previous Stalinist period (Valiavicharska, 2019: 80). By the 1980s BCP had already started posing not as peasants and workers party, but as a "party of the whole people", leading a "unified socialist nation". The BCP's project aiming to present Bulgaria as a post-class and ethnically homogenous nation, which has transcended social antagonisms in a "developed socialist society", went hand in hand with a technocratic managerialism hollowing out the governmental Marxist-Leninist rhetoric of its political meaning (see Popivanov, 2015: 77–90).

Late socialist managerialist technocratic ideas, along with nationalism, could be considered as another instance of post-political denial of social antagonisms (for example, conflicts between industrial managers, workers, and party planners). Even though this is similar in form with the depicted post-1989 moralization of politics, it differs in substance. The post-socialist ones are not simply linked to changes of ownership and privatization, but also to a more general change in developmental strategy. During late socialism Bulgaria attempted to climb up the global value chain via import substitution, stimulating high value-added sectors. The post-1989 adoption of a neoliberal strategy, focusing on low wages and low taxes as a competitive advantage, led to exports of raw products, stimulating investment in low-quality jobs and cutting welfare to create a favorable business climate.

The post-1989 anti-communists, conservative and progressive ones, organized around the Union of Democratic Forces (UDF) right after the changes of 1989. Both the BSP (the heir to the BCP) and the UDF supported a transition to liberal capitalism, leading many Bulgarian sociologists to call the 1990s a period of agreement over the future and disagreement over the past—how to assess socialism, or was there fascism in Bulgaria (see Raychev & Stoychev, 2004). Nevertheless, there were other substantial differences. Generally, the BSP advocated more gradual reforms, while the UDF argued for a shock transition.

The BSP opposed land decollectivization, and wanted to preserve cooperatives. It suggested that land be given to agricultural workers instead of returned to the heirs of the pre-socialist owners. The UDF, on the other hand, called for land restitution and liquidation of assets owned by cooperatives. Thus, rural populations naturally supported the BSP (see Creed, 1997). Nevertheless, in the early 1990s the UDF liquidated the cooperatives' assets, despite the fact that restitution was delayed. Combined with the loss of international markets, this caused a severe crisis in the sector and rising unemployment.

Popular resentment of the disastrous agricultural reform, along with other early policies that rapidly increased inequalities, meant the UDF were unable to form a stable government in the early 1990s. In 1994 the BSP won a parliamentary majority, led by the PM Zhan Videnov. Videnov was on the left of the party and attempted to engineer a left turn that ultimately failed, causing a severe banking crisis and hyperinflation at the end of 1996. Videnov partially reintroduced planning and some governmental control over pricing (for example, the price of bread). It was not a radical break with economic liberalization, but a desperate attempt at a left transition, a "neoliberalism with a human face". The government had neither international support, nor a mobilized wide popular movement to back it up. While some national prices were kept lower than international ones, exports were liberalized (as Bulgaria joined WTO in 1996), which created a severe grain shortage. The BSP went for the so-called "mass privatization", which was presented as an economic democratization, but in practice was a brutal form of primitive accumulation.

The privatization of banking also facilitated the process of primitive accumulation, along with a boom of Ponzi schemes (known as "pyramids" in Bulgaria). This culminated in the already mentioned hyperinflation and banking crisis in 1996. The BSP started negotiations with the International Monetary Fund (IMF) to secure loans and to implement a currency board in order to halt hyperinflation, but the government stepped down in the midst of mass protests at the beginning of 1997. The UDF won the 1997 elections and they finally concluded negotiations with the IMF and imposed a currency board, still in effect today. Between 1997 and 2001 the UDF government seized the moment after the protests and implemented much more radical liberalization, including what they called at the time "accelerated privatization" of public assets.

Videnov's failure dealt a heavy blow to the left in general, which is still felt today, nearly 25 years later. In the 2000s, the BSP adopted a liberal economic program, and since 2016 moved further right. In addition, left policies and ideas were heavily delegitimized. It is important to remember, however, that Videnov's failure was not an effect of the policies themselves (for example, supporting public companies, price controls), but of the particular conjuncture—these measures were implemented without any international or mass grassroots support. This caused the contradictory policies of the doomed attempt to impose neoliberalism with a human face. The tensions within the BSP exacerbated these contradictions, as the party tried to represent both socially marginalized groups, hurt by the first wave of economic liberalization, and the new rich within the party, who pushed for privatization and liberal economic policies. These internal class tensions, still somewhat valid today, led to the BSP being popularly referred to as the "party of the red grannies [standing for marginalized pensioners] and the red mobile phones [owned only by the new rich in the early 1990s]".

The push toward a more radical privatization of public assets, along with wage suppression, austerity, and price liberalization, was conditioned by International Financial Institutions' (IFIs), such as the IMF and the World Bank. The privatization of agriculture and industry led to mass redundancies. For instance, the employment rate among the Roma in 1980 was 84% and by 2001 it fell to 17.9% (Grigorova, 2016: 8). Along with the rise in unemployment, the adjustment programs were accompanied by a rapid rise in inequalities and poverty levels (Vassilev, 2003).

The prevalent critique of the 1997–2001 privatization was framed by the anti-corruption narrative. It claimed that it is not capitalism and privatization to be blamed per se, but only a few bad apples. This, coupled with the exhaustion of the 1990s political confrontation (between ex-Communists and new anti-communists), solidified the widespread desire for efficient and technocratic governance. This promise was embodied by Simeon Saxe-Coburg-Gotha, the former tsar, exiled in Franco's Spain after 1944.

Saxe-Coburg-Gotha founded a political party, National Movement Simeon II (NDSV) in 2001 and won elections on a mandate to apply his business know-how acquired in western Europe to government, get rid of corruption, and "normalize" Bulgaria. His government (2001–2005) furthered the neoliberal course and started privatizing utilities via public–private partnerships. Once more "corruption" became the dominant trope of Saxe-Coburg-Gotha's rule. The 2005–2009 government was led by the BSP, with the support of the NDSV and a liberal pro-minority party. It introduced a flat corporate and income tax of 10% without exempting minimum income earners. VAT, at the same time, was set at 20% with no deduction for basic goods. Heavy taxation of consumption, which affects lower-income groups the worst, renders the Bulgarian system regressive in reality and flat only on paper (Kassabov et al., 2019).

In 2009, after the effects of the crisis started being felt, social discontent was channeled by GERB, a party headed by the charismatic strongman Boyko Borissov—a former bodyguard of both Zhivkov (last communist leader) and Saxe-Coburg-Gotha. GERB's main line of criticism against the BSP was once again anti-corruption, as the government and opposition parties shared identical neoliberal economic programs. Borissov's thuggish attitude embodied the promise for penal, rather than social, justice against those who owed their wealth to privatization. GERB has managed to solidify their rule by remaining in power almost continuously for the past 11 years. The main political slogan of GERB became "stability", and Borissov's style tried to emulate both the technocratic rhetoric of NDSV's cadre and the plebeian style of Zhivkov. GERB introduced more authoritarian policies with the promise to finally crush corruption, and openly cooperated with the far-right.

The economic crisis provoked by deindustrialization was eventually overcome and in the 2000s a process of reindustrialization commenced. But this time Bulgarian businesses specialized in low value-added production, many working as contractors and/or resource producers for larger international capital (Nikolova, 2019). The Bulgarian socialist economy, on the other hand, focused on import substitution and high-tech production. Even though reindustrialization entailed overcoming high unemployment rates (from 20% in 2001 to less than 5% in 2019), these new jobs were of low quality. Income inequalities continued to rise constantly after Bulgaria joined the EU (Eurostat, 2020).

After the heavy land fragmentation and agricultural production decline of the 1990s, it was only in the 2010s that the agricultural sector was resuscitated, but not the sectors which supported it. The import-substitution policies during socialism meant that Bulgarian industry processed its agricultural crops. Agriculture also used fertilizers produced by Bulgarian state-owned chemical plants, which either scaled down their production capacities or went bankrupt after privatization. The 2010s agricultural regime, on the other hand, focused on exports of cash crops and low added value for the national economy. The trend became particularly visible after Bulgaria's accession to the EU in 2007 and is partly due to the EU's agricultural subsidies which tend to support large-scale farming. From 2005 to 2013 the number of farmers decreased by 50%. The concentration of production was accompanied by land grabs—by 2013 only 4% of producers used 85% of the land (Za Zemiata, 2017).

The loss of quality jobs and the upward trend in income inequalities were accompanied by an inefficient austerity welfare regime. The latter was the effect not only of the reaction to the 2008 financial meltdown, as in Western Europe, but of the post-1997 policies, pushed by the IMF and the World Bank (Grigorova, 2016: 11; see Tsoneva, 2018). Welfare was no longer universal, but conditioned by walls of bureaucratic and specific requirements, designed to limit (a fabricated) welfare abuse and corruption. Austerity reforms created a climate of suspicion and competition between citizens. The argument that if someone is denied social assistance, it is the result of free riders abusing the welfare system, led to calls for restrictive measures against so-called welfare free riders. Vanya Grigorova demonstrates that practically all welfare and labor ministries (of various political stripes) had used similar rhetoric against "welfare parasites"—ethnic minorities, people with disabilities, mothers, etc.—in order to transform discontent with the unjust welfare system into calls for further cuts and restrictions. Legitimizing austerity by combining disdain for those in need and anticorruption became a strategy of choice of GERB and its far-right partners.

Anti-corruption rhetoric and the moralization of politics more generally are part of the repertoire of the left, the right, and liberals, but they tend to reinforce the vicious circle of poverty and austerity, with stronger and stronger far-right currents, which has disarmed the left. By the "moralization of politics" I mean the wider shift toward what many have defined as the post-political condition (Mouffe, 2005). After 1989, politics were no longer understood as a conflict between contradictory projects for the future (or between opposing interests), but as the implementation of "good practices" by honest and well-trained experts/managers. Democratic rivalry over different policies was replaced by liberal technocratic administration and a competition between universally beneficial good practices. But even reflexive liberal intellectuals have been discussing the disappearance of the political in a world where it is possible to change the politicians, but not the policies (Krastev, 2002). As mentioned, this depoliticization was partly facilitated by late-socialist developments and articulations between nationalism and managerialism within the BCP's elites. Late-socialist liberalization policies—the hollowing out of Marxist rhetoric—tended to reinforce post-class technocratic imaginaries centered around economic efficiency and national unity. The current to deny the class character of socialist society, and in particular the conflict between "red" managers and workers, made it easier for post-1989 elites (both from the BSP and the UDF) to get support for radical privatization, presented as socialization in the so-called "mass" privatization, or the workers-managers companies. In other words, post-political forms preceded the global technocratic turn that followed the end of the Cold War, despite differences in their substance.

During the 1990 Round Table negotiations Zhelyu Zhelev, the first democratically elected president (backed by the UDF), declared that: "the economy cannot be more or less market-liberal. It is either one or it is not, just as a woman cannot be somewhat pregnant. She is either pregnant, or she is not". Thus, according to him, "the transition should not be partial, it should be wholesale, based on the so-called shock therapy principle". These statements were meant to challenge proposals for a more gradual social-democratic liberalization, espoused by the BSP at the time.

In such narratives—that ultimately became the dominant ones—"there is only one possible history, the history of the victors", presented as a product of natural hierarchies, evolution and the logic of history. The neoliberal transition was presented as inevitable; the institutions of Western liberal regimes as natural, and the socialist legacy as a pathological deviation from the only possible historical movement—the restoration of the past "natural" condition, before the "communist diversion". Paradoxically, what was supposed to be a temporal shift, that is the transition from the past socialism toward the future capitalism, was most commonly depicted in geographical (and thus naturalizing) terms—"Westernization", "Europeanization", adoption of "Euro-Atlantic values", and so forth. Here "Europe" is stripped of its history: conflicts, racism, the Crusades, genocides, nationalist and religious wars. Colonial and other types of violence, which constitute the historical condition of possibility for capitalist development, are erased.

There is not a singular producer of the aforementioned discourse. The first mentions of "Europeanization" came from the left in a mainstream intellectuals-led initiative called "The Road to Europe" in the early 1990s. "Europe" here signified a social-democratic alternative, inspired by the western European welfare models, as opposed to the US-inspired visions of shock therapy neoliberalization, espoused by the UDF elite. Nevertheless, both the mainstream right "Atlantic" and the mainstream left "European" ideals eventually coalesced around "Euro-Atlantic values" and the accession of Bulgaria in both NATO (in 2004) and the EU (in 2007). The "Euro-Atlantic" consensus remained strong even when both the BSP and GERB shifted more openly to conservatism. Even the far-right, which is in coalition with GERB, have not openly questioned EU economic integration and have defended strict budget discipline. The dominant political parties have criticized the EU only when the EU defended workers' rights (for example, 2016 attempts for a common EU social regulation on posted workers) or in the fields of minority rights and gender equality. Those conservative critics of the EU never question liberal economics, but only political liberalism and social rights. Furthermore, they have remained entrenched in the post-political tendencies and the naturalization of class contradictions.

Challenges Before the New Left

Since 1989 there have always been movements, parties, and activists, standing to the left of the BSP, even though their criticisms of the party differed. The UDF itself included leftist, social, and radical democratic currents, particularly while they were in opposition prior to 1997. This make-up reflects most Bulgarians' expectations of the 1989 changes to lead to democratization of socialism, and not an unbridled capitalism.

However, when the UDF took power in 1997, it marginalized internal left dissent and concentrated power around their authoritarian leader.

Some alternative left groups and movements were established in the 1990s, and included restored anarchist organizations, radical environmentalists, and new communist groups. A plethora of post-1989 communist parties appeared, consisting of disillusioned hardliners. These failed to attract new members and some sought to gain popularity by shifting to conservatism.

At the end of the 1990s and more explicitly in the early 2000s, new radical groups were inspired by the alter-globalization movement. They organized protests against international financial institutions, opposed trade liberalization, NATO, took part in the movement opposing the Iraq War after 2003, and organized political education activities—the translation of books, film screenings, discussions, and running various websites.

The label "new left" only started to be used after 2009 in a political education initiative called New Left Perspectives by a small organization I am a member of, but it depicts a much wider group of organizations correctly. It referred to the opposition against the right and liberal economic policies, but also against the rightward shift of the BSP. The critique against the BSP and the "traditional left" targeted the BSP's liberal economic policies, but also its disregard for issues like racism, gender equality, and violence against LGBT people. After 2009, new left groups focused on publishing, research, and establishing social centers both in Sofia and in other cities, hosting discussions, workshops, conferences, and cultural events.

As Boris Popivanov argues in his analysis of the changing images of the Bulgarian left, a strong limitation of the new left groups is their inability to unite, apart from their shared opposition to the BSP's right turn and the rise of the far-right (Popivanov, 2015: 145–176). The strong focus they place on "the inauthenticity" of the BSP is sometimes coupled with a critique of representative institutions like unions. At times, new left groups engaged in unproductive internal fights, fetishizing a kind of a narcissism of small differences. No one quite knows what the "authentic" left is, but everyone is certain that the others are not authentic. A desire for an uncompromising ideological purity fits well with the wider moralization of politics.

Nevertheless, there have been positive developments that counter the moralization of politics and the search for purity. A recently formed queer feminist initiative called LevFem has engaged and collaborated with social movements that were not explicitly left, such as a recent nurses' protest movement (for better working conditions and higher wages). Similarly, Solidary Bulgaria, an influential new left-wing group, formed strong connections with unions, managed to alter part of their concrete policies, and established a strong presence in the public sphere. In the last years there had also been experimentation with the establishment of new left media such as the journal *Dversia* and the online portal *Barikada*. The intellectual background of the new left allows them to produce engaged research that is mobilized in concrete political campaigns. This element of producing governance knowledge and policy expertise is particularly effective, bearing in mind that hitherto the font of "good practices" and sought after expertise, used by political elites, tends to be monopolized by neoliberal think tanks.

There is no easy way out of the vicious cycle of dominant technocratic neoliberalization and discontent with levels of corruption. This is seen in practically every massive protest mobilization in Bulgaria, whose attacks against economic elites is mainly driven by the resentment of political elites connected to businesses. Protests commonly call for changes to the political system (for example, for various electoral or constitutional reforms), but rarely for amending the economic system or granting more social and workers' rights.

This difficulty is objective in the sense that liberal anti-corruption activists tend to be much better organized and funded, with a stronger media presence. Liberal critiques, including social liberal ones, however, have one great drawback in the context of liberal capitalism, where real power is concentrated in private hands and is not directly visible in the sphere of political representation. Historically, liberalism developed as a critique of monarchical absolutism and favored feudal lords and the nascent bourgeoisie's "natural rights". This is why it is ill prepared to articulate effective critiques of the inconspicuous private power. Post-socialist liberalism, similarly, was formed as an attack on "totalitarianism"—the extreme concentration of power in the visible public domain during socialism and the fusion of economics and politics. However, the "transition to democracy" saw the opposite process—the fragmentation of sovereignty in (sometimes conflictual) private networks of interests, and the economic elites capturing public institutions. This is why when liberals attack the current system and its inherent problems they have to rephrase their critiques in terms of the past—as a "return to totalitarianism" (hence their anti-communism, which today, paradoxically, is directed toward economic elites).

This is precisely the lacunae the left can address in the popular liberal anti-corruption discourses. Being prepared with the right policy proposals, knowledge, along with having an, however, may turn the tide when the next opportune moment comes. Nevertheless, what should not be forgotten, is that not everything that appears as public authority or as coming from the state is public in essence and not solely in words. Public authorities, as we currently find them, if captured by private interests, may seem irredeemable. The left can go beyond defending the public in its existing (and sometimes privatized) forms or their idealized past (before neoliberalism), and re-imagine it anew in radically democratic and inclusive ways, in order to provide a viable counter-narrative to the dominant moralistic anti-corruption ideology.

References

Baeva, I., & Kalinova, E. (2006). *Bulgarskite prehodi 1939–2005*. Paradigma.

Buden, B. (2016). *Zone des Übergangs—Vom Ende des Postkommunismus*. Suhrkamp.

Creed, G. (1997). *Domesticating revolution: From socialist reform to ambivalent transition in a Bulgarian village*. Penn State University Press.

Draganov. N. (2019, October 16). Nearly 80% of incomes in Bulgaria are under 900 BGN. *Baricada*. https://baricada.org/2019/10/16/dohodi-2018/. Accessed February 20, 2021.

Draganov, N. (2020, February 12). Nearly 400 BGN needs to be added to the average wage to sustain a living. *Baricada*. https://baricada.org/2020/02/12/knsb-izdrujka/. Accessed February 23, 2021.

European Commission. (2019). *Country report Bulgaria 2019*. https://ec.europa.eu/info/sites/info/files/2019-european-semester-country-report-bulgaria_en.pdf. Accessed February 20, 2021.

Eurostat. (2020). *Income quintile share ratio (S80/S20) by sex*.

Grigorova, V. (2016). Bulgaria: A testing ground for the international monetary fund and the world bank. *Eurodad*. https://eurodad.org/files/pdf/20160122-bulgaria-full-report.pdf. Accessed February 20, 2021.

Hruby, D. (2019, September 30). How to slow down the world's fastest-shrinking country. *BBC*. https://www.bbc.com/worklife/article/20190913-how-to-slow-down-the-worlds-fastest-shrinking-country. Accessed February 23, 2021.

Kassabov, O., Atanasov, I., & Grigorova, V. (2019). *Flat tax or democracy? Towards a progressive tax reform in Bulgaria*. KOI Books.

Krastev, I. (2004). *Shifting obsessions: Three essays on the politics of anticorruption*. CEU Press.

Krastev. I. (2002). The Balkans: Democracy without choices. *Journal of Democracy, 13*(2), 39–53. https://doi.org/10.1353/jod.2002.0046.

Marinos, M. (2015). Anti-neoliberal neoliberalism: Post-socialism and Bulgaria's "ataka" party. *Triple C, 13*(2), 274–297. https://doi.org/10.31269/triplec.v13i2.641

Mouffe, C. (2005). *On the political*. Routledge.

Nikolova, M. (2019). Outsourcing exploitation to Europe's periphery (Interviewed by Loren Balhorn). *Rosa Luxemburg Stiftung*. https://www.rosalux.de/en/publication/id/39946/outsourcing-exploitation-to-europes-periphery?cHash=ec9b8c4f71c442405ce9770388002fd3. Accessed February 24, 2021.

Petrov, V. (2018). Communist robot dreams. *Aeon*. https://aeon.co/essays/how-communist-bulgaria-became-a-leader-in-tech-and-sci-fi.

Popivanov. B. (2015). *Changing images of the left in Bulgaria*. Ibidem.

Raychev, A., & Stoychev, K. (2004). *Kakvo se sluchi? Razkaz za prehoda v Bulgaria i malko sled nego 1989–2004*. Iztok-Zapad.

Tsoneva, J. (2017). Quantity vs quality. Citizens and anti-citizens in the Bulgarian protests of 2013. *Socio.Hu*, Special Issue, 111–130. https://doi.org/10.18030/socio.hu.2017en.111.

Tsoneva, J. (2018). Bulgarian welfare does not combat poverty but the poor. *Rosa Luxemburg Stiftung*. www.rosalux.rs/en/bulgarian-welfaredoes-not-combat-poverty-poor. Accessed February 21, 2021.

United Nations. Department of Economic and Social Affairs. Population Division. (2019). *World population prospects 2019: Highlights (ST/ESA/SER.A/423)*. https://population.un.org/wpp/Publications/Files/WPP2019_Highlights.pdf, p. 12. Accessed February 21, 2021.

Valiavicharska, Z. (2019). Post-Stalinism's uncanny symbioses: Ethno-nationalism and the global orientations of Bulgarian socialism during the 1960s and 1970s. *Dversia*, Special issue on Decolonial theory and practice for Southeast Europe, 79–99.

Vassilev, R. (2003). The "third-worldization" of a "second-world" nation: De-development in post-communist Bulgaria. *New Political Science, 25*(1), 99–112. https://doi.org/10.1080/0739314032000077400.

Vassilev. R. (2005). Bulgaria's demographic crisis: Underlying causes and some short-term implications. *Southeast European Politics, VI*(1), 14–27.

Vatchkov, D., & Ivanov, M. (2012). *Bulgarskiyat vunshen dulg 1944–1989*. Ciela.

World Population Review. (2020, February 17). *Death rate by country 2020*. http://worldpopulationreview.com/countries/death-rate-by-country/. Accessed February 20, 2021.

Za Zemiata. (2017). *Kontsentratsiya na zemedelieto—neobhodimite reformi. Za Zemyata*. https://www.zazemiata.org/wp-content/uploads/2019/08/Koncentracia-na-zemedelieto_Neobhodimite-reformi.pdf. Accessed February 20, 2021.

The New Protest Movements and the Left in Russia: To Overcome the Crisis of Hegemony

Oleg Zhuravlev

Introduction

Thirty years ago Soviet people were coming to the streets to protest against the authoritarian communist regime. These events clearly demonstrated the erosion of the communist hegemony (Yurchak, 2006). Protesters who celebrated the death of communism believed they did not need a new hegemonic political program of social change. Instead, they thought that the society would become better just by the fact of the soviet state dissolution (Prozorov, 2008). Today politically engaged Russian citizens are facing the similar dilemma. Nowadays we observe the political crisis in Russia that is accompanied by mass protest against the authoritarian regime of Vladimir Putin. While many believe that a regime change is the main political goal with regard to a further social change, from the perspective of the Left, current political mobilizations can lead to democracy only if protesters will articulate a vision of the future. Only an articulation of a political vision of the future can overcome the crisis of hegemony which has been lasted since the dissolution of the Soviet Union.

O. Zhuravlev (✉)
Public Sociology Laboratory, Moscow, Russia

A. Gagyi and O. Slačálek (eds.), *The Political Economy of Eastern Europe 30 years into the 'Transition'*, International Political Economy Series,
https://doi.org/10.1007/978-3-030-78915-2_12

This chapter will analyze the nowadays protest dynamics that emerged out of the big eventful protest against electoral fraud in 2011 in Russia. The protest of 2011–2012 was the first mass protest movement since 1993 when the conflict between the neoliberal President and pro-Soviet Parliament happened. At that time the president Boris Yeltsin violently suppressed the parliament. Then the period of depoliticization started in Russia that meant stigmatization of the very genre of contentious politics. From my point of view, the 2011–2012 protests informed contentious politics with new legitimacy within the condition of depoliticization. At the same time, these protests presented the society with a dilemma similar to the one it faced 30 years ago. I will also touch upon the role of the left in these dynamics. First of all, I should describe briefly what are the Russian left and trace the main events of the protest dynamics that started in 2011.

The Russian Left

The leftist movements in Russia can be divided into "systemic" and "non-systemic" organizations. The main representative of the first group is the Communist Party of the Russian Federation (CPRF), the successor of the Communist Party of the Soviet Union. This party was the main opponent of the Boris Yeltsin's regime during the 1990s. Although the party controlled the Parliament in 1990s, it refused to struggle for power seriously. Many experts believe that in 1996 the party's leader Gennady Ziuganov won the presidential elections. However, he refused to dispute the falsification and Boris Yeltsin was officially reelected. Since that time, the party has become dependent on the Kremlin.

From the point of view of the leftist values of internationalism and democracy, the Communist Party of the Russian Federation cannot be called leftist in the full sense of the word. They reproduce the Kremlin's conservative agenda, and support the aggressive foreign politics of Putin's regime. What is more important, the CPRF is nowadays totally dependent on the Putin administration.

The independent leftist movements can be divided into several categories. First, there are organizations that are oriented toward the Soviet ideological tradition. These movements are often called "left patriotic". Second, there are the "democratic leftist" movements that are rather oriented toward the global left trends. Some of them are part of the Trotskyist Fourth International. Third, there are some anarchist activist movements. The independent leftist organizations are weak both because of the stigmatization of the Soviet legacy, and the fact that Putin's regime has captured the social agenda and attracted the socialist electorate. At the same time, the independent leftist movements compete with each other, and are not able to enter electoral politics. Some of these "movements" are, rather, reading groups and interest clubs. Some organizations in the Russian socialist movement have connections with independent trade unions, and are involved in local activism as well as campaigns for the defense of labor rights.

During the massive 2011–2012 protests for fair elections, the Left Front, a prominent independent leftist movement, took part in all the rallies "for fair elections". Its leader, Sergey Udaltsov, played a leading role in these protests. Being both charismatic and politically flexible, Udaltsov became the only prominent leader from the left in public politics. After the Bolotnaya movement evaporated, the public prosecutor's office banned the Left Front, and Udaltsov was imprisoned until 2017.

The "Bolotnaya" Protests and Aftermath

In December 2011, a wave of huge rallies, marches, and "Occupy" camps began to emerge in Russia, triggered by the fraud in the 4 December Duma elections. There had been no strong opposition parties, either within or outside Parliament, that would have prepared or organized the protest. But, after social media (such as Facebook and vkontakte.ru) had been flooded by independent observers' reports of the fraud, and the ruling "United Russia" party showed historically low results even after the fraudulent boost, thousands of people—many of them youngsters participating in protests for the first time—took to the streets. On the following Sunday, about 100,000 people gathered for an authorized rally in the center of Moscow (with smaller but still considerable rallies in other big cities). The main slogans of the protesters included fair elections, a rerun of the December vote, and the denunciation of corruption; honesty and dignity were the main values involved. The protesters, heterogeneous as they were, represented on average a richer and more educated strata of the population (for the numbers, see Volkov, 2012).

On the 6th of May 2012, police brutally dispersed the mass rally. Many rank-and-file protesters were accused of attacking the police and imprisoned. At the same time, Putin won the presidential elections. In addition, the movement faced a severe internal crisis as it failed to propose a clear political program and agenda. People demobilized, while the state became more authoritarian. Since then, new protest campaigns have mobilized almost every year, the most prominent in 2017 against corruption.

Over the past two years, public protests have become increasingly common in Russia: a conflict over the Shiyes landfill site in Russia's far north; a campaign against an Orthodox church being built on a city square in Ekaterinburg; protests in Moscow in support of investigative journalist Ivan Golunov, and over city council elections. These actions have become milestones in the recent history of protest politics in the country. Or at least, that's how it feels for activists, interested observers, and expert commentators.

The Argument

In this chapter, I will analyze the paradoxical process of the emergence of hegemonic politics in Putin's Russia—a country that has been characterized by the permanent crisis of hegemony. I will use the data collected by the Public Sociology Laboratory (Zhuravlev et al., 2019). Following the argument developed by myself together with Volodymyr Ishchenko about the post-Soviet societies, I will show that the major protests against the political regime of 2011 in Russia broke with the post-Communist depoliticization, and gave rise to the struggle for hegemony between the state and the oppositional movements. The paradox is that by now this struggle has led rather to the reproduction and strengthening of the crisis of hegemony than to its resolution (Ishchenko and Zhuravlev, forthcoming). To be more precise, my argument is that the recent dynamics of collective action in Russia generated both the "conditions of possibility" and the demand for hegemonic politics. However, neither the state nor the opposition has yet managed to become a hegemonic force, which opens up some opportunities for the left. This conclusion allowed to redefine the last 30 years of the post-soviet condition in terms of a permanent crisis of hegemony. Indeed, 30 years ago soviet citizens celebrated the death of the communist hegemony and of the communist party. But did they think what was to replace communism?

Before 2011: The Crisis of Hegemony

Post-Soviet Russia has been considered by researchers as a depoliticized society. This condition of depoliticization was caused by the permanent crisis of hegemony that came after the decline of Communist hegemony. As political theorist Sergey Prozorov put it, post-Communist depoliticization meant the impossibility of establishing any hegemonic political project (Prozorov, 2008).

In Marxist theory, hegemony is a moral and political dimension of class formation. On the one hand, hegemony is a process within which social groups articulate their interests and demands politically. On the other hand, hegemonic politics informs these demands with a moral universalism. In contrast with the 1990s, in Putin's Russia public politics became increasingly indifferent toward social divisions, social conflicts, and social demands. At the same time, independent trade unions as well as many other class-based organizations avoided politicization. As a result, both state and oppositional politics did not represent class struggle, while the process of class formation and re-formation lacked a political dimension. As Prozorov wrote,

> it is therefore possible to speak of a mutual exclusion of the state and society from each other's respective domains, whereby formal politics and social life unfold at such a distance from each other that it is increasingly impossible to conceive of any possible relation between them. (2008: 214)

Antonio Gramsci described a crisis of hegemony as a crisis of representation, and a lack of universal political ideas. Post-Communist depoliticization led to a distrust of political representation, and the negation of any political teleology. As Sergey Prozorov wrote on the post-Soviet condition, the latter is characterized by the

> messianic suspension of all teleology, whereby the sacrifices of the past and the dreams of the future are all equally redeemed in the timeless now (…) With the end of the Soviet order history ended not because of the ultimate supremacy of Western liberalism, but rather because the pitiful demise of the Soviet order made the very idea of rivalry between grand teleological metanarratives inconceivable. (2008: 214)

"Putin's bureaucratic depoliticization"—the author argues—"suspends the legitimacy of all political options (witness the decline of all ideological parties, from liberals to communists) without itself occupying a substantive ideological locus" (Prozorov, 2008: 220). Indeed, the "formal politics" of the state was aimed at the "economic performance of the regime" rather than at the establishment of a hegemonic rule. That is why the regime's legitimacy was analyzed in terms of "resigned acceptance" by political scientists (Gel'man, 2010). At the same time, the stigmatization of the Soviet legacy made the very notion of ideological language illegitimate. In the context of the crisis of ideology, hegemonic politics was hindered.

However, every time the society faced a major economic or political turbulence or crisis, those who suffered from the crises felt that these crises were somehow revealing the more general and permanent systemic crisis. Many posed the question: how it could be possible that so different and many protesters unexpectedly and enthusiastically engaged in a protest with the very abstract slogans? It was so not because the protesters were "middle class" and "liberals" who were interested in bourgeois parliamentary democracy or individual rights (Bikbov, 2012). Rather, such abstract slogans and symbols could mobilize and temporarily unite atomized people from different strata with different interests who were deprived of collective identities and political representation but who felt that the country needs fundamental social and political change in order to fulfill their aspirations (Budraitskis, 2014). The protest of 2011–2012 was both the response to the demand for hegemonic politics and the mechanism that formed this demand. The problem was the protest could not satisfy it.

In what follows, I will show that in Russia we can observe the strange reverse logic of a hegemonic politics. Despite what the theory of hegemony says, the revolutionary protests, the Bolotnaya Square demonstrations in Moscow, were not the result of counterhegemonic dynamics, but a starting point for them. The "Bolotnaya" series of demonstrations was an "eventful" protest with a populist agenda. However, this agenda was not a result of the articulation and integration of particular social demands set up by civil society and political parties. Instead, the "Bolotnaya" itself generated new politicized civil society and oppositional movements, that, articulating criticism of those in power, transformed the permanent crisis of hegemony into an "organic crisis" in the sense of Antonio Gramsci. Counterhegemonic politics in Russia intensified and reproduced the crisis of hegemony, rather than overcoming it. I believe that this condition of permanent crisis of hegemony that protest movements make more visible, instead of resolving, is what can strengthen the left. Indeed, within these circumstances contentious politics generates more demand for social change, but cannot propose a convincing vision of this change.

The "Bolotnaya" rallies produced new forms of political legitimacy, based on criticism of those in power and an eventful experience of collective protest action. After the protests subsided, this legitimacy was inherited by the post-protest movements that tried to develop new hegemonic agendas. At the same time, the state in its attempt to de-legitimize the protests, responded to them by repression, on the one hand, and developing its own claim to propose a hegemonic politics, on the other. However, neither the state nor the oppositional movements managed to mobilize popular support around their agendas that would be enough to score a political win against the opponent.

The Eventful Protest

The protests for fair elections of 2011–2012 generated new populist legitimacy while failed to articulate a hegemonic political agenda. It is not a surprise as the protests were not a result of developed grievances but rather an attempt to articulate them as well as to legitimate contentious politics as such in Russia. That is why I consider the rallies in terms of eventful protest (della Porta, 2008; Sewell, 1996).

The "Bolotnaya" demonstrations have been described as unexpected by many researchers and bystanders. Indeed, on the verge of the protest political scientists suggested that a mass protest was not going to happen (Gel'man, 2011). The number of protesters was huge; it was the biggest protest since 1993. However, what was even more intriguing was that the protest suddenly took the shape of a revolutionary rhetoric. Although started as a critical opposition against the electoral fraud, the rallies then focused on regime change. Protesters mainly opposed the corrupt authoritarian regime in power, and wanted political change. They claimed that if the elections had been fair, Putin would not have been reelected. At the same time, the protesters positioned themselves as "the people". Analysis of the slogans showed that to directly refer to the subject of the action, participants of the meetings used several vague categories such as "the nation", "citizens", "the country", "Russia", and "146%". At first glance, it seems that they referred to concrete groups, albeit broad undefined ones, such as, for example, "residents of a single country". In addition, they have their own goal of not indicating a specific group, but asserting the community at large, by using universal categories that include all members of society. Thus, the dominant frame of the protesters was "good citizens" that constitute the "people" against a corrupt and immoral authoritarian elite. Indeed, several leftist researchers claimed that the protests should be termed “populist”. For example, Artemy Magun asserted that “(t)ogether, the constitutional framework of liberal democracy, a special situation in which politicization impacted a deeply apolitical society, and the current global anti-authoritarian trend has produced a movement that combines the features of middle-class liberal and westernizing politics with populism” (Magun, 2014: 185). Sociologist Natalya Savelyeva even said that “although the theory of populism was criticized as being not realistic, in the Russian case we deal precisely with populism as it was defined by Laclau” (Savelyeva, 2013: 74).

Thus, what was surprising with the Russian protest “For fair elections” was not only the unexpectedly large number of protesters, but also the rapid radicalization and universalization of the agenda. The cross-class character of the protest, the universality and revolutionary radicalism of its agenda, as well as the belief that a majority of the country would join the protest made it look hegemonic. Indeed, Ernesto Laclau believed that such populist protests were the most important forms of hegemony of our time (Laclau, 2005). However, the “Bolotnaya” movement based its legitimacy not on social and political demands and articulated programs, but on the “authentic” experiences of protesters themselves. The feelings of insult from those in power who had stolen the votes, as well as the experience of unity in the streets, produced new forms of political legitimacy. This legitimacy was the result of the universalization of the singular eventful experiences and meanings. In a sense, the dominant identity of the protest was self-referential, as it expressed not just belonging to a social group or a commitment to an articulated common interest, but rather the experience of togetherness itself. At the same time, this identity was based on the populist opposition between morally defined citizens and ethically stigmatized elites headed by president Putin. That is why I think that the “Bolotnaya” movement was populist, but it was “as if” hegemonic, rather than hegemonic in the full sense of the word.

In Marxist theory what makes a movement hegemonic is an integration of different social demands into a universalistic political agenda. This agenda is a result of the discursive practice of articulation. Ernesto Laclau suggests that what makes populism hegemonic is an establishment of chains of equivalence between social demands:

The subversion of difference by an equivalential logic does not take the form of a total elimination of the former through the latter. A relation of equivalence is not one in which all differences collapse into identity, but one in which differences are still very active. The equivalence eliminates the separation between the demands, but not the demands themselves. If a series of demands—transport, housing, employment, and so on, to go back to our initial example—are unfulfilled, the equivalence existent between them—and the popular identity resulting from that equivalence—requires very much the persistence of the demands (2005: 46).

By contrast, the "Bolotnaya" populism avoided articulation of any particular demands. As Natalia Savelyeva argues in her analysis of the "Coordinating Council of the Opposition", "the members of the council did not have a task to create something new for the movement, to articulate a political program of the protest. Alternatively, the only goal they had was to find out the goals that allegedly had already been evident for the participants" (Savelyeva, 2013). As one respondent, a rank-and-file rallies' participant, said:

I understand, that people who come to the rallies are different and that they will behave differently, and I'm tolerant. But I like that people are united by the common necessity to come to the streets for some reason. (the interview with the rally participant collected by PS Lab).

If in Western theory, populism is the result of how the protest unfolds, in Russia populism is a prerequisite, a starting condition for protest. If theorists emphasize the productive process that combines various groups and formulates general demands, then in our case populism does not follow this process, but instead precedes it. In post-Soviet Russia—with the declassing of social groups and the atrophying of class consciousness, the vilification of everything "Soviet" and "ideologies" in general, the undermining of parliament and the degradation of the party system—the conflict between the "people" and the "authorities" provides an easily accessible, elementary language of protest politics. One could term this kind of contentious politics "populism by default".

The very experience of the eventful protest constituted this tacit knowledge of the common ground of the protest movement, which presupposed the rejection of the very practice of hegemonic articulation. Moreover, as we showed elsewhere, the protesters deliberately refused to include particular social demands into the movement's agenda (Zhuravlev et al., 2019). The answers we received to the question about new demands led us to conclude that the protesters consciously did not want to include concrete demands into the movement's agenda because of the fear of singling out specific collective identities within the movement and fracturing the eventful "we" of all the protesters, which was considered a guarantee of solidarity and the durability of the movement. Here is a typical example:

> *Q.*: Do you think the movement for fair elections could possibly include any social demands?
>
> *A.*: The movement "For Fair Elections" is good because it unites a lot of people. And if it is changed in some way to include some social or political demands, anything other than fair elections, this would just divide people. Some people would support some of the demands, some people are on the left, some are on the right, some are against private property, somebody wants something else, and so on. It would just divide people, it would not be such a strong movement, and everything would die off (the interview with the rally participant collected by PS Lab).

The hegemonic ambition of the movement, together with the fact that its legitimacy was rooted in the singularity of the event, opened up the opportunity for the regime to start its own criticism of the protest movement.

Politics of Authenticity and the State's Response

Why did the protest movement not generate a new political legitimacy while it also failed to become a hegemonic political force? It was because a hegemony is based on an articulation of an agenda of social change while the protests' legitimacy was rooted in the emotional experiences that blocked such an articulation. The Russian protests of 2011–2013 represent what I call the politics of authenticity, which generates its legitimacy as a truth of an experience of a unique moment of politicization and awakening of civic consciousness (Zhuravlev et al., 2019). Protesters oppose themselves to political elites as well as to "politics" per se, claiming they are constituting an authentic realm of fair collective action. This political culture is what characterizes not only post-Soviet but also "western" protests. Indeed, as Sidney Tarrow wrote on the Occupy Wall Street movement, its legitimacy derived from an occurrence of co-presence experienced by participants during collective action. He termed this kind of political culture in terms of a "we are here" movement: "By their presence, they are saying only, 'Recognize us!' If Occupy Wall Street resembles any movement in recent American history, it would actually be the new women's movement of the 1970s (...) their foremost demand was for recognition of, and credit for, the gendered reality of everyday life" (Tarrow, 2011). In other words, the "Bolotnaya square" protest was rather a "common place", i.e. emotionally invested space, both symbolic and physical, than a mechanism of articulation of an idea of "common good" (Thévenot, 2015). Although celebrated by protesters themselves, such an eventful legitimacy can be either de-legitimated or, alternatively, captured by elites.

Leftist cultural historian Ilya Kalinin shows how Putin's state managed to re-legitimate itself opposing its populist discourse to the discourse of the "cultural leaders" of the "For fair elections" movement. Kalinin argues that:

> the absence of any articulated political programme ultimately rendered the protest movement relatively harmless for the regime, which could coopt or moot the majority of the protest agenda (...) the stylistic and cultural element of the protest movement interpreted by the 'creative class' as its main achievement on the road to new forms of self-representation, possessed a completely idiosyncratic character (...) It was this artistic-stylistic specificity that in the main prevented the movement into development into a truly mass social protest. And it led to reinforcement of the logic of cultural distinctions (...) The turn of the regime, in response, to the language of culture (...) possessed a more inclusive character and was far more successful. (Kalinin, 2017)

Political scientist Ilya Matveev writes that the protest movement reinforced the image of "two Russias", that divides the country into enlightened minorities and ignorant majorities. Matveev argues that the "(l)eaders of the opposition movement still do not focus their efforts on organizing various groups of the Russian population; they still speak of the two Russias. And the Kremlin continues to mirror this discourse with that of 'ordinary working people'" (Matveev, 2012: 190). The Putin regime's response to the mass protest politicization of 2011–2012 was the attempt of counter-politicization and counter-mobilization of 2014, under populist nationalistic slogans. Thus, on the one hand, the regime managed to marginalize the protest agenda. On the other hand, it mirrored the very strategy of politicization in 2014, the strategy that again became legitimate due to the protest movement after the long period of depoliticization in Russia. More importantly, the Putin's regime responded with its own populist agenda in the form of state nationalism. However, even if Putin's administration managed to marginalize the protest it failed to re-legitimize the regime in the long-term perspective. The Crimea effect turned out to be short-run (Rogov, 2016). At the same time, the protest movement re-grounded itself in different forms and continued to effectively delegitimize Putin's regime.

Indeed, the "Bolotnaya" did not disappear after the rallies for fair elections declined. The protests' legitimacy was inherited by the new post-protest activist groups and by Alexei Navalny's mass populist movement which, in their turn, criticized the Putin's regime as not truly popular.

The Struggle Continues

The protesters became disappointed in the movement "For fair elections" because the latter failed to articulate a clear political program. At the same time, it was repressed by the state and many activists were imprisoned. However, encouraged by their experience of the public events, some of the people involved in them, sensing that the protest rallies were becoming less and less meaningful, decided to organize neighborhood associations. On the one hand, these would enable them to realize their desire to engage in public work, and, on the other, render collective action more specific, tangible, and effective. In what follows I will show that both the politicized post-protest local activism and the Navalny's movement contributed to further de-legitimization of the Putin's regime while failed to propose a hegemonic politics.

Protesters became activists. However, these activists got together not in order to solve an urgent problem (as local activists in Russia used to do before the protests of 2011), but because they had already been energized by the public protest; the specific agenda was secondary. Despite the outward resemblance to ordinary local activism (after all, the post-Bolotnaya Square local groups engaged with the exact same issues: the deforestation of public parks, runaway urban development, and road construction that impinged on forests and neighborhoods), they were engaged in a different sort of activism. It was not provoked by immediate troubles such as a public park near a home being clear cut, as had been typical in Russia in the cases described by Clément et al. (2010) and Gladarev (2011), but by the experience of the previous mobilization.

Thus, post-protest activism integrated the local sphere of urban collective action with the nationwide public sphere of contentious politics. This integration allowed protesters to reproduce and spread the very strategy of criticism of those in power being engaged in local activism.

The strategy of the post-protest local activists was to "solve particular problems" and to "get real things done" in order to engage "the citizens", "the people" in the struggle against the local offices of the ruling party, "United Russia". As one of our informants says:

> My task [as an activist] is twofold. On the one hand, I want to preserve my town. (...) On the other hand I want people's mentality to be changed. This is what Navalny has done and I want to continue(...) The most important thing for us is to inspire people to unite, to do something, to act collectively. In this case we will preserve the town (the interview with the rally participant collected by PS Lab).

Thus, the post-protest local activism became a laboratory in which the techniques of de-legitimization of the regime had been developed, reproduced, and widespread. Activists accused those in power of being not interested and incapable of solving local problems and troubles. At the same time, Alexey Navalny, one of the leaders of the 2011–2012 protests, who is now imprisoned, managed to use this protest's "authentic" political culture to develop his own political agenda aimed at de-legitimization of the regime. Analyzing Navalny's success, political scientist Ilya Matveev writes:

> the displacement of [ideologies and] discursive politics likewise generated a demand for authenticity. (...) Alexei Navalny's popularity is largely based on the fact that all his statements are exposés featuring inevitable demonstrations of the alleged evidence: scanned copies of documents, video clips, etc. These pieces of evidence do not serve as proof, they rather generate an aura that makes the utterance universally valid. (...) Authenticity's "apolitical" aura provides confidence in it. (...) [Navalny] divined it was the right time to toss aside labels and -isms, and speak only of "concrete" problems. (Matveev, 2012)

Navalny who managed to become the main leader of the opposition in Russia integrated the "authentic" emotional and moral populism of the protests with political claim that the regime is illegitimate and even criminal (Zhuravlev and Medvedev, 2021). However, neither the politicized local activism nor the Navalny's movement managed to propose a consistent program of a social change for the society.

In the context of depoliticization the "Bolotnaya" informed the populist critics of those in power with the legitimacy based on authentic experiences and "facts". Then this critique was reproduced and spread through cities and regions. As a result, protests and criticism engaged more and more people, making the protest slogans increasingly popular while making those in power illegitimate. At the same time, the state responded to the protests by the attempt to politicize itself and to develop its own hegemonic agenda. Putin's regime articulated its own populism in the form of state nationalism. However, neither the state that is losing legitimacy due to the protests' critique, nor the opposition repressed by the state, managed to become a truly hegemonic political force. As a result, we can conclude that the dynamics of collective action analyzed above contributed to both the development of legitimate democratic politics in Russia and, at the same time, to the reproduction and intensification of the crisis of hegemony. These conditions open up some opportunities for the left.

The Current Crisis and the Navalny's Movement

Nowadays the political crisis is reaching its new peak in Russia. Alexey Navalny's poisoning, his return to Russia, and then his imprisonment and publication of his investigation about Vladimir Putin's palace in Gelendzhik caused the mass mobilization across the country. I believe that leftists can gain legitimacy for their hegemonic agenda by taking part in democratic movements in Russia. However, there are different positions among the Russian left concerning a strategy toward the emerging movement. While some call to boycott the rallies led by the bourgeois authoritarian leader and to focus instead on a theoretical work in Marxist reading groups, others insist on developing a leftist protest movement independent from the Navalny's one (for example, in collaboration with the official Communist Party).[1] Finally, the majority of the Russian left, including Russian Socialist Movement and well-known speakers such as

[1] See, for example, the position of the Left Front leadership https://jacobinmag.com/2021/01/alexei-navalny-russia-protests-putin.

Boris Kagarlitsky,[2] claim it is necessary to propagate their agenda among the protesters, arguing that Navalny is rather a symbol than a leader of the protest[3] While I share the first two groups' vision of Alexey Navalny as a political figure, I support the strategy proposed by the last group although I do not always agree with their argumentation.

Navalny is undoubtedly the leader of the protest, whether we on the left like it or not. He is the main organizer of protest rallies. His articulated goal is to become the president of Russia. Finally, his symbolic, not programmatic role in the protest is paradoxically a key to his success in asserting a political leadership over the protest movement. Indeed, precisely because the protest is not programmatically defined and remains ideologically vague, it is vulnerable to a possible appropriation by an authoritarian leader. Protest with particular demands and program is much less easy prey for those who seek to capture the leading role, than a shapeless movement that stands against authoritarianism in general.

Recent populist uprisings from the Arab Spring to Ukrainian Euromaidan have shown that a revolutionary legitimacy can be appropriated by authoritarian leaders and the very elites protesters opposed during the mobilizations. This happened precisely because the protesters refused political self-determination in favor of maintaining moral unity of the revolutionary movements, because they did not want to participate in the "big" politics, preferring to focus on what was going on in the streets (Gopal, 2020; Krastev, 2014; Zhuravlev & Ishchenko, 2020). Recently we saw an example of how even in the context of the oligarchization of party systems, democratic leaders can embody political parties and ideas. Bernie Sanders and Jeremy Corbyn each returned democratic-socialist politics to the public sphere in the United States and Britain respectively. Yet, in the Russian case of what I termed above "populism by default", Navalny does not offer a coherent political program, simultaneously combining opposite rhetoric, from the left- populist to the neoliberal. Like Putin, he offers himself, not an idea or program. Thus, the class and ideological "neutrality" of modern protests, paradoxically, it itself

[2] http://rabkor.ru/columns/analysis/2021/01/25/from_protests_to_revolution/.

[3] See one of the discussions here https://lefteast.org/left-perspectives-on-the-protests-in-russia-and-navalny/.

becomes part of their ideological appropriation and—more precisely—part of the mechanism by which these "neutral" uprisings are captured by far from neutral leaders and elites.

What Is to Be Done

Although unconditional support of the Navalny's movement would be a mistake that was already made 30 years ago, the arguments for non-participation are even less persuasive. They draw on the traumatic experience of revolutions and coups over the last 30 years, ending with a neoliberal offensive and territorial disintegration—as in Russia in the early 1990s, as in the case of Maidan or in various countries in the Middle East. But we must not forget that very real problems in post-Maidan Ukraine, which so worry Russians, are presented by the official Russian media in a hyperbolic and distorted form. All these factors have ultimately pushed a huge part of the pro-Soviet or simply conservative audience into outright political paralysis.

Meanwhile, the active part of society is immersed in the reality of arrests and repression, including many against people who think rather like we do on the Left.

Cautioning against participation in the protest movement, many on the left say: Navalny's left-populist rhetoric hides a neoliberal program, so why should we want to bring its implementation closer by our participation, and what we can put up against a leader with such resources? Indeed, in addition to his nationalist past and populist strategy, Navalny has a neoliberal agenda, which not so many people know about. Yes, the resources of the Russian left are now incomparable with Nalvany's. However, in my opinion, by participating in the protest movement, the left can become stronger, thanks to Navalny's neoliberal program. Despite the personalist and populist nature of the current struggle between power and opposition, one of the latest trends in Russian protest politics is a public attention to political programs that no one would have read or discussed ten years ago. However, Navalny's program is contradictory and not well developed. While supporting the campaign for Navalny's release and an investigation into his poisoning, the left must argue with Navalny supporters about his program and articulate in these disputes our own program. This is an opportunity to mobilize those who have appeared on the public stage in recent years: leftist political scientists, sociologists, and economists of the new generation. This will make it possible to compensate for the temporary weakness of the left in street mobilization, through competent analysis of the economy and society and the programmatic defense of the economic interests of the majority.

References

Bikbov, A. (2012). Representation and empowerment. *Logos, 4*(88), 43–54.

Budraitskis I. (2014). The weakest link of managed democracy: How the parliament gave birth to nonparliamentary politics. *South Atlantic Quarterly 113*(1), 169–185.

Clément, C., Miryasova, O., & Demidov, A. (2010). *Ot obyvatelei k aktivistam. Zarozhdaiushchiesia sotsialnye dvizheniia v sovremennoi Rossii. [From ordinary folk to activists: Emergent social movements in modern Russia].* Tri kvadrata.

Della Porta, D. (2008). Eventful protests, global conflicts. *Journal of Social Theory, 9*(2), 27–56.

Gel'man, V. (2010). Regime changes despite legitimacy crises: Exit, voice, and loyalty in post-communist Russia. *Journal of Eurasian Studies, 1*(1), 54–63.

Gladarev, B. (2011). Istoriko-kulturnoe nasledie Peterburga: rozhdenie obshchestvennosti iz dukha goroda [Petersburg's cultural heritage: The emergence of a public from the city's spirit]. In O. Kharkhodin (Ed.), *Obshchestvennogo k publichnomy [From the social to the public]* (pp. 69–304). EUSP Press.

Gopal, A. (2020). The arab thermidor. *Catalyst, 4*(2).

Ishchenko, V., & Zhuravlev, O. (forthcoming). *Post-Soviet vicious circle: Conserving or intensifying the crisis of hegemony?* (Unpublished manuscript).

Kalinin, I. (2017). Why "two Russias" are less than "United Russia". Cultural distinctions and political similarities: Dialectics of the defeat. In B. Beumers, A. Etkind & O. Gurova (Eds.), *The shrew untamed: Cultural mechanisms of political protest in Russia.* Routledge.

Krastev, I. (2014). *Democracy disrupted.* University of Pennsylvania Press.

Laclau, E. (2005). Populism: What's in a name? In F. Panizza (Ed.), *Populism and the mirror of democracy.* Verso.

Magun, A. (2014). The Russian protest movement of 2011–2012: A new middle-class populism. *Stasis, 2*(1). http://www.stasisjournal.net/index.php/journal/article/view.67.

Matveev, I. (2012). Effekt podlinnosti [The effect of authenticity]. *Russkii zhurnal*, March 12, 2012. http://www.russ.ru/Mirovaya-povestka/Effekt-podlinnosti. Accessed March 5, 2021.

Prozorov, S. (2008). Russian postcommunism and the end of history. *Studies of Eastern European Thought, 60*, 207–230.

Rogov, K. (2016). "Crimean Syndrome" Mechanisms of Authoritarian Mobilization. *Russian politics and law, 54*(1). https://www.tandfonline.com/doi/abs/10.1080/10611940.2015.1160710?journalCode=mrup20.

Savelyeva, N. (2013). Edinstvo raznykh: Representatsiia i populizm v dvizhenii 'Za chestnye vybory' [The unity of different people: Representation and populism in the fair elections movement]. *Sotsiologiia Vlasti, 4*, 59–78.

Sewell, W. (1996). Historical events as transformations of structures: Inventing revolution at the Bastille. *Theory and Society, 25*(6), 841–881.

Tarrow, S. (2011). Why occupy Wall Street is not the tea party of the left. *Foreign Affairs*. October 10, 2011. https://www.foreignaffairs.com/articles/north-america/2011-10-10/why-occupy-wall-street-not-tea-party-left. Accessed March 5, 2021.

Thévenot, L. (2015). Voicing concern and difference: From public spaces to common-places. *European Journal of Cultural and Political Sociology, 1*(1), 7–34.

Volkov, D. (2012). Putinism under siege: The protesters and the public. *Journal of Democracy, 23*(3), 56–62.

Yurchak, A. (2006). *Everything was forever, until it was no more: The last Soviet generation*. Princeton University Press.

Zhuravlev, O., & Ishchenko, V. (2020). Exclusiveness of civic nationalism: Euromaidan eventful nationalism in Ukraine. *Post-Soviet Affairs, 36*(3), 226–245. https://doi.org/10.1080/1060586X.2020.1753460

Zhuravlev O., & Medvedev, K. (2021). Alexei Navalny's Movement Reflects the Weakness of Russian Democracy. Jacobin. https://jacobinmag.com/2021/03/alexeinavalnyrussiaopposition?__cf_chl_managed_tk__=pmd_881956a2a28252b93d6893ce1e786d3b8f430afe-1628945743-0-gqNtZGzNAyKjcnBszQmi.

Zhuravlev, O., Natalya, S., & Svetlana, E. (2019). The cultural pragmatics of an event: The politicization of local activism in Russia. *International Journal of Politics, Culture, and Society, 33*, 163–180.

Fear, Doubt and Money. War of Ideas, Production of Ignorance and Right-Wing Infrastructures of Knowledge and Hegemony in Poland

Andrzej W. Nowak

Introduction: Pastor in the Borderlands and the World Youth Day

In September 1989, I enrolled in a technikum, a vocational school where I was meant to become a chemical technician. Shortly after the "fall of the Berlin Wall", I heard the English language "live" for the first time. My friends invited me to a meeting, which, as it turned out, was hosted by a US Protestant pastor who was trying to convince the audience to go to the USSR (still existing at that time) and to preach "the word of God" out there. It was also the first time that I had shared the space of the railway station with homeless people, while commuting to school every day.

The chemical school was strongly immersed in the passing mythology of Communist modernity: pipes, chemical kombinats, laboratory equipment, white coats. Like the Communist promise itself, it too quickly

A. W. Nowak (✉)
Faculty of Philosophy, Adam Mickiewicz University, Poznań, Poland
e-mail: awnowak@amu.edu.pl

A. Gagyi and O. Slačálek (eds.), *The Political Economy of Eastern Europe 30 years into the 'Transition'*, International Political Economy Series,
https://doi.org/10.1007/978-3-030-78915-2_13

became outdated. When I finished school, there were no more factories in which I could work as a chemical technologist. Shut down factories, the pastor and the homeless at the railway station are my snapshots of the 1989 transition. It was not until many years later that I realized that they were connected much more than I had thought or than I would like them to be. I did not know at the time how it was also connected to the Amway recruitment meeting, which I accidentally attended a few years later looking for a part-time job. The above remarks are a kind of sketch auto-ethnography, a sharing of experience that has made sense thanks to the theoretical analyses I want to discuss later in this chapter.

In her book about the Black Protest in 2016,[1] the author, Klementyna Suchanow (2020),[2] presented a kind of complementary auto-ethnography. The protest and the women's strike in Poland were against the tightening of the abortion law and against the law that allowed for the punishment of miscarriage. This fundamentalist religious law was largely the product of the right-wing think tank Ordo Iuris. Suchanow's investigation into the capture of the Polish public sphere and law by this think tank led her to Spain and the organization Hazte Oir ("Make yourself heard"). The Spanish organization was founded in 2001 as an offshoot of Latin American right-wing Catholic organizations, and became more visible in 2005 during the Zapatero government, when it opposed the law on same-sex marriages. However, as Suchanow writes, interesting threads appear when we trace the personal connections[3]—so we will take a look at the affiliation of its president, Ignacio Arsuga, and the other prominent members. Arsuga, in his memoirs, highlights how important it was for him to participate at the World Youth Day in Poland in 1991, at

[1] On October 3, 2016 women in Poland organized a nationwide strike following a Polish parliamentary decision to consider a ban on abortion and criminalization of all terminations. The day became known as Black Monday.

[2] In Autumn 2020 She became one of leaders of Women Strike (Ogólnopolski Strajk Kobiet http://strajkkobiet.eu/) against radical assault on women reproductive rights in Poland. Since the decision of the Polish Constitutional Tribunal (Trybunał Konstytucyjny or TK) on October 22, 2020—restricting one of the most restrictive anti-abortion laws in Europe–Poland experience enormous demonstrations and civic protests in most cities (even small ones). Mass protests despite the pandemic, gathering tens of thousands of people, where consciously formulated against the hegemony of the right and the Catholic Church described in the chapter (Rogowska, 2020).

[3] I am close to the approach of C. W. Mills, of making power analysis always an analysis of "the people of power".

which Pope John Paul II appeared (Mata, 2015; Suchanow, 2020: 50). The meeting of the Catholic youth of Jasna Góra in Częstochowa was an electrifying event for the whole of Poland. World Youth Day also then became—unnoticed by the public—a knot that connected Polish anti-Communists with Spanish post-Francoists and the Latin American right, and would become part of the (Vatican inspired) right-wing hegemonic strategy later known as Agenda Europe (Datta, 2018, 2019).

Suchanow recalls that she did not care much about this event at the time, she preferred to go to concerts of alternative bands. But, a year earlier in 1990, obligatory Catholic religious lessons had been introduced in Polish schools and she remembers her distress when it turned out that her whole class unresistingly went to lessons with a priest (Suchanow, 2020: 50). She discovered the sinister nature of World Youth Day and its importance only in 2018, when she was collecting material for her book on the Black Protest and Women's Strike.

Poland in the 1990s was still re-enacting the post-socialist patterns. Although many of us in our youth had a critical attitude toward so-called "real socialism", we lived in a modernist—still secular—world, although increasingly decaying. The remnants of the faded Enlightenment still formed the foundations of the lifeworld (Nowak, 2020c). The collapse of the USSR and the post-Soviet sphere was accompanied by the disintegration of enlightenment embodied in official "scientific socialism". The former Soviet Union and "Eastern bloc" were an arena of the explosion of irrationalism, with figures like Bulgarian Baba Vanga or Kashpirovsky (Michalik, 2020) a part of a collapse of Communist hyper-normalization of reality (Velminski, 2017; Yurchak, 2013). Unfortunately, the consequences and beneficiaries of this can only be clearly seen from today's perspective. Both stories, events that were then taking place on the margins of our lives, almost thirty years later became its center. What appeared to be harmless right-wing religious eccentricity normalized, and began to define reality.[4] However, if we look at transition retrospectively, it is clear that it has been co-evolved since the 1980s by an alliance of Catholic fundamentalism and neoliberalism (Kościelniak, 2018b).

[4] The defense of modernity here results from the specific Polish context. Due to the institutional strength of the Catholic Church and its influence, the criticism of modernity formulated in the critical and emancipatory approach becomes ambiguous when it accelerates the dismantling of modernity (Nowak, 2020a).

Therefore I would like to show that those stories with which I open this chapter are not just anecdotes, but symptoms of the international networks of anti-Communism (Dean, 2019: 16). They revealed the foundations which were laid for the mixture of religious and fundamentalist dystopia—epitomized by Gilead in Margaret Atwood's "The Handmaid's Tale" (Atwood, 1986),—and a new Gilded age[5]—a world in which free-market capitalism has "freed itself" from political or social control (Giroux, 2008; Kotz, 2017: 181–196). The rhetoric of the "natural order" which is promoted by Ordo Iuris and similar organizations is the quintessence of anti-Communism. Because communism legitimized itself as a project, necessarily exceeding the status quo, right-wing rhetoric demands the erasure of everything that such an order questions: "Anti-communism thus serves to structure the political field by establishing the terrain of possibility: what is available, what is off the table, what is impossible—is unthinkable" (Dean, 2019: 17). In this text, I only want to briefly point out that the building of this anti-Communist, reactionary anti-International was not started recently as a reaction to the transformations after 1989 (Golinczak, 2019), but that it has been going on since the Cold War and even earlier, it has just become more evident.[6]

Turning point of 1979/80—and long durée of transition.

Although we have celebrated the thirtieth anniversary of the transition, we should look for its origins prior to 1989, from at least the turn of the 1980s, or even earlier. The pastor I met was only a small symptom of the

[5] According to Nick Fisher, American anti-Communism was forged in the Gilded Age of the late nineteenth century, ahead of the birth of Communism itself. For my text, Fisher's main line of argumentation is important, showing the importance of institutional and financial connections organizing anti-communist networks. The "Anticommunist Spider Web" (1919–1941) he analyzed, crucial for the interwar period, shaped the subsequent networks of anti-communist influence (up to the "Kochtopus" discussed below): "The Spider Web also melded anticommunism and evangelical Christianity, seeding the modern Religious Right. And elements of the Spider Web helped found the American Nazi movement and perpetuate racist eugenics research into the twenty-first century" (Fischer, 2016: xvii).

[6] As Agnieszka Mrozik points out: "Anti-communism is as old as communism, maybe even older. In the Communist Manifesto Marx writes about the 'spectre of communism' which 'haunts Europe' and against which 'all powers of old Europe' have united: 'Pope and Tsar, Metternich and Guizot, French Radicals and German police-spies'" (Mrozik, 2019: 178). In a sense, in the text I return to such a "conspiratorial" way of thinking, and want to sketch out the vastness of the right-wing infrastructure of knowledge and hegemony.

emergence of a neoconservative and religious counter-revolution, which was marked by such emblematic figures as Karol Wojtyla (John Paul II) in Poland who, along with his friend Ronald Reagan, formed a broad anti-Communist front. Wojtyla seduced the Polish anti-Communist Left (see Michnik and his 1993 book, *The Church and the Left*) just as Khomeini seduced Foucault. As Kacper Pobłocki points out (Pobłocki, 2017), the key symbolic date was 1980, the year that ended almost twenty years (1956–1978) of unprecedented economic growth, industrialization and mass construction.[7]

On the other hand, the decades of the 1980s and 1990s are economically more similar to each other than we would like to admit. It was only the 2000s that brought about a radical change, as Poland began to develop under the influence of the so-called Asiatic reorientation of the world economy together with the rise of financialization. A more detailed analysis of transition of central and eastern Europe from the turning point of 1979/80 is provided by the perspective proposed by Agnes Gagyi, and her suggestion of "external penetration as an internal force" as a proper frame of analysis (Gagyi, 2016).

At the turn of the 1980s, modernity—understood as a high modernism or high modernity—both in the West and the East (Rupprecht, 2011) had reached its peak and entered its twilight period, intertwined with the growing neoliberal dismantling of it. The decline of modernity is marked by the collapse of faith in the possibility of stabilizing reality (connected with the trust in science and state), and the open horizon of the future. The failure of "real socialism" is a part of the exhaustion of the rationalistic and revolutionary sequence opened by the 1789 French Revolution (Ponerau, 2020). It is worth noting that many attempts at reforming socialist modernity were actively destroyed during the Cold War. This was the case with Chile and the attempts to create CYBERSYN, the cybernetic ancestor of the Internet, which, through network management, was supposed to solve the problems of central planning and open the way to democratic socialism. This project embodied the Enlightenment, at least in its cyber-socialist version and tried to control reality

[7] Even according to Polish liberal economist Marcin Piątkowski Polish "real socialism" proved to be ambiguous force of progress: I go to argue that the Second World and—above all—Communism was the external shock that helped push Poland and the rest of CEE to a new inclusive equilibrium, which laid the foundation of the country's post-1989 economic achievements (Piatkowski, 2019: 2).

but in a way that would be sensitive to feedback, and not manifest one-way instrumental rationality (Medina, 2011). This project was destroyed by Pinochet's military coup d'état in 1973. In this symbolic way, the destruction of this "Cybernetic Revolution" Project opened the way to neoliberalism—the annihilation of all attempts to correct the capitalist self-organization of the market. A similar attempt to correct socialist modernity was proposed in the Czech Republic by a team led by Radovan Richta (2018). His proposal (Bendyk, 2020: 71; Boucas, 2020), was an attempt to save socialist modernity through its democratization, covering both the political and technical-scientific spheres.

This attempt was destroyed with the Prague Spring in 1968.

In Poland, the symbolic moment of this shift is what happened between 1978 and 1979. In 1978 the first Polish cosmonaut, Mirosław Hermaszewski, flew into space. It was an event that attracted the attention of millions of Poles, arousing national pride. It also briefly diverted attention from the economic and political problems of Gierek's government. Unfortunately, the election of Wojtyła as Pope in 1979 launched another machine—this time non-scientific hegemonic—and the Catholic Church and its resources proved to be stronger in the positional war (Egan, 2016a, 2016b). This meant that in the face of building a hegemonic advantage through the strategic and organic takeover of civil society, the strength and resources of the Catholic Church grew stronger with society's support, while the Communist Party was losing ground. The 1970s was a period of educational, transformational and symbolic exhaustion of the Communist Party's influence on civil society; they were left with power over the state apparatus (and its coercive part—police [milicja] and army).

Solidarity as a workers' movement was multidimensional and initially dominated by left-wing mindsets. Seen as a true workers' voice, it was it that, above all, made the communist party politically delegitimized (Kowalewski, 2011). As such, it embodied the grassroots labor movement dreamed of by Kuroń and Modzelewski (Kuron & Modzelewski, 1975). This is how it was perceived in the West, and that is why in the 80s and 81s left-wing political parties, anarchists, Trotskyists and trade unions massively sent aid, both material and financial, to Poland. Unfortunately, as Zbigniew Marcin Kowalewski points out, this left-wing voice of support was soon replaced by the right-wing narrative. Reagan, the bourgeois political parties in the West, and the Catholic Church took over the voice of Solidarity as early as 1982. The symbol of this was the letter to Reagan adopted at the First National Congress of Delegates of "Solidarność" (Kowalewski, 2006: 105–107). This could be treated as a symbolic moment when John Paul II and Reagan combined the resources of the Catholic Church and neoliberalism: "This nation that wants to stand on its own feet can also fall on its knees", as France catholique, Ecclesia commented at the time on role of the church and religious symbols in the strike (Kościelniak, 2018b).

The Solidarity talks in Gdańsk, "observed" by Lenin's bust, dominated by Catholic symbolism, from Mary at the breast of Wałęsa to crosses, masses and paintings of saints (Kubik, 2010) at first, they seemed only exotic, as did the fact that aid sent by Western anarchists and Trotskyists was distributed by parishes (Kowalewski, 2006: 104). The alliance of neoliberalism and the Catholic Church was largely legitimized by Reagan's "moral crusade", which was also undertaken by some of Solidarity's circles (Kościelniak, 2018a) and whose main actor was the "conceived child", (Nowak, 2020a) i.e. the war on reproductive rights and abortion (Kościelniak, 2020), which marks the Polish political landscape to this day and was the cause of the Women's Strike (Korolczuk, 2017).

This symbolic moment was the end of a certain arrangement that had dominated for several decades. Science, including social science, had achieved its high esteem and role in organizing knowledge climaxing in the 1960s (Lee, 2011: 6; Lee & Wallerstein, 2004: 229) and declining after 1968 (Lee, 2011: 67). This period is also the peak of the ambiguous relationship between the universality achieved by science, and the role of science in stabilizing power systems: referring to Robert McNamara, Boltanski and Chiapello claim that "(f)or management in the 1960s, the association of reason and freedom, in opposition to passion and barbarism, goes without saying" (Boltanski & Chiapello, 2018). The failure of Johnson's policy in Vietnam was not only a failure of American imperialism, but also a failure of the alliance of the state as a vehicle for progress embodied in the unfulfilled plan of the Great Society (Johnson was representative of the New Deal elite).[8] The American alliance of science, the Keynesian state and imperialism symbolically ended in Vietnam, with McNamara becoming a symbol of this negative, instrumental role of science (Twomey, 1999). The stabilizing role of science

[8] This help to fuel the unmaking the New Deal as a source of the legitimation of American politics (Storrs, 2013).

was important for high modernism in its capitalist version, but even more inextricably intertwined with the fate of socialism (and socialist high modernism), science and progress. Since the 1950s "the counterculture" emerged, reflecting symptoms of this crisis of the role of science (and social science and humanities). Despite a positive emancipatory moment—the counterculture as a rejection of what they called the "system" in the 1960s—it developed into a broader rejection of "objectivity" and positivism, meshing with an attack on reason. The ambivalence of the relationship between science as a universality, and the legitimacy of the system of power, has also extended to its criticism. Countercultural criticism, by combating the system of power, simultaneously delegitimized science as a medium of universality (and reason). The crisis of structures of knowledge intertwined with the burgeoning of a new spirituality—which strongly moved through the "1968 revolt generation"—strengthened this process. The 1970s in the USA and the rest of the West were a period of cuts in expenditure on science, and the slow beginning of the neoliberalization of scientific institutions, the effects of which we are experiencing today (Crouch, 2016; Mirowski, 2011). This was in line with the "new spirit of capitalism", and the transition from a Fordist to a flexible neoliberal model of capitalism (Boltanski & Chiapello, 2018) driven by "Californian ideology" (Barbrook & Cameron, 1996; Maliński, 2017):

> The original promise of the Californian Ideology was that the computers would liberate us from all the old forms of political control, and we would become Randian heroes, in control of our own destiny. Instead, today, we feel the opposite—that we are helpless components in a global system—a system that is controlled by a rigid logic that we are powerless to challenge or to change. (Curtis, 2011)

"War on Gender" and the "latinization" of Poland

The Polish "war on gender" (Duda, 2016; Graff, 2014; Graff & Korolczuk, 2017; Kuhar & Paternotte, 2017; Nowak, 2020a; Peto et al., 2016; Szwed & Zielinska, 2017) and the process of taking over the law and the state by the free market and fundamentalist Catholic right-wing started to become perceived as a kind of "Latinization" of Poland, that is, the relationship between capital, church and state has started to resemble that of Latin America (Korolczuk, 2016). Both main parties—PO (Civic Platform) and PiS (Law and Justice)—were dependent on the church as a political factor. Their attitude to neoliberalism differed in rhetoric. The PO was openly neoliberal. Law and Justice used anti-liberal sentiment but did not change the neoliberal rules of the game in practice. While the social support transfers of the Law and Justice party helped—especially in the rural areas—at the same time, the lack of structural reforms and financial expenditure on health care and education in practice resulted in "a second wave of privatization" (Pawłowski, 2020). The neoliberal dismantling of the state has not stopped, but was only covered by a temporary measure. We can argue that the PO proposed an individualistic neoliberalism, while the PiS proposed a family-based neoliberalism (Cooper, 2017). In practice, the state's care functions were provided by conservatively understood families and churches. It is no coincidence that the strong free-market Ordo Iuris coexists perfectly with the allegedly "social" Law and Justice.

The "Latinization of Poland" could only remain a metaphor, strengthened perhaps by references to literature on the theory of dependence or the theory of the modern world-system, indicating similarities between these semi-peripheral areas (Boatcă, 2006). However, I am interested in pointing out the institutional connections among the Right which were established, some of them with beginnings in the Cold War period. This is important in as much as it shows that the waves of Polish—and, more broadly, central European—cultural wars are a repercussion of a broader pattern (Kaoma, 2009).

In 2016 (and again in Autumn 2020), Poland was shocked by the above mentioned Black Protest organized by women and feminist activists, the largest mass protest after 1989. This protest and the subsequent Women's Strikes caused the government to retreat, and freeze the restrictive anti-abortion law. It is worth mentioning that these events have illuminated the hitherto invisible process of winning hegemony by right-wing power and knowledge networks. This was because in the struggle on the streets it was revealed how far the legal system, discourse and state apparatus had been taken over by the right-wing "march through the institutions".[9]

[9] Polish "Black Protest" showed power and fragility of networked protest exactly as described by Tufekci. Even if it could be claimed as a big success, it doesn't counter the institutional and legal hegemony of the fundamentalist and religious right (Tufekci, 2017).

These events have been extensively analyzed recently by Klementyna Suchanow—an activist, writer, Latin American specialist and Gombrowicz biographer—who undertook an extensive investigation, which resulted in a book of over 600 pages (Suchanow, 2020) with the title To jest wojna. Kobiety, fundamentaliści i nowe średniowiecze ("This is war: Women, fundamentalists and the new Middle Ages"). Suchanow in her investigation traces the links of networks connected to an initiative named Agenda Europe. Analyses of Agenda Europe (Datta, 2018; Kontrewolucja kulturowo-religijna: Czy Polsce grozi prawo podporządkowane ideologii chrześcijańskich fundamentalistów, 2020), lead us from Spain to Latin America, and through the United States to Russia. A crucial hub is the international organization "Tradition, Family and Property"[10] (TFP) established in Brazil in 1960 by Plinio Corrêa de Oliveira, and inspired by his book Revolution and Counter-Revolution (Oliveira, 1993). It was created as a strongly anti-Communist organization, fighting against all left-wing movements, with the aim of protecting the "natural order", that is, a mixture of references to monarchism and aristocracy together with the promotion of the free market. The activity in Latin America manifested itself, among other things, in combating the Theology of Liberation, for example, in 1968 the Brazilian TFP gathered two million signatures in a continent-wide petition campaign against Communist infiltration of the Catholic Church, In Chile, The TFP fought the government of Salvador Allende and supported the Pinochet junta.[11] It has also been active in South Africa since 1984, acting as a counter-revolutionary force on nearby Portuguese-speaking and socialist Mozambique (in which a civil war was waged between the socialist government and South African-supported right-wing militia RENAMO). In the USA, it was founded in 1973 by people affiliated with the journal Crusade for a Christian Civilization (founded in 1971). Since 1977, they have existed in France under the TFP label, and before that, since 1975, they operated as Jeunes Français pour une Civilisation Chrétienne ("French Youth for a Christian Civilization"). The disintegration of the Eastern bloc was a chance for the aforementioned expansion to the east. Since 1999, its influence in Poland

[10] http://www.tfp.org.br/.

[11] In 1999, Polish politicians Michał Kamiński and Marek Jurek, along with the journalist Tomasz Wołek, visited London to present a gorget embossed with an image of the Virgin Mary to former Chilean dictator General Augusto Pinochet. This is a symbolic example of the "latinization of Poland".

has been connected with the Fr Piotr Skarga Association of Christian Culture (Stowarzyszenie Kultury Chrześcijańskiej im. ks. Piotra Skarga) and, since 2013, with the Ordo Iuris Institute for Legal Culture (Instytut na rzecz Kultury Prawnej Ordo Iuris); they have been present in Croatia since 2016 (Suchanow, 2020: 582).

The views of Plinio Corrêa de Oliveira can be described as a kind of right-wing Leninism, reading Oliveira one gets the impression of certain Lenin motives of political struggle copied and "reversed". It is a combination of fundamentalist and monarchist Catholicism, praise of the free market and political violence. Additionally, it contains a lot of organizational guidelines for the counter-revolutionary movement. In this sense, it can be described as a functional ideology for the Cold War junta and military dictatorships. For the analysis of central Europe, the remarks in the following sections of Oliveira's book are interesting: Part III, Chapter 2, commentary Perestroika and Glasnost: Dismantling the Third Revolution or Metamorphosing Communism? and Postface (Oliveira, 1993: 108) where the collapse of the USSR is defined as the End of the Third Revolution, However, at the end of the book Oliveira (who died in 1995) writes:

> After reading the previous words, the reader will necessarily wonder where the revolutionary process stands today. Is the Third Revolution still alive? Or does the collapse of the Soviet empire permit us to affirm that the Fourth Revolution is erupting in the deepest levels of the political reality of Eastern Europe, or even that it has won? (Oliveira, 1993: 107)

Conservative Anti-international

The Cold War ended only for one side—the losing Communist one. The emancipatory policy critical of state socialism after 1989 has succumbed to an anti-socialist sentiment, expressed in support of the liberal myth of "civil society", an oversimplified vision of a monolithic state, and in support of romanticized anarchist ideals and practices (Ross, 2008). It has a strategic implication—the Left deprived of its weapons—both in theory and practice. The other side did not have reservations in taking over the "abandoned" and "drifting" state apparatuses (Althusser et al., 2014), despite describing themselves as anti-statist.

As mentioned above, the meeting of the Catholic youth of Jasna Góra in Częstochowa was moment that started contacts between Polish anti-communists with Spanish post-Francoists, and the Latin American right (Suchanow, 2020: 49) and through the Phoenix Institute and the Pan-American Institute for Political Studies in Notre Dame, with Protestant and ultra-Catholic US neoconservatives (Suchanow, 2020: 55). It is important to note that the Spanish organization Hazte Oir was linked with the Mexican paramilitary group, the National Organization of the Anvil (El Yunque) supposedly formed in the early 1950s and described as ultra-Catholic, anti-Communist, with fascistic attributes by, Alvaro Delgado, author of the 2003 book El yunque: La ultraderecha en el poder (Suchanow, 2020: 74). In Spain, Hazte Oir itself is also linked to the right-wing party Vox and the ultraconservative advocacy group CitizenGo (Suchanow, 2020: 93–100).

Another important link leads us to the Kremlin, where in 2012–2013 President Putin began to further legitimize his power through a religious-conservative turn[12] (Suchanow, 2020: 118–119). As an example, one could point to important Russian figures like Igor Belobrodov being involved in the fight against abortion (Suchanow, 2020: 125) which resulted in organized by him the pilgrimage of the Polish icon of the Black Madonna of Czestochowa.[13] This powerful religious symbol was run from "ocean to ocean", linking most of the post-soviet countries. Using the connections developed from the very beginning of the fall of anti-communism, US-inspired global "culture war" (Kaoma, 2009) on women's and LGBT + rights started to flood central Europe via the Kremlin[14] (Peto et al., 2016).

The next important institutional hub which gathered the right-wing "anti-Internationale" was the World Congress of Families (WCF), organized for the first time in Prague in 1997 (Suchanow, 2020: 177–205). It was co-created by Allan Carlson, a leading and controversial US antiabortionist and ultra conservative who started his relationship in Soviet time

[12] http://en.kremlin.ru/events/president/news/19243.

[13] http://primorye24.ru/news/post/51540-ot-vladivostoka-do--portugalii-proydet-krestnyy-hod-protiv-abortov.

[14] In May 2020, following a trial initiated by Ordo Juris, a court forbade feminist activist Marta Lempart: "to disseminate information that the Ordo Iuris Institute for Legal Culture Foundation is a Kremlin paid fundamentalist body". This has triggered the "Barbara Streisand effect" in Polish media and social networks—people started the mass publication of this phrase. https://oko.press/sad-zabronil-marcie-lempart-mowic-ze-ordo-iuris-to-oplacani-przez-kreml-fundamentalisci/.

in 1995 where idea of WCF was born. Besides Prague (1997), the World Congress of Families has also been organized in central and eastern Europe in Warsaw, Poland (2007); Tbilisi, Georgia (2016); Budapest, Hungary (2017); and Chisinau, Moldova (2018). It is worth noting that the planned WCF meeting in 2014 in Moscow was canceled due to the sanctions after the Russian invasion of Ukraine, but instead an alternative meeting was held under the name Large Families: Future of Humanity[15] (Suchanow, 2020: 190). This meeting was also important because it was a moment where the WCF, Russian were linked up with The Family (or The Fellowship). This right-wing US organization was recently made famous by the Netflix documentary based on Jeff Sharlet's book (Sharlet, 2008), and is known as the organizer of the National Prayer Breakfast.[16] This last event has been going on since Abraham Vereide's organization in the 1930s, and has been a powerful political lobbyist hub in Washington since 1953,[17] creating a meeting-point for free-market, neoliberal and religious fundamentalists.

Weaponized Philanthropy: The "Kochtopus" and the Long Shadow of the Cold War

For more than 40 years, starting in the 1970s, American think tanks have been supporting the financial policies that have created the current, neoliberal, financially based phase of capitalism. A group of extremely wealthy capitalist tycoons at the beginning of the 1970s, started to believe that the USA was going in the wrong direction—student revolts, the achievements of the civil rights movement, an emerging environmental movement. These movements shared one common factor—they created limitations for big businesses and corporations, and increased the bargaining power of the workforce. As a counter strategy, the uber-rich "weaponized philanthropy"[18] (Mayer, 2017: 391). This created a fresh stream of funding to build right-wing infrastructure: politicians,

[15] http://anton-shekhovtsov.blogspot.com/2014/09/a-rose-by-any-other-name-world-congress.html.

[16] https://en.wikipedia.org/wiki/National_Prayer_Breakfast.

[17] Every American president since Dwight D. Eisenhower has participated in the annual event.

[18] Contemporary report see https://ips-dc.org/wp-content/uploads/2016/11/Gilded-Giving-Final-pdf.pdf.

"think tanks", AstroTurf "grassroots" groups, friendly media, and legal and research institutions.

What is crucial is that their crusade against "statism" and regulation took place both directly and indirectly. The former is obvious—it is the financing of neoliberal institutions to promote libertarianism, to create a network to support "classical economics" and the Chicago Boys" as the only economic option. This has been brilliantly reconstructed by Susan George in How to Win the War of Ideas: Lessons from the Gramscian Right (George, 1997), and by Jane Meyer in her book Dark Money: The Hidden History of the Billionaires Behind the Rise of the Radical Right (Mayer, 2017). As both demonstrate, the major players have pumped millions of dollars into promoting the neoliberal right: American Enterprise Institute, Heritage Foundation, billionaires like the Koch brothers (oil industry), Scaife, Olins (chemical, munitions), Mellon (steel), DeVos (Amway), and the Bradley brothers. This money was used to strengthen the power of the right, and to take over the universities. In response to the 1968 revolt, the billionaires' goal, as they themselves say, was to create a right-wing counter-intelligentsia (Mayer, 2017: 111).[19] This was needed to neutralize, and then take over the, university campuses which had become radicalized in the 1960s and early 1970s. The plan was that this would be done, not by shooting students as was done during the suppression of strikes and riots, but in a non-controversial and unnoticed manner (Mayer, 2017: 108). So that by financing books, sponsoring grants, and paying for research, the ideas that dominated campuses would be changed. Generous funding has been given to such right-wingers as Allan Bloom (a $3.6 million grant from Olin), author of the famous book The Closing of the American Mind, important for both the American and the Polish right. It is worth mentioning that Tadeusz Zysk—the Polish publisher of Bloom's books—is also a politician of the Polish ruling party PiS (Prawo i Sprawiedliwość, or Law and Justice).

The meeting of the "American dark money" and the Polish right became visible at the time of Solidarity. It is crucial to highlight that the money to support the Solidarity trade union was largely distributed through a network of Catholic church parishes. What is more, the anti-communist alliance between John Paul II and Ronald Reagan not only

[19] See also the lecture by Jane Mayer, *The Koch Brothers and the Weaponizing of Philanthropy* https://www.youtube.com/watch?v=AFaSCOqumpM&feature=share&fbclid=IwAR3Dyq0enIlBDHspKOXUs5-uWKcTbgBrrByb_jZ6npFPgNWH1UCqCI6D7Tg.

resulted in the legitimacy of this practice, but also triggered additional sources of funding. Representative of this was the activity of Father Jankowski (Aksamit & Głuchowski, 2019), who in Gdansk became the chaplain of Solidarity on was responsible for redistribution of money. This made it possible to sponsor the activities of the right wing both during the communist and post-communist periods.[20] A thorough analysis of the financial resources of the Polish right is beyond the scope of this chapter. However, it is worth mentioning an example of "weaponized philanthropy", which is much closer in time and closely related to the "war on gender".

In Poland, in the years before PiS took power in 2015, an example of such weaponized philanthropy was a network of credit unions—a member-owned financial cooperative—the SKOK.[21] Referring to the tradition of the Second Republic of Poland, those credit unions drew their legitimacy from the past, and used the language of "conservative social solidarity". In practice, however, they were a profitable banking venture. Grzegorz Bierecki was—and still is—the president of the SKOK credit unions.[22] He is a millionaire and "sponsor" of the Polish right. He was associated with the anti-communist opposition in the 1980s, and is today a PiS senator. SKOK and, especially, the Stefczyk cash unions in the years preceding the PiS victory in 2015, sponsored many right-wing magazines and initiatives. Interestingly, right-wing, nationalist, pro-state and Solidarity rhetoric did not prevent the registration of activities abroad in Luxembourg to avoid control. Moreover, PiS and SKOK actively blocked state supervision over their operations.[23] Furthermore, like Ordo Iuris, they used the legal system to suppress press criticism of SKOK's activities.[24] SKOK Holdings held shares in the businesses of

[20] Father Jankowski, accused of paedophilia, became a figure of controversy. Its symbolic moment was the overturning of his monument by three activists. https://www.nytimes.com/2019/05/17/world/europe/poland-priests-sex-abuse-film.html.

[21] https://www.skok.pl/.

[22] https://www.polityka.pl/tygodnikpolityka/rynek/1520042,1,jak-senator-pis-wzbogacil-sie-na-skok-ach.read?fbclid=IwAR12kxLYYMwM82G1C8seeL55NfBP3n8ySQNHkQ4ZKpxtvMbRzH9zyhSCauY.

[23] https://oko.press/piec-bitew-o-skok-jak-bierecki-kaczynski-duda-i-politycy-pis-blokowali-nadzor-nad-kasami/?fbclid=IwAR2rMPNcBE_nQxbWvghflZvz147cDrEgGFcK0_Xf8tnaQ-Z_lVwBzHpNAug.

[24] https://wyborcza.pl/1,75398,10999878,SKOK_i_przegraly_z___Polityka__.html.

Father Tadeusz Rydzyk—Geothermia Toruñ and the cellular network "In our family". Bierecki's companies were also the main advertisers of Gazeta Polska, Gazeta Polska Codziennie, Nasz Dziennik and the Niezalezna.pl website. Moreover, Stefczyk.info closely cooperates with the service of the Karnowski brothers, Wpolityce.pl (media backer of the political success of PiS), and SKOK Stefczyka—the largest cash union in Poland—funds scholarships for right-wing Catholic students and academics.[25] SKOK is the Polish equivalent of the "Kochtopus", which paved Law and Justice's (PiS) way to power, and caused a hegemonic takeover of the media sphere prior to 2015. The media supported the spread of moral panic against refugees, LGBT, "cultural Marxism" and other "fears" popular among the international radical right. Below I will show how the merchanting of doubt has become a tool of right-wing domination.

In the Mist of Doubts, Might Is a Winner

Anticommunism has been a strategy of spreading fear from its very beginning (Dean, 2019: 19), since the times of the Red Scare. What the strategy of right-wing think tanks described above has added to this is the "merchanting of doubts" (Oreskes & Conway, 2011). As a result, the strategy itself became less obvious and has been allowed to "consume" the critical impulse. We saw this in the Brexit campaign, for example, where supporters of staying in the EU were accused of spreading fear, and supporters of Brexit presented themselves as being reasonably skeptical. The struggle against "statism" and left ideas by the Kochtopus was carried out by supporting fringe movements that proclaimed the need for the abolition of state control, and opposed modernity (and enlightenment), disguised as skepticism and criticism. This resulted in an attack on the broad scientific consensus and the destruction of the social circulation of scientific facts (Mooney, 2005). The latter—that is, the circulation of facts—is crucial in the modern world because it sustains and stabilizes the modern social ontology. This is because after the disenchantment of the world, the destruction of old mythical and religious ways of binding of the society, the process of rationalization can only be reflexive, but not undone, as long as we want to preserve modern achievements (Nowak

[25] https://www.newsweek.pl/skok-grzegorz-bierecki-sponsorem-prawicy-w-polsce/9gmlwsd.

et al., 2016). Moreover, when the circulation of scientific facts is interrupted at all levels (from the laboratory to education and popularization), science, instead of helping bind society together, becomes a cause of alienation.

This particularly applies to the promotion of "FUD", a strategy of selling Fear, Uncertainty and Doubt. It's a specific equivalent of Naomi Klein's "shock doctrine", only in the realm of knowledge. The aim of "fear- and doubt-mongering" is to undermine trust in public experts, science as a stabilizer of the public sphere, and a source of public trust.[26] Spreading fear, increasing social atomization, and undermining social trust in public institutions is functional for a world ruled by the "Right of Might". This is because in a world of destroyed trust (in the state, science, society, rationality) there is no place for the creation of solidarity and resistance based on progressive politics—nor on a vision of such a future. In a world of scared and doubting monads, only a reactionary revolt is possible,[27] which neither refutes the mighty nor helps the weak and frightened.

The origins of "merchanting of doubt" strategies date back to the 1950s, and the lawsuits for compensation for the discovery of the link between smoking and cancer (Oreskes & Conway, 2011: 10). In order to avoid responsibility, tobacco magnates hired PR companies to create a campaign, which was later labeled the "tobacco strategy".[28] This strategy was used to create and fuel controversies around tobacco, acid rain, the ozone hole, global warming and DDT. This "fog of doubts" helps to indirectly promote free-market fundamentalism, aided by a too-conforming media. The "Tobacco Strategy" is intended to create and maintain the controversy, then to create a substitute for public debate and keep it thriving. The main goal is not to win the argument, but to promote disagreement, as they described it—"doubt is our product" (Oreskes &

[26] One of a striking example of such standpoint according to COVID pandemic was series of articles by Giorgio Agamben, see Nowak (2020b).

[27] https://www.lrb.co.uk/the-paper/v33/n16/slavoj-zizek/shoplifters-of-the-world-unite.

[28] https://www.merchantsofdoubt.org/.

Conway, 2011: 16).[29] In later years, this became the matrix used by corporations and right-wing think tanks to seize and retain power:

> From the late 1980s, one of the major sources of sceptical and contrarian claims about global warming was the George C. Marshall Institute, a think tank in Washington DC. The institute was founded in 1984 by Frederick Seitz, a solid-state physicist and one-time president of the National Academy of Sciences, Robert Jastrow, an astrophysicist and head of the Goddard Institute for Space Studies, and William Nierenberg, a nuclear physicist and head of the Scripps Institution of Oceanography. All three were successful, prominent and brilliant. And all three spoke strongly against communism and in favour of free enterprise. In 1984, the men joined forces to defend then US president Ronald Reagan's Strategic Defense Initiative (popularly known as Star Wars). (Oreskes & Conway, 2010: 686)

It is no surprise that this strategy was linked to an anti-communist, Cold War agenda. "Merchants of doubt", by undermining confidence in science and public debate, created a veil of doubt, infected the audience with "bad" skepticism, which did not lead to increased critical thinking but blinded them (Nowak, 2020b). This allowed them to paralyze the work of government agencies that wanted to regulate big business. And in a world without regulation, they could create their neoliberal mayhem—a world without control and without responsibility, in which industry and business can accumulate but do not pay for the damage they cause—because the "fog of doubt" and the lack of regulation make it impossible to curb (Mayer, 2017: 129).[30]

This "neoliberal mayhem" was supported by a kind of manufactured scientific illiteracy (Mooney & Kirshenbaum, 2009), simultaneously used as a weapon and a tool for installing an anti-socialist, pro-neoliberal agenda. Space constraints do not allow this point to be elaborated, but is

[29] This strategy can be treated as something equivalent to known CIA advice on how to sabotage organizational meetings https://www.cia.gov/news-information/featured-story-archive/2012-featured-story-archive/CleanedUOSSSimpleSabotage_sm.pdf.

[30] The associations of the Polish fur industry in the right-wing parties *Konfederacja* or *Kukiz 15* are intriguing. These strongly right-wing, free market parties have combined with the fur industry to cultivate an aversion to environmental or state regulations. Extreme right-wing movements have proved to be a functional ally for "Latifunders". https://jutrobedziefutro.pl/2019/11/02/futrzarze-oplacili-hejt-na-politykow-dziennikarzy-aktywistow-i-organizacje-pozarzadowe/.

necessary to signal this extensive anarcho-capitalist network of institutions and think tanks, promoting a kind of anarcho-totalitarianism (Mayer, 2017: 11). Importantly, this network—that pumps millions of dollars into the spread of neoliberal ideology and irrationalism—benefits from financialization. "Empty", "cheap" speculative money is spent to accelerate and promote neoliberalism, to counter statism and other forms of control of capital, and as a result are used to strengthen processes which help to reinforce the spiral of speculation and accumulation of capital (Patel & Moore, 2017).

The Unfulfilled Promise of "Real Socialism"

The march of irrationalism, as I mentioned above, has been even more catastrophic for the Eastern bloc than the West. The promise of real socialism was more intricately linked to science and progress than Western, Fordist modernity. The left-wing promise of dignity and recognition realized the secular fulfillment of religious promises. It did not do this perfectly, of course, but it did so with that goal in mind. "We will be better" was a slogan that organized everyday life; Gramota—put' k komunizmu ("Literacy—a path to communism") was the slogan from the famous poster.[31] Real socialism, as a forced state-driven modernization leap, was able to industrialize, rebuild cities ruined after the war, satisfy fundamental needs such as education or health, but it never fully offered an alternative model to the capitalist center. The countries of the Eastern Bloc chased the West, forced by their dependence within the structures of the global capitalist world-system to participate in a game which they eventually lost. By sharing the same fate with the capitalist center (Gagyi, 2020), the countries of "real socialism" shared the problems of global systemic crises. Their destiny became what is well described by a cruel Polish proverb: "where the fat man will lose weight, the skinny one will die".

Intertwined with the fall of the Second World is the disintegration of a cynical "hegemonic machine" of late socialism, legitimized by the narrative of scientific socialism. Socialism was supposed to be scientific, to replace superstition, hunger, war, and religion thanks to scientific knowledge. This had its serious philosophical function; socialism/communism

[31] https://digitalcollections.nypl.org/items/510d47de-83b2-a3d9-e040-e00a18064a99.

was to replace the old religious promises by showing that is able to fulfill them (Kohonen, 2017). Even in such a literal field as ensuring the specific immortality of Lenin's body (Yurchak, 2015). Of course, science in the USSR and satellite countries was involved in the arms race, and scientists were useful to industry, but it remained an important element of legitimacy, of a certain universal promise (Vasilyeva, 2012). The symbol of this remains as the collective portrait of idealistic scientists in the Chernobyl television series, symbolized by Ulana Khomyuk. What is crucial for me is the collapse of the legitimizing function of science understood in this way. We can describe it as a symbolic duel between two anti-communist strategies: that of Sakharov, and that of Solzhenitsyn. The former wanted to reform communism, he dreamt of a humanistic scientific utopia, the latter criticized the USSR from national-religious positions. As we know, the latter won. Sakharov's accelerationist dream remained unfulfilled (Sakharov & Salisbury, 1974).[32]

Let's Talk About Logistics

In Poland after 1989, left-wing thinking—because of the memory of the exploits of the Communist Party—was heavily poisoned with anti-statism and resentment for organizing into political parties, for institutional thinking, for careers in the bureaucratic machinery, and for taking over the state apparatus. The other side did not have such resentments though. Using both the powerful administrative apparatus of the Catholic Church, and the "ammunition" derived from "culture wars" in the West, they took over the state.

Even if, in radical terms, the Eastern Bloc countries—after short periods of autonomy—were part of the modern world-system, and even if the Soviet Union with its state capitalism did not fulfil its socialist promise, still, during "real socialism"—in order to keep the nomenklatura and Communist parties in power, both the USSR and the socialist bloc allocated significant amounts of money and support to left-wing movements, and an ideology of universalism, science and progress. Although I'm not so cynical as to say pecunia non olet, it makes a big difference in which direction the bullet sponsored by capital is shot. Once, the Kremlin sponsored the Left—even if it was cynical, and maintained

[32] http://wilsonweb.physics.harvard.edu/sakharovconference/76953998.pdf.

the hyper-normalization of the oppressive structures of the patriarchal power of the nomenklatura and the Politburo (Yurchak, 2013). The situation was radically different from today, when the Kremlin (in alliance with US neocons) supports the free market and religious right. And now it supports the hyper-normalization of neoliberal mayhem and interregnum.[33]

When discussing 30 years of post-communist transformation in Poland, we should recall David Ost's book *The defeat of solidarity: Anger and politics in postcommunist Europe* (Ost, 2005). As Ost writes, the right has gained influence "by organizing the anger of the economic 'losers' along non-economic lines, Polish political and trade union leaders impeded the development of the emerging democratic system, which has wide relevance to the rest of the postcommunist world" (Ost, 2005: 2). What I wanted to show in this text is a wider background, thanks to which this "organizing anger"[34] was possible. It is crucial for me to analyze on two parallel levels: the epistemological—the level of "war of ideas"—and the ontological—institutional, financial and personal background—which makes it possible to mobilize the resources and means to conduct such a "war of ideas" (George, 1997). The anger described by Ost was not born in a vacuum, nor were the ideas on which it was redirected. This "vacuum" is not natural, but it was also produced. The undermining of faith in the stabilization of the future, the alliance of science and progress, and the belief in the possibility of a collective change of reality causes that anger, which instead of being a constructive driver of transformation becomes only an epiphenomenon of desperation and impotence. The triad in the title—fear, doubt, and money—is intended to point out precisely the factors that in a sense precede this recognized moment—the anger of the abandoned and alienated, which is captured by the right. In summary, the "redirection of class anger" described by Ost is the completion of a long process, the "gathering of what is sown" in the long process of installing right-wing, hegemonic structures.

One may ask if I want to praise cynicism in this article? No, I want to praise political realism, only one that will be subordinated to the utopian dreams of humanistic socialism. The "merchanting of doubts",

[33] https://www.culturematters.org.uk/index.php/arts/films/item/2483-hypernormalisation.

[34] The thesis about redirecting class anger is quite well recognized, both in the context of Poland and the USA. Frank (2004), Hochschild and Toren (2017).

fear-mongering and the production of ignorance is part of neoliberal hyper-normalization. I do not want to mourn a glorious leftist past (Traverso, 2016) and to praise The Right with the fascination of a witness (Dean, 2019: 21). To counter the Right we have to learn from how the enemy acts as a "dialectic of war on position and war of manouevre" (Egan, 2016a): to combine activism driven by values and emotion with cynical Machiavellian strategies. As Judi Dean states: the Left needs to be the communists the Right fears. Such a move of identification occasions the practical work of building power. Rather than power being the object of a fantasy, it's a capacity to be built and exercised (Dean, 2019: 21).

What we can learn from the Right is that "Amateurs talk strategy. Professionals talk logistics" (Srnicek & Williams, 2015). To have a more just and equal future, we have to gather the resources, power and infrastructure to provide it.

References

Aksamit, B., & Głuchowski, P. (2019). *Uzurpator: Podwójne życie prałata Jankowskiego*. Agora.

Althusser, L., Balibar, E., Bidet, J., & Goshgarian, G. M. (2014). *On the reproduction of capitalism: Ideology and ideological state apparatuses*. Verso.

Atwood, M. (1986). *The Handmaid's Tale*. Penguin.

Barbrook, R., & Cameron, A. (1996). The Californian ideology. *Science as Culture, 6*(1), 44–72.

Bendyk, E. (2020). *W Polsce czyli wszędzie: Rzecz o upadku i przyszłości świata*. Polityka Sp. z o.o. S.K.A.

Boatcă, M. (2006). Semiperipheries in the world-system: Reflecting Eastern European and Latin American experiences. *Journal of World-Systems Research*, 321–346. https://doi.org/10.5195/jwsr.2006.362.

Boltanski, L., & Chiapello, È. (2018). *The new spirit of capitalism* (New updated edition). Verso.

Boucas, D. (2020). Theory, reality, and possibilities for a digital/communicative socialist society. TripleC: Communication, capitalism & critique. *Open Access Journal for a Global Sustainable Information Society, 18*(1), 48–66. https://doi.org/10.31269/triplec.v18i1.1140.

Cooper, M. (2017). *Family values: Between neoliberalism and the new social conservatism*. Zone Books.

Crouch, C. (2016). *The knowledge corrupters: Hidden consequences of the financial takeover of public life*. Polity Press.

Curtis, A. (2011). *All watched over by machines of loving grace: Part I love and power*. BBC. https://www.bbc.co.uk/programmes/b011k45f. Accessed January 28, 2021.

Datta, N. (2018). *"Restoring the natural order": The religious extremists' vision to mobilize European societies against human rights on sexuality and reproduction*. https://www.epfweb.org/sites/epfweb.org/files/rtno_epf_book_lores.pdf.

Datta, N. (2019). Modern-day crusaders in Europe. Tradition, family and property. *Političke Perspektive, 8*(3), 69–105. https://doi.org/10.20901/pp.8.3.03.

Dean, J. (2019). Anti-communism is all around us. *Praktyka Teoretyczna, 31*(1), 15–24. https://doi.org/10.14746/prt.2019.1.1.

Duda, M. (2016). *Dogmat płci: Polska wojna z gende*r. Wydawnictwo Naukowe Katedra.

Egan, D. (2016a). *The dialectic of position and maneuver: Understanding Gramsci's military metaphor*. Studies in critical social sciences, volume 94. Brill.

Egan, D. (2016b). Gramsci's war of position as siege warfare: Some lessons from history. *Critique, 44*(4), 435–450. https://doi.org/10.1080/03017605.2016.1236486

Fischer, N. (2016). *Spider web: The birth of American anticommunism*. University of Illinois Press.

Frank, T. (2004). *What's the matter with Kansas? How conservatives won the heart of America*. New York: Metropolitan Books.

Gagyi, A. (2016). "Coloniality of power" in East Central Europe: External penetration as internal force in post-socialist Hungarian politics. *Journal of World-Systems Research, 22*(2), 349–372.

Gagyi, A. (2020). *February 20. Socialism and development: seven theses on global integration*. https://www.criticatac.ro/lefteast/socialism-and-development-six-theses-on-global-integration%ef%bb%bf/. Accessed January 28, 2021.

George, S. (1997). How to win the war of ideas: Lessons from the Gramscian right. *Dissent, 44*(3 Summer). https://www.tni.org/en/archives/act/1447.

Giroux, H. A. (2008). Beyond the biopolitics of disposability: Rethinking neoliberalism in the new gilded age. *Social Identities, 14*(5), 587–620. https://doi.org/10.1080/13504630802343432

Golinczak, M. (2019). Communism as a general crime: Applying hegemony analysis to anti-communist discourse in contemporary Poland. *Praktyka Teoretyczna, 31*(1), 94–117. https://doi.org/10.14746/prt.2019.1.5.

Graff, A. (2014). Report from the gender trenches: War against 'genderism'in Poland. *European Journal of Women's Studies, 21*(4), 431–435.

Graff, A., & Korolczuk, E. (2017). "Worse than communism and Nazism put together": War on gender in Poland. In R. Kuhar & D. Paternotte (Eds.),

Anti-gender campaigns in Europe: Mobilizing against equality (pp. 176–194). Rowman & Littlefield International.

Hochschild, A. R., & Toren, S. (2017). *Strangers in their own land: Anger and mourning on the American Right*. [Ashland, Oregon]: Brilliance Audio.

Kaoma, K. (2009). *Globalizing the culture wars: US conservatives, African churches, and homophobia*. Political Research Associates.

Kohonen, I. (2017). *Picturing the cosmos: A visual history of early Soviet space endeavor*. Intellect.

Kontrewolucja kulturowo-religijna: Czy Polsce grozi prawo podporządkowane ideologii chrześcijańskich fundamentalistów? (2020). Wielka Koalicja za Równością i Wyborem.

Korolczuk, E. (2016). The Vatican and the Birth of Anti-Gender Studies. *Religion and Gender, 6*(2), 293–296. https://doi.org/10.18352/rg.10181.

Korolczuk, E. (2017). *Explaining "Black protests" against abortion ban in Poland: The power of connective action*. https://www.researchgate.net/publication/314232114_Explaining_black_protests_against_abortion_ban_in_Poland_the_power_of_connective_action.

Kościelniak, M. (2018a). Krucjata moralna Solidarność. *Teksty Drugie*, 5, 25–44. https://doi.org/10.18318/td.2018.5.2.

Kościelniak, M. (2018b). Revolution in the cross's shadow: Solidarity as performance. *Polish Theatre Journal (PTJ), 2*(6), 1–24. https://www.polishtheatrejournal.com/index.php/ptj/article/view/181/880.

Kościelniak, M. (2020). Transformacja i aborcja.: Genealogia „kompromisu aborcyjnego. *Widok. Teorie I Praktyki Kultury Wizualnej*, (27).

Kotz, D. M. (2017). *The rise and fall of neoliberal capitalism* (First Harvard University Press paperback edition). Harvard University Press.

Kowalewski, Z. M. (2006). Solidarność zachodniej lewicy z "Solidarnością": Opowiem jak było. *Rewolucja, 4*, 100–108.

Kowalewski, Z. M. (2011). Give US back our factories!: Between resisting exploitation and the struggle for workers' power in Poland, 1944–1981. In I. Ness & D. Azzellini (Eds.), *Ours to master and to own: Workers' councils from the commune to the present*. Haymarket Books.

Kubik, J. 2010. *Power of symbols against the symbols of power: The rise of solidarity and the fall of state socialism in Poland*. Penn State Press.

Kuhar, R., & Paternotte, D. (Eds.). (2017). *Anti-gender campaigns in Europe: Mobilizing against equality*. Rowman & Littlefield International.

Kuron, J., & Modzelewski, K. (1975). *A revolutionary socialist manifesto: An open letter to the party*. Pluto Press for the International Socialists.

Lee, R. E. (2011). *Knowledge matters: The structures of knowledge and the crisis of the modern world-system. Creative Economy Series*. Routledge.

Lee, R. E., & Wallerstein, I. (2004). Structures of knowledge. In J. R. Blau (Ed.), *The Blackwell Companion to Sociology* (pp. 228–235). Blackwell Publishing Ltd. https://doi.org/10.1002/9780470693452.ch16.

Maliński, J. (2017). Neoreakcyjny Utopizm. *Sensus Historiae, 26*(1), 97–110.

Mata, S. (2015). *El Yunque en España: La sociedad secreta que divide a los católicos*. Amanecer.

Mayer, J. (2017). *Dark money: The hidden history of the billionaires behind the rise of the radical right*. Anchor Books.

Medina, E. (2011). *Cybernetic revolutionaries: Technology and politics in Allende's Chile*. MIT Press.

Michalik, G. (2020). *Kaszpirowski: Sen o wszechmocy* (Wydanie I). Agora.

Michnik, A. (1993). *The church and the left*. University of Chicago Press.

Mirowski, P. (2011). *Science-mart: Privatizing American science*. Harvard University Press.

Mooney, C. (2005). *The republican war on science*. Basic Books.

Mooney, C., & Kirshenbaum, S. (2009). *Unscientific America: How scientific illiteracy threatens our future*. Basic Books.

Mrozik, A. (2019). Anti-communism: It's high time to diagnose and counteract. *Praktyka Teoretyczna, 31*, 178–184.

Nowak, A. W. (2020a). „Dziecko poczęte" jako obiekt ontohegemoniczny.: Obiekty, materialność i wizualizacja a procesy ustanawiania hegemonii. *Avant, XI*(3), 1–26. http://avant.edu.pl/wp-content/uploads/A_W_Nowak_Dziecko_poczete.pdf.

Nowak, A. W. (2020b). *Philosophical necromancy or accelerationist hope?* https://www.criticatac.ro/lefteast/necromancy-or-hope-response-to-agamben/. Accessed January 28, 2021.

Nowak, A. W. (2020c). *The unbearable lightness of critique of the enlightenment. Reading the invention of Eastern Europe 25 Later*. https://www.criticatac.ro/lefteast/the-unbearable-lightness-of-critique-of-the-enlightenment-reading-the-invention-of-eastern-europe-25-later/. Accessed January 28, 2021.

Nowak, A. W., Abriszewski, K., & Wróblewski, M. (2016). *Czyje lęki? Czyja nauka? Struktury wiedzy wobec kontrowersji naukowo-społecznych*. s. 233.

Oliveira, P. C. de. (1993). *Revolution and counter-revolution* (3rd English ed.). American Society for the Defense of Tradition, Family, and Property.

Oreskes, N., & Conway, E. M. (2010). Defeating the merchants of doubt. *Nature, 465*(7299), 686–687. https://doi.org/10.1038/465686a. Accessed January 28, 2020.

Oreskes, N., & Conway, E. M. (2011). *Merchants of doubt: How a handful of scientists obscured the truth on issues from tobacco smoke to global warming*. Bloomsbury Publishing USA.

Ost, D. (2005). *The defeat of solidarity: Anger and politics in postcommunist Europe*. Ithaca: Cornell University Press.

Patel, R., & Moore, J. W. (2017). *A history of the world in seven cheap things: A guide to capitalism, nature, and the future of the planet*. University of California Press Books.

Pawłowski, Ł. 2020. *Druga fala prywatyzacji: Niezamierzone skutki rządów PiS* (Wydanie pierwsze). Biblioteka Kultury Liberalnej, Vol. 15. Fundacja Kultura Liberalna.

Peto, A., Grzebalska, W., & Post, H. (2016). How Hungary and Poland have silenced women and stifled human rights. *Transitions Online*, (10/25), 28–31.

Piatkowski, M. (2019). *Europe's growth champion: Insights from the economic rise of Poland*. Oxford University Press.

Pobłocki, K. (2017). *Kapitalizm: Historia krótkiego trwania*. Fundacja Nowej Kultury Bęc Zmiana.

Ponerau, F. (2020). *The political (auto)biography of a generation*. https://www.criticatac.ro/lefteast/political-autobiography-generation1989/. Accessed January 28, 2021.

Richta, R. (2018). *Civilization at the crossroads: Social and human implications of the scientific and technological revolution*. International Arts and Sciences Press, Routledge.

Rogowska, G. (2020). *Women strike back turning Polish society upside down*. https://visegradinsight.eu/women-strike-back-poland-abortion/. Accessed October 28, 2021.

Ross, S. (2008). The strategic implications of anti-statism in the global justice movement. *Labour, Capital and Society/Travail, Capital Et Société, 41*(1), 6–32. www.jstor.org/stable/43158322.

Rupprecht, T. (2011). Socialist high modernity and global stagnation: A shared history of Brazil and the Soviet Union during the cold war. *Journal of Global History, 6*(3), 505–528. https://doi.org/10.1017/S174002281100043X

Sakharov, A., & Salisbury, H. E. (1974). *Sakharov speaks*. Edited and with a foreword by Harrison E. Salisbury. Collins & Harvill Press.

Sharlet, J. (2008). *The family: The secret fundamentalism at the heart of American power* (1st ed.). HarperCollins.

Srnicek, N., & Williams, A. (2015). *Inventing the future: Postcapitalism and a world without work*. Verso Books.

Storrs, L. R. Y. (2013). *The second red scare and the unmaking of the new deal left. Politics and society in twentieth-century America*. Princeton University Press.

Suchanow, K. (2020). *To jest wojna: Kobiety, fundamentaliści i nowe średniowiecze*. Warszawa: Agora SA.

Szwed, A., & Zielinska, K. (2017). *A war on gender? The Roman Catholic Church's Discourse on Gender in Poland*. https://doi.org/10.1057/978-1-137-43751-8_6

Traverso, E. (2016). *Left-wing melancholia: Marxism, history, and memory. New directions in critical theory*. Columbia University Press.

Tufekci, Z. (2017). *Twitter and tear gas: The power and fragility of networked protest*. YALE University Press.

Twomey, C. P. (1999). The McNamara line and the turning point for civilian scientist-advisers in American Defence Policy, 1966–1968. *Minerva, 37*(3), 235–258. www.jstor.org/stable/41821147.

Vasilyeva, Z. (2012). DO-IT-YOURSELF PRACTICES: Technical knowledge in late Soviet and post-Soviet Russia. *Tsantsa, 17*, 178–181.

Velminski, W. (2017). *Homo sovieticus: Brain waves, mind control, and telepathic destiny* (E. Butler, Trans.). The MIT Press.

Yurchak, A. (2013). *Everything was forever, until it was no more: The last Soviet generation*. Princeton University Press.

Yurchak, A. (2015). Bodies of Lenin: The hidden science of communist sovereignty. *Representations, 129*(1), 116–157.

Conclusion: Seven Excursions into the Ideological Landscape of Eastern Europe

Ondřej Slačálek

In their *Manifesto of the Communist Party*, Karl Marx and Friedrich Engels provide a moving depiction of the "most revolutionary part" played historically by the bourgeoisie and capital. The idea that "the bourgeoisie cannot exist without constantly revolutionising the instruments of production, and thereby … the whole relations of society" applies universally, and during the last three decades we have witnessed it globally. But for inhabitants of postsocialist societies[1] these revolutionary forces has been more than evident as they have undergone a monumental social

[1] To formulate conclusions touching three decades in a very differentiated region, I need to use terms which are for many contexts unsatisfactorily generalizing, like "postsocialist" or "neoliberal" in their most common meanings and postpone for the purpose of this text the debates that the label "postsocialist" is outdated and only reifies the subordinate positions of these countries, or that "neoliberalism" is a relatively vague label covering quite a broad variety of approaches. The same applies about speaking too generally about "region", "countries" and "societies"—I underline that what I generalize under those terms are general tendencies and the results of complicated social processes and often struggles, not some necessary and homogenous "essences".

O. Slačálek (✉)
Department of Political Science, Faculty of Arts, Charles University, Prague, Czechia
e-mail: Ondrej.Slacalek@ff.cuni.cz

A. Gagyi and O. Slačálek (eds.), *The Political Economy of Eastern Europe 30 years into the 'Transition'*, International Political Economy Series,
https://doi.org/10.1007/978-3-030-78915-2_14

revolution whereby old values were rapidly sunk in the "icy water of egotistical calculation", and which has almost "left remaining no other nexus between man and man than naked self-interest, than callous 'cash payment'".

The political aspect of social transformation in the Eastern Europe has been the democratic revolutions in 1989–1991. Sooner rather than later, however, the transformation to a "market society" (in the Polanyian meaning) was declared a necessary precondition of democracy. This had to work both in economic and cultural terms. The market had to create wealth for all (let's remember the popularity of the "trickle-down effect" in the ideology of the time). But its function was also to re-educate the spoiled children of state socialist dictatorship to become responsible individuals, adult enough to be democratic citizens. Democratic revolutions soon became bourgeois revolutions. Fairly strange bourgeois revolutions, as they started almost without a real bourgeoisie (with scarce and mostly illegal exceptions). The creation of a real bourgeoisie was something like a "work in progress" or desired goal, as well as a new and more intense reintegration into global capitalism.

This social revolution corresponded to globalization and the boom in personal computers and the internet. Of course, most of these changes were global, and postsocialist Europe was not their central point. But there was an Eastern contribution, since the definitive fall of the Eastern bloc led to triumphalist capitalism globally (Mark et al., 2019). The former Eastern bloc countries underwent many processes connected to global or Western dynamics (typically: selective de-industrialization or the liberalization of markets), but their subordinate position and transition meant these processes had a different intensity and temporality. Fresh experience of "social revolution", of large-scale societal change, was an important part of societal imagination with many, sometimes unpredictable results.

Very often, these revolutions were considered by various actors to be "unfinished" or "betrayed": the capitalism and democracy built in these new countries is not "real" and "true" (meaning of the "Western" type), corruption and the illiberal forces in power are considered to be evidence of "unfinished" transformation or "backsliding". Chapters of this book propose a different reading: these revolutions were quite successful, they created a bourgeoisie and market society. Popular dissatisfaction, problems with quality of democracy as well as an unequal position in the EU and the strength of authoritarian conservatives are the results of relatively *successful* neoliberal revolutions, not unsuccessful ones.

The Left found itself in a somehow paradoxical role. While its genealogy bore strong imprints of revolutionary ethos, it now had to be somehow alien to these revolutions, at the latest from the moment when they visibly changed from democratic revolutions to neoliberal ones.

There were of course many possibilities for left-wing forces. Some of them took a conservative, even reactionary stance. The most notable cases are probably the various neo-Brezhnevist communist parties in their embrace of nationalism and various "red and brown alliances". Others, opportunist post-communists, social democrats and left-liberals, tried to saddle the wild horse of market revolution, sometimes they struggled for the position of its main riders or they tried to mute its impacts. Other versions of the left tried to formulate radical criticism by using various (mostly Western) concepts for criticism of transformations—something that made them (us) relatively radical and relatively alienated from their (our) domestic societies.

This book aims to capture the experience of the left-wing part of the "first postsocialist generation" (see Dana Domșodi's and Florin Poenaru's chapter for more on this). Most of the authors participated in various New Left milieus which needed to find a new orientation. The stories they tell originate from various national contexts; partly because of the relatively low level of communication across the region (in comparison with the level of acceptance of Western impulses) this is one aspect of the postsocialist condition which is being overcome relatively slowly. Many of those milieus were reacting to similar or the same impulses, however. We can identify the three most important influences as: first, the legacy of left-wing dissent under state socialist dictatorship; second, alterglobalist movements; and third, global capitalist crisis. It is too soon to judge if the next strong common experiences will be the climate change movement or socioeconomic crisis coming with the COVID-19 pandemic.

The *legacy of left-wing dissent* has provided both contributions to the analysis of state socialist dictatorships from within and a strong moral commitment of resistance to bureaucratic dictatorships and of building an emancipatory alternative under harsh conditions (Ernu & Budraitskis, 2017; Kuroń & Modzelewski, 1966; Kužel, 2017; Uhl, 1980).

The alterglobalist movement opened many debates and connected them with the politics of social movements and the global perspective. The movement made a major contribution to the transfer of critical concepts and social movement practices which meant a partial "globalization from below". However, these were mostly concepts transferred largely via Western activism with a focus on "Third World countries". While the failures of neoliberalism in some postsocialist countries made moderate left-wing *convertitos* of neoliberal hardliners like Jeffrey Sachs, the decimated Eastern European Left did not contribute substantially to the ideas of the "movement of movements".

The *global capitalist crisis* in 2008 made criticism of capitalism mainstream even in the core countries. *Something happened* and many neoliberal "truths" were lost. Still, the Left was generally much less skilful in politically exploiting the crisis in comparison with various versions of the Right. It was the Right which mostly met with success—with various versions of Thatcherism on steroids, combining the triple aggressiveness of neoliberal individualism + value conservativism + vague and negativist neonationalism. Of course, this development was not endemic to Eastern Europe.

...

As various chapters of this book describe important aspects of their national contexts, their description captures some characteristics applicable more broadly. In the rest of this conclusion, I will trace seven aspects of ideology in Eastern Europe present in the chapters which I consider to be the most important. These seven aspects will be divided into three sections, based on their relation to time, space and depoliticization.

The chapters mostly criticize and deconstruct these ideologies. I will summarize and discuss the basic aspects of this criticism. At the same time, I will try to develop a dialectical approach to these aspects of ideology in two steps. In the first step, together with a recapitulation of the criticism, I will pose the question whether we can find some "moments of truth" there. In the second step, I will examine the possibility for dialectical synthesis, which merges these moments of truth with critical anti-thesis by negation into a new proposal.

Temporal Imagination

The postsocialist decades meant temporal destabilization, especially at the beginning. Liberalism was presented both as the gate to endless progress and as the "end of history" at the same time. Many suppressed traditions came out from semi-oblivion to struggle for space and attention, while decades of defeated "ancién regimes" were sometimes declared to be "lost" or "void" time, and sometimes to be the source of "real" and "authentic" experience of resisting those regimes. The patterns of temporal destabilization differed within the region, but there are two more general aspects:

1. ***Anti-communism***. One important cut in temporal imagination was made by anti-communism (see Domsodi and Poenaru's chapter, also Praktyka Teoretyczna, 2019; Traykov, 2019). It declared state socialist dictatorship to be "criminal" as a whole, the equivalent of Nazism. This played the role of excluding "Communism" (described as one single devilish phenomenon, from Marx to Stalin and various "communist" regimes and parties) not only from political legitimacy, but also from legitimate historical time. Together with communism, there was a broader set of what could be excluded because of contamination by Communist Evil. This set of various—often contradictory—topics and actors could include social democracy, left-wing or centrist liberals, nationalism (as connected to Communism in some countries), anti-nationalism (as critical to anti-Communist nationalists in others), feminism, progressive taxation, any regulation of free trade, environmentalism (described as the "new red menace"), anti-environmentalism (described as a continuation of "communist" technocracy), any form of police violence, or state surveillance...

   Anti-communism could take the form of liberal legitimization of transformation, of an anti-totalitarian narrative and a discourse of liberalism triumphant. But it could also merge with conservative nationalism to become part of an anti-liberal ideology exploiting the resentment caused by transformation to bring about projects of "illiberal democracy". But almost always, anti-communism meant the delegitimization of left-wing ideas and forces and a schematic Manichean image of the communist "ancién regimes". Conflict with anti-communism was a precondition for the Left in postsocialist countries to achieve political space, as well as to re-evaluate the legacy of the historical Left.

   However, argumentation against the anti-communism imprisoned some parts of the Left in the logics of polemics. This is not limited to the region. Sometimes, the Left loses its materialism by defending an almost Platonic "idea of Communism" which can be judged without any reference to the role of these ideas in relationship to real movements and historical forces. In other cases, the Left reacts to Manichean perceptions of "ancién regimes" by apologetics of them. While anti-communists often absolutize a moralist view of history, the Left is sometimes tempted to exclude moral questions from its view of history or to pose these questions selectively.

In order to challenge liberal and conservative anti-communism and not rehabilitate state socialist dictatorships, we need to develop analyses of those dictatorships. Chapters by Domşodi and Poenaru, Simovic and Vuksa, Krzan and Birac, and Gagyi and Gerőcs contribute to such analysis. Together with various particular analytical insights, they share two tendencies instructive for any further analysis: spatial and temporary difference from implications of speaking about "previous" era and "Eastern bloc".

(1) Speaking about temporality, the image of a social revolution of "post-communist" transformation evoked above leads to the idea that there was a clear division between "then" and "now", and that we have to start our analysis with the *anni mirabiles* of 1989–1991. But there is no such clear cut. Any revolution can be understood only from its roots and causes, and thus the history of our present in fact starts in the final decades of the state socialist dictatorships. (2) Concerning spatial dimension, as all four chapters show, it is hard to draw a precise border between "capitalism" and "socialism" when we consider the capitalist relationships inside state-socialist dictatorships as well as the role of the state-socialist bloc in the capitalist world-system. As especially Gagyi and Gerőcs show us, a conceptual transfer from the global South can be fruitful here to understand state socialist dictatorships as a form of developmentalist dictatorship, with a characteristic combination of emancipatory and oppressive moments. It is only within these comparisons that the state socialist legacy can be understood as a global phenomenon which cannot be separated and excluded from history as "criminal" and "illegitimate", but which also does not need to be defended or apologized.

2. ***Irrationalism and refusal of progress***. From a different point of view, the negation of communism and its attempted erasure from history can be viewed as a subchapter of a much broader phenomenon, of an attack on rationality and progress or, in other words, the legacy of enlightenment. This view is powerfully

presented in Andrzej W. Nowak's chapter. Many of his insights can be generalized. The fall of communism coincided with the explosion of the fashion for vulgar postmodernism attacking the "arrogance of reason" and making it impossible to judge between values on the basis of any "Truth". At the same time, the homogenized empty space of discredited late socialist modernity was marked by many "born again" traditions, sometimes by very aggressive particularist traditions. While enlightened reason was pushed onto the defensive (often for good reasons, articulated from Adorno to contemporary decolonial critique), particularist traditions, especially nationalist and religious ones, were relatively successful in filling the free space.

The Left had to react here and defend reason and progress. But paradoxically, even this reaction led the Left to become a somehow conservative and nostalgic force, longing for a *return* to progress and the unconditional authority of reason. The accent on reason and progress thus paradoxically looks like a declaration of identity and belonging to some particular tradition.

The Left needs to defend rationality and future-oriented thinking as a condition of its very possibility. But this defense will be futile unless it integrates self-criticism of both rationality and a future-oriented horizon. Its materialism has to be historical, integrating historical lessons to transcend its former illusion (including illusions of automatic progress or overly-ambitious enlightened reason).

There is another context, somewhat paradoxical. Anti-communism is a form of the politics of memory. In postsocialist Europe, the politics of memory is used mostly by the political Right. In western Europe and the US, it is often employed by liberals (with usage of the memory of the holocaust and discourse of totalitarianism in general as an important source of the legitimacy of the liberal order) and both in the global West and global South, the politics of memory is very often part of the ideology of the Left (a reconstruction of the memory of the oppressed). From our context we can see some problems of the politics of memory in a sharp light (maybe too sharp). From this point of view, Walter Benjamin's great thesis "On the Concept of History" ("working class['] ... hatred and its spirit of sacrifice... are both nourished by the image of enslaved ancestors rather than that of liberated grandchildren") almost directly prefigures the turn in the Left since the 1960s: from the concept of social justice as a universal transformative vision for the future to the focus on past grievances and their reparations, from militants to victims. The left-wing analysis definitely needs to uncover various versions of oppression and left-wing culture has as its function to recognize and give voice to the victims of this oppression—but above all to help them cease to be victims, not through liberal "compensation", but through the ethos of struggle for social justice. "Liberated grandchildren" maybe do not produce such strong images as "enslaved grandfathers", but it is their liberation that is the center of gravity of left-wing politics.

Self-critical and future-oriented reason stands in front of us as a task for the development of our historical materialist and moral/political imagination. Such reason needs to be capable of avoiding both an arrogant belief in automatic progress and nostalgia for unreformed enlightenment, and at the same time to avoid the dominance of the politics of memory. If we are to have learned any lesson from the twentieth century, it is not that we should prefer the past to the future. It is much more that we can never sacrifice present emancipation to future emancipation. Future emancipation needs to be a continuation of the emancipatory praxis of today.

Spatial Imagination

The spatial imagination also differs throughout the region. Some parts of postsocialist Europe could dream (in ideological phantasies like that of "Central Europe") that they would relatively soon become an unproblematic part of the West. They could dream of only partial and temporarily limited subordination, which would be compensated by full identification with the West, without any of the usual borders which prevent it (race, geographical distance and so on). The expansion of the West had to be their "emancipation". It was mostly after this "successful integration" that they were forced to recognize not only their continuing subordinate position, but that there was never such a thing as "the West", an ideological phantasy created from various aspects of a few Western societies transferred to others.

Other parts of postsocialist Europe were recognized to have been left "somewhere else" (especially some parts of Balkan and post-Soviet Europe) or to construct their own alternatives, mostly with reactionary content (the most important being Putin's Russia). The power of the

Western institutions often had colonial aspects, but its intensity differed—from the "protocoloniality", described by Majstorović and Vukovać in the case of Bosnia and Herzegovina, to countries which have formal veto power in the European Union and sometimes use it.

Various versions of Western dominance and local humiliation were produced not only by the West, but also by various other parts of postsocialist Europe, which compete with each other to be "more developed", "more modernized" and "more Western" (Bakić-Hayden, 1995; Todorova, 2009). The same applies to internal competition inside the societies, especially between the more Europeanized segment of middle classes and other strata.

These differences have created very different settings across the region and pose different questions. Nevertheless, the two poles of many dilemmas have some important common characteristics:

3. ***Westernism***. At the beginning of the postsocialist period, a subordinate position was accepted as transitory. The West seemed to be promising that everything was better there, even a better Left and better socialism. The East was labeled using the metaphor of postsocialist children who have to grow up with their "infant and fragile" democracy (Buden, 2009). But sooner or later (depending above all on regional position) it became clear that this hope was actually not true. Transitory childhood transformed into eternal subordination.

   Agnes Gagyi (2016) described the option of identifying with the promise of Western-led development as "self-colonizing emancipation": in many cases, Western institutions *really* proposed more developed standards, norms or concepts. They promised even better concepts for criticism of the West than the concepts that were available "ready-made" domestically. But this all had its price: an acceptance of unjust structural hierarchies which systematically imposed a subordinate role on their own societies. Social movements and NGOs thus could, for example, criticize their own societies for racism (which was a completely legitimate criticism in most cases) but by doing so, they confirmed an oppressive stereotype about their own societies.

   Western superiority as a condition of the possibility of the emancipatory values is directly based on a political and economic set-up which integrates lower standards for semi-peripheries and peripheries (both in the economic sphere and in the quality of democracy). As Gagyi's and Gerőcs's chapter shows (as does Yurchenko's chapter from a different angle), we cannot think of "nationalist authoritarianism" outside "Western liberal empire", as its challenger, in spite of the way that both Westernist and nationalist protagonists depict themselves. In fact, the nationalist reaction is a specific part of the relationships of the matrix of external-internal capital relationships. Not only do nationalist authoritarians *ideologically* struggle for a "better" ("illiberal" or "Christian democratic") West, but above all *economically* they are part of the Western order.

4. ***Nationalism***. Thus, nationalism can only very partially pretend to be an alternative to Westernism. In fact, their relationship is complicated from the beginning. Revolts against Soviet rule (or against Yugoslavia and the Soviet Union) had both strong democratic and strong nationalist dimensions. Nations were in most cases reconstructed as subjects which want to "return to Europe" (in the case of "Central Europe") and/or to accept (Western) "universal" values of market society and liberal democracy. Nationalism now is in most cases connected to authoritarian and xenophobic approaches, and can thus be easily condemned. But it brings the Left many practical—and some theoretical—difficulties. Agnes Gagyi (2016) posed it in opposition to "self-colonizing emancipation", as "anti-colonial self-love". Nationalist critique has its "moment of truth" in tracing some power relationships and underlining the position of people who cannot (or do not want to) escape from their place. In their unpleasant way, nationalists underline one important local dimension of solidarity, communications and democracy. While nationalists obscure the domestic relationships of dominance and exploitation, they visualize the clearly exploitative nature of some international relationships. The Left cannot escape from these nationalist "moments of truth" and has to include it in its analysis. At the same time, it needs to rid these elements of their exclusivist and particularist contexts and implications by placing them in a new context of other local, as well as regional and universalist, dimensions of its analysis.

The most visible alternative to Westernism and nationalism consisted of some form of sympathy with "third world" countries, whether (mostly paternalist) charity in the case of NGOs or (sometimes romanticized) solidarity, as in the case of the alterglobalist movement. This view of the global South was of key importance in the development of broader analysis and international solidarity. But sometimes it could also work for some parts of the Eastern European Left as a way of escaping the imperative to formulate *its own* experience.

In her article quoted above, Agnes Gagyi (2016) found an alternative both to self-colonial emancipation and anti-colonial self-love in the Fanonian path to universalism through locally-recognized chances for emancipation from oppression. The Left cannot give up on the universalist horizon and universalist categories of analysis. But local experiences are always needed in order to be corrective of them, and only their dialogue can produce any emancipatory theory and praxis.

Anti-political Imagination

The postsocialist condition meant the discrediting of un-democratic politics and the relegitimization of democracy. The hopes which were over-invested in democracy (as well as often very unclear and competing understandings of it) along with its identification with market competition of political parties on the "political market", complementing market competition in the economy, led to disillusionment with democracy and politics. An important part of the ideological imagination in postsocialist Europe thus also included the negation of politics and a vision of corrections of democracy. The Western gaze is often focused on the authoritarian nationalist form of these corrections, and thus confirms its image of "backwardness" and low quality of democracy in eastern Europe. In contrast to this, many chapters of this book focused on those versions of depoliticization connected with their liberal opponents.

5. ***Anti-corruption***. As we have seen in the chapters by Georgi Medarov and Madlen Nikolova, and Daniel Šitera and Ondřej Slačálek, the discourse of corruption becomes a form of perverse self-criticism in the postsocialist condition: various countries are in this image of the world perceived outside of international structural relations. The blame for bad domestic conditions and the

lack of fulfillment of some promises of transformation is distributed fully into domestic societies, both their pathological contemporary political structures and norms, and their historical legacy. Here anti-corruption discourse meets anti-communism, as corruption is considered to be the legacy or remainder of communism. Even in cases where the connection is not made explicit, the anti-corruption discourse shares with anti-communism a common denominator in moralism. In the words of Georgi Medarov and Madlen Nikolova, this discourse shifts our attention to the "moral integrity of politicians rather than the political integrity of policies".

The moment of truth in the ideology of anti-corruption is of course visible, maybe too visible. The discourse of corruption describes relatively correctly many practices present during the original accumulation of capital in postsocialist states, and also their continuation in various oligarchical networks, state captures and so on (Magyar, 2016). It is probably impossible to conduct class analysis in postsocialist countries without speaking of criminal networks and their activity (although this applies to class analysis globally). But the political discourse of corruption does not only suggest that corruption is endemic in the East, while the West does not suffer from it nearly as much. It also focuses on the illegal exchange of economic power for political influence, thus indirectly legitimizing the legal dominance of big money over politics. It also replaces class analysis with detective stories. This discourse also focuses attention more on the receivers of corruption (state, politicians and officials) rather than on those who corrupt (private business). Thus disillusionment with political democracy at the same time obscures capitalist relationships.

6. ***Civil society***. A key mobilizing image present in political mobilizations is the image of civil society. Sometimes it is connected with the image of demonstrations which toppled the state socialist dictatorships in 1989–1991 and with trying to revive their "lost spirit". Often this kind of mobilization paradoxically combines mass meetings (images of crowded squares as a direct challenge to the legitimacy of power) with some kind of elitism (the civil society often sees itself as the "better part" of society, with a better education and/or a moral presupposition to be accepted in a privileged way). This combination becomes typical of the middle class.

As Joe Feinberg's chapter shows us, the ideology of civil society is often connected with "post-dissent" mentality and re-evoking the "last war" of "democracy" against totalitarianism" (this mortal enemy is now sometimes rebranded as "populism"). This form of depoliticization means a temporal escapism from contemporaneousness, as well as escape from the role of capitalist economy in society. Addressing people only as citizens means hiding their role in the political economy. It is connected with the "politics of authenticity", described by Oleg Zhuravlev in a chapter based on direct emotional experience of resistance against power. However, this basis can be alienating to those who do not share this experience and the class conditions which often make this experience possible. This concept of (anti)politics is also anti-institutional and based on spontaneity, and thus it has problems both with continuity in the medium and long term, as well as problems with internal democracy (in a way corresponding to Jo Freeman's 1971 "tyranny of structurelessness"). This self-image of civil society also does not correspond to the *real* organizational form of a huge part of civil society, which is NGOs and their "transactional activism" (Císař, 2010; Fagan, 2005; Shevstova, 2017). This combination of the spontaneist ideology of "civil society" with the real bureaucratic world of NGOs, and often also with their dependency on foreign funding, leads to problems with the democratic legitimacy of this ideology of civil society. These problems are often used by their authoritarian opponents in various propaganda strategies.

There is more: as Khelaia and Chivadze's chapter—but also Feinberg's chapter—show in particular, "civil society" is not necessarily in opposition to nationalism. Historically, the years 1989–1991 often combined the ideology of "civil society" with the ideology of "nation". And logically, the "politics of authenticity" corresponds to the vision of a people/nation which is "finally speaking" without mediating institutions. Thus, we can find common ground both for nationalism and for this concept of "civil society". For a long time, some political science authors were cautious enough to differentiate between "civil society" with liberal values of civility and "uncivil society" with an exclusivist particularist ideology (Kopecky & Mudde, 2003). In fact, however, it is impossible to hide this common ground held by both of them.

7. ***Technocratism.*** The last form of depoliticization is a leaning toward technocratic politics, based on "competence" and a "problem solving" approach, instead of competing political visions. As Daniel Šitera's and Ondřej Slačálek's chapter and to some extent Yuliya Yurchenko's chapter show, very often this technocratic depoliticization becomes a mask hiding another form of depoliticization: oligarchization. The oligarchs are exactly those who are able to produce the necessary expertise outside of classical political institutions, and their success also embodies not only the ideology of a market Darwinist "survival of the fittest", but also the ideology of "reality": in a capitalist society, big money often easily seems the only realistic way to any change.

   Demand for technocracy has a strong logic not only in disillusionment with corruption (in fact, in its oligarchical form, it institutionalizes corruption). It also has its moment of truth: "standard" politics of left-versus-right competition undergoes its crisis, which makes demand for centrist and technocratic solutions stronger. This crisis can be especially powerful in the region where such competition was renewed in a relatively short historical period.

Behind all these three forms of depoliticization we can see above all the paradoxical relationship between liberal democratic politics and economics. Liberal democratic politics is dependent on the market economy, but at the same time it excludes it from the sphere where it is sovereign. By being depoliticized, the market economy is considered to be "free"; in fact, with the working of market forces, it is mostly a sphere of apolitical coercion. Three ideologies of depoliticization aim to "liberate" society from "political games", but in fact, they continue the basic game of liberal democracy (depoliticizing the economy) and they even make it stronger.

Is there any negation of negation which might be proposed for this competition? We could formulate it as democratic socialist repoliticization. But to propose it means going beyond the concept of democracy that was the final result of the democratic revolutions of 1989–1991. It means arriving at a concept of democracy which strongly politicizes various spheres of life, and the economy above all. It is democracy understood in terms of socialism as a synthesis of the legacies of both left-wing dissidents in the East and the progressive Left in the West and South.

This book should be a contribution to the development of this legacy from a region where various versions of depoliticization have attempted, explicitly or implicitly, to exclude this vision from the sphere of thinkable alternatives.

References

Bakić-Hayden, M. (1995). Nesting orientalisms: The case of former Yugoslavia. *Slavic Review, 54*(4), 917–931.

Buden, B. (2009). *Zone des Übergangs: Vom Ende des Postkommunismus*. Suhrkamp.

Císař, O. (2010). Externally sponsored contention: The channelling of environmental movement organisations in the Czech Republic after the fall of communism. *Environmental Politics, 19*(5), 736–755.

Ernu, V., & Budraitskis, I. (2017). Dissidents among Dissidents: Interview with Ilya Budraitskis about his recent book, *Lefteast*. http://www.criticatac.ro/lefteast/dissidents-among-dissidents-interview-with-ilya-budraitskis-about-his-recent-book/. Accessed February 1, 2021.

Fagan, A. (2005). Taking stock of civil-society development in post-communist Europe: Evidence from the Czech Republic. *Democratization, 4*, 528–547.

Gagyi, A. (2016). 'Coloniality of power' in East Central Europe: External penetration as internal force in post-socialist Hungarian politics. *Journal of World-Systems Research, 22*(2), 349–372.

Kopecky, P., & Mudde, C. (Eds.). (2003). *Uncivil societies in Eastern Europe*. Routledge.

Kuroń, J., & Modzelewski, K. (1966). *A revolutionary socialist manifesto, written in a Polish prison*. Socialist Review Publishing.

Kužel, P. (2017). Social self government is a dream i haven't given up on, interview with Petr Uhl. *Kontradikce*, 2, 169–184.

Magyar, B. (2016). *Post-communist mafia state: The case of Hungary*. Central European University Press.

Mark, J., Bogdan, C. I., Rupprecht, T., & Spaskovska, L. (2019). *1989: A global history of Eastern Europe*. Cambridge University Press.

Praktyka Teoretyczna. (2019). *Anti-communisms: Discourses of exclusion, 31*(1). https://pressto.amu.edu.pl/index.php/prt/issue/view/1361. Accessed February 1, 2021.

Shevstova, M. (2017). Friends or foes? Foreign donors' role in the formation of civil society in Ukraine. *Socio.hu, 7*(5), 53–70.

Todorova, M. (2009). *Imagining the Balkans*. Oxford University Press.

Traykov, B. (2019). From anti-communism to fascism: Ideological crusaders of the Bulgarian passive revolution versus socio-economic reality. *Dversia: Special Issue on Decolonial Theory and Practice in Southeast Europe*. https://dversia.

net/4644/dversia-decolonial-theory-practice-southeast-europe/. Accessed February 1, 2021.
Uhl, P. (1980). *Le socialisme emprisonné: Une alternative socialiste à la normalisation*. Stock.

Index

0–9

1989, revolutions of, 9, 17, 18, 20–22, 24–26, 29–33, 36, 46, 47, 61, 62, 74, 75, 89, 137, 152, 154, 156–158, 160, 161, 165, 187, 188, 192, 193, 197–199, 223, 224, 226, 231, 233, 242, 252, 256, 262–264

A

accumulation regime, 115, 116, 119, 126

anti-communism, 3, 8, 11, 12, 23, 36–39, 138, 142, 143, 154–156, 176, 178, 181, 182, 193, 195, 201, 226, 227, 232, 234, 236–238, 240, 242, 255–257, 262

B

Bosnia and Herzegovina, 9, 81, 259

Bulgaria, 11, 187–196, 198, 200

C

capital, 10, 25, 27, 28, 31–34, 43, 44, 50, 53, 56, 59, 61, 67, 70–72, 77, 78, 91, 97–101, 103–105, 109–111, 116, 119, 121–124, 126, 127, 135, 138–140, 146, 157–159, 161, 173, 174, 177, 178, 195, 230, 241, 242, 251, 260, 262

capitalism, 5, 8, 9, 11, 24–26, 29, 33, 38, 43, 47, 48, 50, 60–62, 66, 68–74, 76–78, 89, 91, 93, 97, 99–102, 116, 134, 135, 147, 155, 160, 161, 165, 173, 193, 194, 198, 200, 226, 230, 235, 242, 252, 254, 256

Catholic church, 12, 72, 228, 229, 232, 236, 242

class, 2, 10, 19, 24–28, 33–35, 37, 45, 50, 52–55, 59, 61, 66, 68–74, 76, 78, 85, 87–89, 99, 103, 104, 110, 116, 118, 121, 123, 135, 138, 139, 143, 146, 160, 162, 163, 165, 173, 177,

A. Gagyi and O. Slačálek (eds.), *The Political Economy of Eastern Europe 30 years into the 'Transition'*, International Political Economy Series,
https://doi.org/10.1007/978-3-030-78915-2

187, 190, 192, 194, 197, 198, 209, 210, 212, 213, 215, 219, 225, 243, 257, 262, 263
communism, 8, 11, 17, 18, 20, 22, 24–26, 28–37, 43, 51, 52, 62, 98, 101, 103, 138, 143, 145, 154–157, 160, 161, 163–165, 170, 173, 192, 198, 199, 205, 206, 208, 209, 223, 225, 228, 232, 233, 237, 240–242, 251, 253, 255–257
conservativism, 254
corruption, anti-corruption, 8, 11, 12, 76, 109, 137, 139–142, 146, 148, 151–153, 155, 162, 164, 176, 177, 181, 183, 184, 187–191, 194–196, 200, 201, 207, 208, 252, 261, 262, 264
crisis, 1, 6–10, 12, 20, 22, 25–31, 33, 34, 36, 38, 41, 42, 48, 57, 61, 68, 69, 72, 73, 75, 78, 93, 102, 103, 106, 109, 115–118, 120, 124, 126, 127, 134, 135, 138, 140–143, 147, 188, 193–195, 205, 207–210, 218, 230, 253, 254, 264
crisis of 1970, 7, 10, 12, 26, 27, 30, 31, 33, 38, 55, 57–59, 68, 69, 89, 116, 117, 126, 192, 215, 228, 230, 235, 236
crisis of 2008, 9, 28, 38, 78, 116, 120, 122, 124, 126, 137, 140, 142, 183, 254
Croatia, 9, 58, 68, 75–79, 233
Crony capitalism, mafia capitalism, 139, 156
Czechia, 133, 134, 138, 139, 141, 142, 145–147, 191

D
decoloniality, 91, 93, 257
democratization, democracy, 1, 7, 8, 10, 11, 21, 42, 44–46, 53, 88, 101–103, 133, 134, 138, 142–145, 161, 162, 164, 165, 172, 175, 177, 180, 181, 193, 198, 200, 205, 206, 210, 212, 228, 252, 255, 259–264
depoliticisation, 10, 11, 183, 187, 189, 191, 197, 206, 208, 209, 216, 218, 254, 261, 263–265
dissent, legacy of, 11, 153, 156, 160, 161, 164, 165, 253

E
European Union (EU), 9, 11, 36, 68, 70, 72, 73, 78, 82, 83, 85, 92, 93, 104–107, 120, 121, 123, 125, 127, 133, 134, 138–140, 142, 145, 146, 163, 187, 188, 196, 198, 238, 252, 259

F
far right, 188, 189, 195–199
Foreign direct investment (FDI), 10, 78, 100, 119, 120, 126, 135, 139–141, 146

G
generation, 3, 9, 18–20, 29, 33, 35–39, 180, 221, 230, 253
Georgia, 11, 109, 170–173, 175–184, 235
Germany, 92, 122, 144
globalisation, 22, 157, 199, 252, 254
global South, 4, 8, 26, 29–31, 256, 257, 261

H
Havel, Václav, 137, 139–141, 143–145, 152

hegemony, 3, 8, 11, 12, 27, 29, 39, 69, 71, 88, 116, 118, 154, 171, 172, 174, 175, 183, 184, 205, 208–210, 212, 214, 218, 231
Hungary, 4, 10, 23, 70, 115–120, 124–127, 134, 141, 154, 156, 189, 235

I
illiberalism, 2, 9, 20–24, 36
imperialism, 23, 97, 99, 229

K
Klaus, Václav, 137, 138, 140, 142–146, 156, 160

L
liberalism, 1, 2, 20–25, 36, 70, 134, 154, 157, 162, 163, 178, 188–190, 198, 200, 209, 254, 255

M
market reforms, 44, 55, 58, 59, 61, 67, 68, 81, 156, 162
Marxism, 87, 238

N
nationalism, 8, 10, 12, 23, 58, 68, 88, 94, 138, 146, 148, 178, 190, 192, 197, 216, 218, 253, 255, 260, 263
Navalny, Alexei, 216–220
neoliberalism, 4, 26–28, 33–36, 38, 71, 76, 101, 102, 142, 154, 158, 188, 193, 194, 201, 225, 228, 229, 231, 241, 254
new left, 3–6, 8, 12, 78, 144, 189, 198–200, 253

O
oligarchy, oligarchs, 86, 98, 99, 102, 103, 106, 108–110, 134, 137, 141, 142, 147, 148, 161, 162, 264
Orbán, Viktor, 22, 23, 189

P
peripherality, 9, 81–84, 91, 93, 94
Poland, 12, 70, 125, 134, 141, 154, 156, 224, 225, 227, 228, 230–232, 235, 237, 238, 242, 243
politics of authenticity, 11, 214, 263
privatization, 4, 41, 42, 44, 46, 49, 61, 62, 70–72, 74–77, 81–85, 88–91, 93, 98, 118–120, 126, 138, 139, 141, 155, 157, 160, 162, 188, 192–197, 231
protest, 10–12, 38, 57, 77, 82–86, 93, 104, 108, 109, 120, 122, 135, 139, 140, 142, 147, 153, 155, 163, 170, 176, 179–182, 190, 191, 194, 199, 200, 205–208, 210–220, 224, 225, 231
Putin, Vladimir, 2, 12, 23, 107, 182, 191, 205–209, 211, 212, 215, 216, 218, 219, 234, 258

R
racism, 93, 145, 198, 199, 259
regime change, 7, 22, 107, 133, 152, 205, 211
Romania, 5, 9, 18–20, 25, 30, 31, 33, 36, 37
Russia, 2, 22, 23, 35, 97, 99, 101, 102, 104, 105, 107, 124, 141, 178, 182, 205–211, 213, 216–220, 232, 258

S

Slovakia, 11, 134, 151–159, 162, 163, 191

Slovenia, 9, 58, 69–71, 73, 75, 79

social movements, 1, 135, 144, 180, 200, 253, 254, 259

Soviet union, 50, 53, 66, 117, 176, 178, 182, 205, 206, 225, 242, 260

state socialism, state socialist dictatorships, 252, 253, 255, 256, 262

U

Ukraine, 10, 97–111, 220, 235

Z

Zelensky, Volodymyr, 10, 106, 110

The manufacturer's authorised representative in the EU is Springer Nature Customer Service Centre GmbH, Europaplatz 3, 69115 Heidelberg, Germany. If you have any concerns regarding our products, please contact ProductSafety@springernature.com

Printed and bound by CPI Group (UK) Ltd, Croydon, CR0 4YY
30/09/2026
02225700-0005